The Economic Decline of Empires

The Economic Decline of Empires

edited with an introduction by
CARLO M. CIPOLLA

METHUEN & CO LTD
11 NEW FETTER LANE · LONDON EC4

1970

First published in 1970
by Methuen & Co Ltd
Introduction © 1970 by Carlo M. Cipolla
Printed in Great Britain by
The Camelot Press Ltd
London and Southampton

SBN (hardbound) 416 16090 5
SBN (paperback) 416 18210 0

Distributed in the USA
by Barnes & Noble Inc.

Contents

Acknowledgements

The editor and publishers wish to thank the following for permission to reproduce material from the publications listed below:

Professor Aurelio Bernardi for an article in *Studia et Documenta Historiae et Iuris*, Vol. XXXI, 1965; Editore Boringhieri for an article in *Storia dell' economia italiana*, 1959; Harvard University Press for *Studies on the Population of China, 1368–1953* by Ping-ti Ho; Hutchinson Publishing Group Ltd for *The Arabs in History* by Bernard Lewis; Hutchinson Publishing Group Ltd and Alfred A. Knopf, Inc. for *The Dutch Seaborne Empire 1600–1800* by C. R. Boxer; Oxford University Press for *The Emergence of Modern Turkey* by Bernard Lewis; Past and Present for an article in *Past and Present*, No. 20, 1961; Princeton University Press for *An Economic History of Spain* by Jaime Vicens Vives; Rutgers University Press for *Byzantium: Greatness and Decline* by Charles Diehl; and The Viking Press, Inc. and Chatto and Windus Ltd for *Aspects of Antiquity: Discoveries and Controversies* by M. I. Finley.

Editor's Introduction

Why do empires decline and fall? What 'laws' or 'mechanisms' regulate that seemingly inescapable cycle which appears to reproduce on a large scale the ontogenetic cycle of life and death? The problem has bothered philosophers and historians of all times. And, among others, it has bothered me, as a native of a country which twice in her history has been in decline.

Whenever we look at declining empires, we notice that their economies are generally faltering. The economic difficulties of declining empires show striking resemblances. It is not unreasonable to try to identify these similarities provided that we keep in mind that individual histories are characterized by important elements of originality.

At first sight it may seem that economic decline can be easily defined as the reverse of economic growth. This would not be logically circular because in recent times economic growth has been defined with satisfactory precision, but it would not be correct. Theoretically, growth can go on indefinitely. Decline cannot: beyond a certain point the declining society would simply die out. Examples of societies whose *per capita* incomes diminished over periods of time are not impossible to find in recorded history. In the case of seventeenth-century Italy and Spain absolute decline must have lasted from about the 1620s to the 1680s or 1690s. After the 1690s, however, the trend was supposedly reversed. But since other countries were growing faster, Italy and Spain not only did not recover their pre-eminence but they progressively lost more ground. In this last phase of their economic history, Italy and Spain were declining in relation to other countries while they were growing in absolute terms. In the long view of history, when societies do not die out, all cases of decline turn out eventually to be cases of relative decline.

If we can have decline while we have growth, it is obvious that we cannot define one as the reverse of the other. On the other hand, the concept of relative economic decline is ambiguous. If existing societies grow at different rates, all but one – the one with the highest rate of growth – are relatively declining. This would bring us too far. Therefore, in the following pages, the word 'decline' is used in a broad sense to mean, roughly, a loss of pre-eminence. The term 'empire', as I use it here, is not an exclusively political description. It refers also to an economic or cultural predominance, like that of the Italian states in the Middle Ages and the Netherlands in the seventeenth century.

The most simple declines to be analysed would be, of course, those related to a catastrophe of some kind. If the legendary Atlantis ever existed, it would supply us with the best example of catastrophic decline. In the industrial world we are becoming uncomfortably accustomed to the idea that countries could be wiped out by an atomic bang. However, an external calamity cannot always be assumed as a sufficient cause of the decline of a civilization. More often than not, the question is complicated by the lack of an adequate response to the challenge, and the lack of response must be explained. On the other hand, catastrophes are not always truly exogenous factors. A number of calamitous events that at first sight look exogenous may have their roots in the history of the society which they upset. Foreign invasions may be invited by internal political and social unrest. The story of China shows that even floods cannot always be considered exogenous factors. Flood may be the consequence of lack of public works or excessive deforestations which in their turn may be attributed to bureaucratic inefficiency or to bad social, political and economic conditions. At any rate, disappearances of empires due to catastrophes have been extremely rare in history, and none of the examples of decline analysed in this volume belongs to the catastrophic type.

Before it can decline, an empire has first to grow. Growth means an increase of incomes. It also means an increase of consumption both private and public. In general it can be assumed that improvements in standards of living are initially experienced by small and relatively privileged circles, but the process is bound to extend eventually to progressively larger sectors of the population. Ingrained habits and sets of values may slow down the change in patterns and levels of consumption of the many. Moralists may preach the ethical value of low and stable standards of living. Selfish oligarchies may try to keep only for themselves the gains of economic development. Religious zealots or other groups of fanatics can make life poisonous to themselves and others by trying to channel all additional income either into the building of temples and churches, or into armament and machinery. But eventually, in the long run, the masses are bound to overcome such resistance. It may happen that in the course of time the oligarchies lose their strength or that the myths on which they base their power wear out. Or people may get tired of hardships which they no longer consider either necessary or unavoidable. They will demand to share the amenities enjoyed by the *élite* and in one way or the other they will press towards such a goal. The broken temples of the Mayas possibly indicate that at a given moment in their history the Maya peasantry violently refused to pay their tribute of hardship and labour for the benefit of the priesthood and through violent revolution demanded an improvement in their standards of living. In the late Roman Empire the masses of the large towns pressed successfully upon the administration for liberal supplies of food, public schools and public amusements. In the later Middle Ages the less privileged groups of urban craftsmen learned how to organize themselves, often through violent action, in order to increase their bargaining power and improve their standards of living. The story of Italy in the later Middle Ages and in the Renaissance and the story of Spain in the sixteenth century are no exception to the general rule.

The improvement in standards of living is generally reflected, among other things, by the least attractive jobs tending to be deserted. With a falling off in the labour of the mines, the late Roman Empire had to freeze the existing workers and to recall to the mines workers who had found other employment. The next step was to tie the children of miners to the industry. In fifteenth- and sixteenth-century Italy, very few people were still willing to serve as oarsmen on the galleys, and what had been in the twelfth and thirteenth centuries a job for free men increasingly became the dreaded punishment of convicts and prisoners of war.

The degree and the speed at which the lower strata of a population succeed in sharing the material gains of economic progress vary drastically from one society to another. But even in the least open societies, some benefits eventually reach to the lowest part of the social ladder. Strictly speaking, to consider slaves as part of an agricultural society is no more correct than to consider automobiles as members of an industrial society. However, it is worth pointing out that, even in societies based on slavery, in the course of time the material gains of economic progress were eventually felt by the least fortunate members too. By the time of Augustus, the manumission of slaves in Rome had reached a rate which the emperor thought too high. In fifteenth- and sixteenth-century Italy, personally owned domestic slaves enjoyed on the average better living standards than the serfs of the eighth or the ninth century.

There is nothing inherently wrong in the growth of consumption. From an economic point of view, it could be maintained that under certain conditions, higher consumption might create better opportunities and stimulate production. On a broader level, it can be maintained that by devoting additional wealth to the welfare of its constituents, a society fulfils the ethical concept that the dignity of human personality is all that eventually matters.

Of course, perversions and excesses are bound to occur. As a counterpart to the tendency of those who would like to chain a population to primitive standards of living for the sake of a privileged group or of some remote ideal, there is a natural tendency in any population to move towards excesses and to strive for abnormal sensations and unnatural experiences once elementary and normal needs are satisfied. Reasonableness and self-control are not common virtues. Men like Pliny and the Emperor Vespasian, who, although in closest touch with the excesses of a mature and highly developed society, were capable of retaining a calm, healthy and human routine of life, are relatively rare. In mature empires, extravagances of fashion and licence are bound to develop. Again, the process germinates in upper circles, but in the course of time, extravagances creep down inexorably into the lower strata of the population, acquiring in the process distinct overtones of vulgarity. I am not mentioning these facts here for their ethical significance. I quote them merely to emphasize that while there is a minimum of human needs below which human life is impossible, there is practically no upper limit to human desires. Instinctively and irresistibly people strive towards greater consumption, incessantly creating new needs, no matter how artificial, desultory, or even pernicious, as soon as the old needs are satisfied.

In his pamphlet on the *Death of the Persecutors*, Lactantius charges Diocletian with having quadrupled the armed forces and vastly expanded the civil service to the point that soon, as he concludes, 'there will be more governors than governed'. Bureaucrats swarmed in the late Byzantine Empire, and as Bernard Lewis writes, an 'inflated bureaucracy' plagued the economy of the late Arab Empire. About 1740, Macanaz ranked the excessive number of civil servants first in his enumeration of the causes of the decline of Spain: there are, he says, a thousand employees where forty would suffice if they were kept at work, and the rest could be set to some useful labour. In our day, Mr Parkinson noticed that as the number of battleships in the Royal Navy diminished, the number of admirals was swollen. Complaints of this kind are commonly heard in mature Empires. They cannot be lightheartedly discarded as exaggerations of pessimistic and inveterate grumblers. As a political unity grows and develops, more and more functions become increasingly complex and ramify in various directions. Moreover, as a society develops, it becomes progressively more conscious of social and collective needs which may take the most different forms.

One of the major items of public expenditure for mature empires is, of course, defence. A number of interrelated factors contribute to the expansion of military expenditures. Empires do not exist in a vacuum. They are surrounded by countries that in one way or another gain some advantage from the very existence of the empire itself. The prosperous economy and the progressive technology of a growing empire are bound to radiate beneficent effects beyond its boundaries and contribute to the development of its neighbours. In the course of time these neighbours become a threat and force the empire into greater military expenditure. The story of what Greece did to Egypt, the Germanic tribes did to Rome, early sixteenth-century France did to Italy, and England did to Spain and to Holland are significant in this regard. On the other hand, the growth of living standards within an empire pushes up the cost of an army. In the modern world the economic problems are less that of paying manpower than that of possessing very expensive equipment that becomes very rapidly obsolete. But whatever the specific elements involved, the problem remains essentially the same: military expenditure powerfully contributes to the growth of total public consumption.

We do not have reliable quantitative data that enable us to assess the composition of public expenditure in most of the mature empires of the past, but it is not hard to believe that the structures of public expenditure must have shown remarkable differences. In one place the construction of temples and pyramids may have weighed heavily on the economy; in another place the extravagances of a dynasty of rulers may have burdened the public treasury; in another place military expenditure and administration may have absorbed an increasingly larger share of the gross national product. The fundamental fact remains that public consumption in mature empires shows a distinct tendency to rise sharply.

The phenomenon is reflected in the growth of taxation. One of the remarkably common features of empires at the later stage of their development is the growing amount of wealth pumped by the State from the economy. In the later Roman Empire taxation reached such heights that land was abandoned and many peasants, after paying their rents or taxes, had too little food left to nourish their children. In sixteenth-century Spain the revenue from the two taxes, the *alcabala* and the *millones* (which was introduced in 1590), increased from 1504 to 1596 by more than five times. It is true that in the meantime the general index of prices more than trebled, but it is also true that while the revenue from the *alcabala* represented in 1504 about 85 per cent of the government revenues, in 1596 its yield represented only 25 per cent. Of sixteenth-century Italians, Fynes Moryson wrote that they lived under 'cruell exactions under which they grone as under the bondage of Egypt'. Figures relating to tax revenues, however, do not always tell the whole story. In the later Roman Empire, in the late Byzantine Empire, in seventeenth-century Spain, inflation was rampant. Debasing the currency is just another form of taxation. The Italian decline in the seventeenth century was exceptional in the sense that inflation was not part of the scenario.

At the beginning of the twentieth century some economists advanced the idea that mature economies are bound to stagnate because consumption cannot expand as production does. The crisis of 1929 and subsequent events seemed to support the theories of the stagnationists. There is no doubt that on occasion demand can fall short of productive potential and damage the economy for more than five or ten years – the span of a business cycle.

There may also be long-term disequilibria with overtones of excessive production in some specific sector of the economy. But on the whole, in the long view of history, economic difficulties of mature empires apparently do not stem from insufficient consumption. Quite the contrary! Even if their economic analysis is not unremittingly rigorous, historians have always felt instinctively that the main economic troubles of mature empires stemmed from the side of supply. In trying to explain this fact, most historians pointed to real or imagined bottlenecks such as shortage of slaves, or of population, or of bullion, or to stagnant technology. Some of these arguments are most definitely naïve, but some are not, and the line of thought deserves to be pursued.

'What can be done to revitalize a flagging economy and increase national productivity?' This is a modern expression of the problem that the Spanish *arbitristas* asked themselves throughout the seventeenth century. The economic problem that plagued the late Roman Empire, the late Byzantine Empire, Ming and Ch'ing China, seventeenth-century Italy, and the eighteenth-century Netherlands was not different from that of seventeenth-century Spain. At least in the early phase of a decline, however, the problem does not seem to be so much that of increasing visible inputs – capital or labour – as that of changing ways of doing things and improving productivity. The survival of the empire demands such basic change. But it is typical of mature empires to give a negative response to this challenge.

It is worth noticing that some empires were able to grow and develop without being really innovatory on the economic level. The Spanish empire is an excellent case in point. Spain as a whole, on the eve of the conquest, was fundamentally an underdeveloped country even in terms of the technology and the economy of those days. At the beginning of the sixteenth century, Guicciardini wrote that poverty prevailed in Spain 'not so much for the quality of the country but because the Spaniards by nature are not inclined to the arts and crafts'. In 1552 the Venetian Ambassador Badoer wrote: 'I do not think that there is another country less provided with skilled workers than Spain.' The Spanish Empire grew up on the unexpected and accidental returns of the conquest. The influx of bullion and the induced expansion of global demand had certain positive effects in stimulating the growth of some activities in the course of the sixteenth century. But fundamentally the country failed to change. Spain remained essentially a country of peasants, shepherds and landlords; she remained a militant society imbued, as Professor Elliott writes, 'with the crusading ideal, accustomed by the *reconquista* and the conquest of America to the quest of glory and booty and dominated by a church and an aristocracy which perpetuated those very ideals least propitious for the development of capitalism'. Where some manufactures grew, the methods employed were generally the traditional. In 1603 the Frenchman Joly echoed the remarks made one century earlier by Guicciardini and emphasized the backwardness of the Spaniards in the sciences and the mechanical arts. Quite differently from Spain, the Italian States of the Middle Ages were highly innovatory societies. Yet Italy, too, at a given stage of maturity resisted further needed change and declined. By the middle of the seventeenth century Italian manufacturers were confronted with new types of products and new systems of production that drove Italian products out of one market after another. Adaptation to new and more efficient methods of production was required: the example was there, and Italy was traditionally a country of able businessmen and abundant capital. Yet at that juncture the Italians failed to complete the needed transformation and lost for ever their economic pre-eminence. Similarly, the Dutch of the seventeenth century were great innovators, and their leadership was recognized all over Europe in matters of agriculture, trade, manufactures and shipping. By the end of the eighteenth century they appeared incapable of keeping up with the progress taking place outside their boundaries. Whereas in the second half of the seventeenth century the Dutch had been the undisputed leaders in many fields, a century later they were overtaken and displaced by the English. A conservative mentality was reflected in most branches of Dutch trade and industry during the Periwig Period. The Dutch lost their seventeenth-century lead in maritime cartography and navigational techniques, in the whale fisheries as well as in the textile sector, and they were equally slow to adopt new and improved methods in shipbuilding. In 1775, a Dutchman wrote: 'We are no longer innate innovators and originality is becoming increasingly rare with us here. Nowadays we only make copies whereas formerly we only made originals.'

All empires seem eventually to develop an intractable resistance to the change needed for the required growth of production. Then neither the needed enterprise, nor the needed type of investment, nor the needed technological change is forthcoming. Why?

We have to admit that what appears *ex post* as an obsolete behaviour pattern was, at an earlier stage in the life of an empire, a successful way of doing things, of which the members of the empire were justly proud. The Spaniards had acquired their national unity and built a huge Empire by being soldiers and crusaders, not by being merchants and craftsmen. Their pride was in those belligerent traditions and ideals that had helped them in the *reconquista* of their country as well as in the conquest of the Americas. When the Italians of the seventeenth century were confronted by aggressive competitors with new types of products and new ways of doing things, a few realized the need for change, but the majority resisted innovation. Many textile manufacturers were justly proud of 'the good woollen of the old traditional quality' and they emphasized that the traditional system of production had given the Italian industry an undisputed supremacy: they were sceptical about what was in their eyes a less careful way of doing things. Why should the old, tested, successful methods be given up for the new and dubious ways of aggressive, unscrupulous competitors? Innovations are important not for their immediate, actual results but for their

B

potential for future development, and potential is very difficult to assess. Innovation is to society what mutation is in biology. Not all mutations are good. Some are just poor and unfortunate experiments. Only natural selection (which is not rational although *ex post* it can be rationally explained) will tell over time which are good and which are bad mutations.

The rational element that lies behind the strong conservatism of mature empires is mixed with altogether irrational elements. Success breeds conceit. Self-complacency and readiness to change are mutually exclusive attitudes. In the pages reproduced below Charles Diehl shows how ruthlessly the Italians exploited the economy of the late Byzantine Empire. As A. M. Andreades once wrote, 'the Byzantine shipowners, merchants and manufacturers rooted firmly in antiquated methods of business could not keep pace with the younger Italian competitors'. One of the reasons for this failure was that the Byzantines took no notice of the remarkable developments appearing among the 'Western barbarians' during the twelfth, thirteenth and fourteenth centuries. As Grenier wrote, 'they failed to realize that the barbarians developed after the barbarian invasions'. When at the end of the Middle Ages they made the discovery that the West had something to offer and teach, it was too late. The Chinese refused to take notice of Western military gadgetry until this gadgetry wreaked havoc on their country. This type of 'proud conservatism' is not the original sin of a given people or race. It develops quite naturally after a prolonged period of successful action. Towards the end of the thirteenth century, the Italians were still a highly dynamic and innovating society. When Marco Polo visited China he did not look snobbishly at the natives, nor did he criticize the things which were unfamiliar to him. He came ready to observe, to admire and to learn. Some Italians were like-minded three centuries later, but the country as a whole had turned into a conservative, complacent, narrow-minded society. The Italians, wrote Fynes Moryson at the beginning of the seventeenth century, 'thincke themselves to have so much sweetness, fruitfulness and such monuments of arts and fabricks, as they seldome or never travaile into forayne Kingdomes, but driven by some necessity ether to followe the warrs or to traffique abroad: this opinion that Italy doth afforde what can be seene or knowne in the world, makes them only have homebred wisdome and the prowde conceete of their owne witts.'

It must also be recognized that as there is no such thing as '*homo oeconomicus*', so there is no economic activity divorced from all other forms of activity. When we do business we act in a certain way which reflects our global personality, and the way we carry on business is related to the way we love and hate, the way we eat and rest, the way we think and look at things in general. To change our way of working and doing business implies a more general change of customs, attitudes, motivations and sets of values which represent our cultural heritage. The more a mature empire is proud of its cultural heritage, the more emotionally difficult it is for its people to change to new modes of being and to new ways of doing things, under the pressure of external competition and growing difficulties. Many would feel deeply that to undergo such a change would be like admitting defeat. Then change, which would be the only hope of survival, becomes ironically equated with surrender.

Change implies imaginative effort. Change hurts vested interests. It is not difficult to explain why change is generally opposed. It would be surprising if it were not. The tendency to resist change is strengthened by existing institutions. There is no doubt that institutions in general have a life-expectancy much longer than they deserve, and this is why revolutions take place. Once an institution is in existence, it is very hard to change it or to get rid of it. Owing to its past growth and development, an empire is inevitably character-ized by a large number of sclerotic institutions. They hinder change for their very existence. Moreover, they give invaluable support to that part of the population which opposes change for one reason or another. Institutional rigidities reflect cultural rigidities. Conser-vative people and vested interests cluster around obsolete institu-tions, and each element supports the other powerfully. Innovating minorities are bound to see their efforts frustrated by this combina-tion. In seventeenth-century Italy a few entrepreneurs clearly saw that the only way to save the economy was to adopt the new English and Dutch methods of production, but it was easy for the conservatives to use the guilds and their outdated regulations to oppose any innovation.

Another set of factors must be taken into account, namely that mysterious combination of cultural, biological, social, psychological and economic influences that for want of a better term I might call 'the third generation effect'. In every good family there is the generation that builds up a fortune, the generation that holds on to it, and the generation that dissipates it. In this respect, societies differ little from families. Let us make it clear that any moral judgement is absolutely alien to my argument. In fact, we may have a great deal of sympathy for the 'third generations'. They may be more urbane and polite than the aggressive, bully 'parvenus'. The objective fact remains, however, that 'third generations' seem to lack the characteristic strength of those who build. Sometimes they actually develop a masochistic disposition to self-destruction that psycho-analysts have not yet fully explained. Old myths that helped the 'first generation' to endure hardships wear out progressively and are laughed at. The residents at Carthage were taken by surprise on the amphitheatre when the Vandals attacked. The patricians of Cologne were sitting at a banquet when the barbarians were already near their walls. It takes quite a lack of humour to build an empire. Once an empire is built, humour is bound to develop. People learn to laugh with other people, and eventually they also learn to laugh at themselves. *Don Quixote* was written in a mature empire. Moreover, as old myths wear out and living conditions improve, more people think in terms of 'rights' rather than in terms of 'duties', in terms of 'enjoyment' rather than in terms of 'work'.

The pseudo-biological interpretations of racialist historians of the twenties and thirties were doubly unfortunate. Not only did they nourish stupid racialist preconceptions and favour macabre politics. Because of their unscientific basis and their criminal consequences they also cast a sinister shadow on the study of the biological component in the history of human civilization. We are in complete ignorance of the interaction between cultural and biological development and, unfortunately, not enough scholars dare to venture into this essential field for fear of being accused of racialism, nazism, or some other kind of unpleasant mental disposition. Yet I feel sure that we will not be able to understand fully the decline of empires until a combined effort of historians and biologists has clarified the effects of protracted well-being and high standards of living on the psychological structure of a population and the feedback effects of these changes on the cultural behaviour of the same population.

Economists recognize that there is more to the determination of output than the observable inputs. This boils down to saying that if, for instance, paleolithic hunters had decided to put more people to work and use more stone, this might have delayed their decline, but in the long run it would not have helped them to resist the neolithic invasion. In order to survive they had to stop hunting and had to become agriculturalists; they had to stop producing polished stone and produce ploughs instead. In the cryptic jargon of the economists, they had to jump on to a totally different production function. Ways of doing things are strategically important in determining the performance of a society. If the necessary change does not take place and economic difficulties are allowed to grow, then a cumulative process is bound to be set into motion that makes things progressively worse. Decline enters then in its final, dramatic stage.

When needs outstrip production capability, a number of tensions are bound to appear in the society. Inflation, excessive taxation, difficulties in the balance of payments are just a small sample of the whole series of possible tensions. The public sector presses heavily over and against the private sector in order to squeeze out the largest possible share of resources. Consumption competes with investment and vice versa. Within the private sector, the conflict among social groups becomes more bitter because each group tries to avoid as much as possible the necessary economic sacrifices. As the struggle grows in bitterness, co-operation among people and social groups fades away, a sense of alienation from the common-wealth develops, and with it group and class selfishness. As has been said of the Roman Empire, 'the most depressing feature of the later Empire is the apparent absence of public spirit. The motive forces seem to be on the one hand, compulsion, and on the other hand, personal ambition in its cruder forms.' Public spirit and the spirit of mutual co-operation were the basis of the growth and development of the Italian city-states in the twelfth and thirteenth centuries. They were conspicuous for their absence in the resigned, frustrated, cynical Italy of the seventeenth century.

If public spirit is faltering and the spirit of co-operation is lacking, any programme of renovation has scant possibility of success. In so far as the inadequacy of production is related more to outdated ways of doing things than to inadequate inputs, any programme of austerity can avail little. Moreover, a programme of austerity would be, ironically enough, only a recognition of a situation of decline rather than a means really to avert it. The curtailment of public expenditure can put the country at the mercy of potential invaders or can relegate the country to only a minor role in international affairs. A curtailment of private expenditure in the face of growing private consumption abroad can mean the loss of distinctive features of pre-eminence.

In environments characterized by lack of co-operation among social groups, by emphasis on rights rather than on duties, by a strong leisure-preference, all efforts towards renewal can only develop in the unpleasant direction of compulsion and further taxation. But beyond certain limits, compulsion and taxation nurture corruption, evasion and often a redistribution of income in favour of powerful bureaucrats and of people close to those in power. Feelings of frustration and pessimism are bound to spread, and in this gloomy atmosphere there is little room for innovation. Disinvestment is likely to occur. Land was abandoned in the late Roman Empire as well as in seventeenth-century Castille. Many firms closed in seventeenth-century Italy. If and when things reach this point, decline is bound to take place at an accelerated pace.

While an empire is flourishing, its members show a strong inclination to delude themselves about its life-expectancy. History offers no examples of indestructible empires, yet most peoples are convinced that what happened to previous empires cannot happen to their own. In so doing they just show a lack of imagination, a naïve incapacity to imagine new situations for which their tastes, inclinations and institutions will grow progressively inadequate. Once the decline starts, there are still optimistic people who stubbornly deny reality, but the number of those who realize what is happening is bound to enlarge progressively. Some then try to rationalize the events and to build general theories around them. The theory of

Vico on the ebbs and flows of history was propounded just after the decline of Italy in the seventeenth century. The theories of Toynbee were expressed in twentieth-century Britain. Others refrain from generalizations and focus their attention on the specific situation. It is remarkable to see how relatively numerous in declining empires are the people capable of making the right diagnosis and preaching some sensible cure. It is no less remarkable, however, that wise utterances remain generally sterile, because, as Gonzales de Cellorigo forcefully put it while watching impotently the decline of Spain, 'those who can will not and those who will cannot'.

ONE

The Economic Problems of the Roman Empire at the Time of its Decline[1]

AURELIO BERNARDI

I. THE FALL OF THE ROMAN EMPIRE AND DIFFERENT ATTEMPTS TO ACCOUNT FOR ITS CAUSES

The fall of the Roman Empire as an organized political unity, and along with it the decline of the Hellenistic Roman civilization it had propagated all over the ancient world, had far-reaching consequences for the history of mankind. So strong was its impression upon posterity that each new generation inquires again into the causes that led to this momentous event. 'A revolution that will ever be remembered', Gibbon stated, 'and is still felt by the nations of the earth'. A great historian, E. Meyer, once wrote

> Trajan in his famous decree on the Christians emphasizes that anonymous denunciations could never be taken into consideration: *nam et pessimi exempli nec nostri saeculi est* (Plin. Epist. X, 97). Nowhere else does one feel so vividly the fulness of a great civilized state reaching its culmination. It seemed to be founded to last forever, and yet only one century later the whole majestic building collapsed.[2]

Many other empires have crumbled in the course of history either

[1] This article was first published in *Studia et Documenta Historiae et Iuris*, Vol. XXXI, 1965.
I wish to express my special thanks to my friend Professor Carlo M. Cipolla, who has made many valuable suggestions relating to the economic aspect of the work (however he is in no way responsible for opinions contained here) and to Dr John Meddemmen, Lecturer in English at Collegio Ghislieri, for his patient help in preparing the text.
[2] E. Meyer, 'Die Wirtschaft. Entwicklung des Altertums', in *Jahrbücher für Nationalökonomic und Statistik*, 9 (1895), 733 (=Kl. Schr. 1, p. 79).

because they were overwhelmed by more powerful empires as happened to the monarchies of the ancient East, or because they were established hurriedly by the individual initiative of some impetuous condottieri and had no chance to strike roots deep enough to let them survive. This was the case with the empire of Alexander the Great. The great drama of the fall of the Roman Empire, on the other hand, lies in the fact, and in the fact alone, that it disintegrated not because of other organized rival powers – which actually did not exist on its borders (the barbarian tribes cannot be put in this category and the Persian Empire of the Sassanids had only a very short common border with the Roman) – but by an internal process of disintegration. It was like an organism whose strength suddenly failed.

The first questions which occur to the minds of those who meditate on this event concern the nature of this process of disintegration. However, even when the historical interest was directed at the political and constitutional history only, manifold answers were given at all times to these questions. They depended on the diverse criteria for the evaluation of history from which the respective investigations started. Criteria of a moralistic order – the corrupted customs, the unbridled luxury, etc. – guided the Fathers of the Church. Criteria of a politico-social order – suppression of the republican liberty at the advent of the empire, the gap between senate and people, the predominance of the army and, as a consequence, the disturbed balance of power, the decline of the republican institutions, the gradual elimination of the ruling *élite*, the great power of the lower classes, miscegenation, massive infiltration of barbarians, etc. have impressed many scholars from the Renaissance on. Religious feelings have also to be taken into account; they placed the whole responsibility for the final crash upon the discouraging behaviour of Christianity, which, according to Voltaire's famous dictum 'ouvrait le ciel, mais il perdait l'empire'.[1]

[1] For detailed treatment of modern historiography on the Roman Empire see A. Momigliano, 'La formazione della moderna storiografia sull'Impero Romano', in *Riv. Stor. Ital.* 1 (1936): 1, 35–60; 2, 19–48 (reprinted in *Contributi alla Storia degli studi classici* [1955], 107–164). For a survey of some of the many proposed explanations of the problem of why Rome fell see A. Piganiol, *L'Empire Chrétien*, 1947, 411 ff.; see also chap. XII of M. Rostovtzeff,

The evolutionistic criteria, on the other hand, strengthened through Darwinism, the great fashion at the end of the last century, linked themselves with the ancients' belief in periodic cycles. Such belief already appears in Plato and Polybius and was taken up again by Vico around 1700. For them civilizations come into being, grow and mature, but when their life cycle is completed, they must decline and vanish, also because of the weakening of the instinct of procreation, exactly as happens in biology.[1]

Yet the explanations given on the basis of the criteria which have been briefly compiled here have caught not the causes but the symptoms of a historical situation which the tangle of spiritual and material forces at play made extremely complex. Nevertheless, the variety of explanations had the effect of drawing more and more attention to that great turning-point in the history of mankind reaffirming the principle that in history great effects presuppose great causes and that, in order to search for these, one must penetrate deeper into the very socio-economic structures of nations. Progress in historical investigations has made it possible to get a vivid perception of the socio-economic reality of the Roman world. This task has been facilitated in the last decade by data furnished in ever-increasing quantity by sciences such as epigraphy, papyrology, archaeology, and numismatics that have advanced enormously in recent times.

There has been a tendency to trace one of the causes of the fall of the Roman Empire to a general, progressive, economic decline that allegedly occurred in the ancient world from the third century to

Social and Economic History of the Roman Empire, 2 Ed. 1957. On the influence of the Christianity in Roman Society see J. Gaudemet, *L'Eglise dans L'Empire Romain* (IV–V siècles)[2] 1958; A. Momigliano, *Christianity and the Decline of the Roman Empire*, reprinted from *Paganism and Christianity in the fourth century*, edited by A. Momigliano.

[1] On the biological explanation of the Fall of Rome see E. Ciccotti, 'Motivi demografici e biologici nella rovina della civiltà antica', in *Nuova Riv. Storica*, 14 (1930), 29–62, who discusses the opinions of: O. Seeck, *Geschichte des Untergangs der Antiken Welt*, 6 vol. 1897–1921; T. Frank, *An Economic Survey of Rome*, 5, 1940, chap. XII, p. 213 ff.; M. Nilsson, *Imperial Rome*, 1926, 338 ff. On the idea of decadence see: A. Rehm, *Der Untergang Roms im abendlaendischen Denken*, 1930; Werner, *Der Untergang Roms; Studien zum Dekadenzproblem in der antiken Welt*, 1941; S. Mazzarino, *La fine del mondo antico*, 1959.

the fifth[1] – decline in production, in the means of transport, in the means for payment, in the labour force and its efficiency. For the followers of Marxism, for whom the modes of production in the last analysis condition the processes of social, political and spiritual life, this decline must have been the principal cause. Although various and complex processes such as those that led together to the ruin of the Roman Empire cannot be attributed to one factor only, that is to say to a *causa causarum*, it cannot be denied that the vitality of a political organism is conditioned also by its economic vitality; this, in turn, influences the most various manifestations of life and civilization in a process of constant interaction, where, however, it is difficult to single out any priority.

2. THE EMPIRE'S ECONOMIC EFFICIENCY WITHIN THE FRAMEWORK OF ANCIENT ECONOMY

In the particular case of the Roman Empire in its twilight it must be asked in the first place whether the imperial economy actually suffered a general and prolonged decline of production; whether this decline was due to declining population or to scarcity of natural resources, or to technological or organizational factors; or whether, from a certain moment on, the economy as a whole

---

[1] The fundamental study of the economy of the empire is Rostovtzeff's Work, mentioned above. See also: *Economic Survey of Ancient Rome*, T. Frank, vol. 5, 1936–40; F. Oertel, 'The economic life of the Empire', in *Cam. Anc. Hist.* XII Chap. 7, 1939. The direct or indirect bibliography on the economic causes of the empire's ruin is extensive: the argument is directly debated by: M. Rostovtzeff, 'The decay of the ancient world and its economy interpretations', in *Econ. Hist. Review*, 2 (1929–30), 201 ff.; C. Barbagallo, 'Il problema della rovina della civiltà antica', in *Civiltà Moderna*, 5 (1933), 508 ff.; L. C. West, 'The economic collapse of the Roman Empire', in *Class. Journal*, 28 (1932), 96 ff.; E. Ciccotti, 'Il crollo dell'Impero e della civiltà antica', in *Nuova Riv. Stor.* 19 (1935), 305–332; S. Mazzarino, *Aspetti sociali del IV secolo*, 1951; A. H. M. Jones, 'The decline and fall of the Roman empire', in *History*, 40 (1955), 209 ff.; F. W. Walbank, *The decline of the Roman Empire in the West*, 1953; A. E. Boak, *Manpower Shortage and the Fall of the Roman Empire in the West*, 1955; A. G. M. Jones, 'Overtaxation and the decline of the Roman Empire', in *Antiquity*, 33 (1959), 39–43; id. *The Later Roman Empire 284–602. A Social Economic and Administrative Survey*, 1964, vol. II, chap. XXV.

proved unable to support the policy of universal welfare favoured by the emperors, in the Age of the Antonines and later in the fourth century; or, again, whether the economy of the Empire entered a phase of relative decline in relation to the economics of foreign countries.

This last possibility can be discarded at once. The Empire constituted an enormous and almost closed economic entity. To the west and north it was bordered by the sea; the sands of Africa stretched to the south; in the north-east were the barbarians, in the south-east Persia and beyond it, but far away, India and China. The 'barbarians' did not have a sufficiently organized economy. Their way of life was very modest.[1] An exchange of certain goods did exist at the borders. The Empire exported wine and oil in considerable quantities and manufactured products, especially glassware and ceramics; the imports, on the other hand, did not amount to much.[2] Yet it is impossible to estimate the value of exports and imports; there are no indications in the sources. Nevertheless, the balance of trade was in favour of the Roman at the end of the fourth century, and when the political situation became difficult for the Empire, previous prohibitions were renewed against the exportation of products like wine, oil, arms, grinding stones, grain, gold.[3] The measure was evidently taken in order not to furnish the barbarians with means that could have increased their capacity to attack. Yet the excess of exports over imports could have brought back, in the form of payments, part of the gold which the Roman State considered it

[1] It seems – but has not been proved – that in one field, the working of iron, they had made remarkable progress producing arms of a harder and more resistant steel than that used for the Roman arms: A. Varagnac,' Technique et échanges en protohistoire et dans l'antiquité, in *Annales Econ. Soc. Civil.* 6 (1951), 353. We know however that for the fabrication of weapons the barbarians had recourse to Gallic smiths and techniques copied from Romans: A. Lesmaries, 'Armes gallo-franques', in *Rev. Etud. Anc.* 30 (1928), 222 ff. On the metallurgy of Romans generally see R. G. Forbes, *Metallurgy in Antiquity*, 1950, chap. 3 and 5.

[2] On the trade with *gentes externae* see R. E. Mortimer Wheeler, *Rome beyond the imperial frontiers*, 1954; K. Majewski, 'Récentes découvertes d'importations romaines et leur interprétation', in *Annales Econ. Soc. Civ.* 15 (1960), 314 ff.

[3] Dig. 39, 4, 11; Cod. Iust. 4, 41, 1 and 2; 63. The last passage is significant: *non solum aurum barbaris minime praebeatur, sed etiam, si apud eos inventum fuerit, subtili auferatur ingenio.*

advantageous to give to barbarian tribes, partly to keep them away from the borders, partly to compensate them for outright collaboration in the defence against other tribes who were in migration from more distant regions. In any case, the State never encouraged intensive trade with the barbarians on its frontier. Actually, the customs duties levied at all times on exports and imports – 5 per cent[1] while the internal ones did not exceed $2\frac{1}{2}$ per cent – led to the conclusion that this difference of the rate was an obstacle deliberately put up against an excessive expansion of such trade.[2]

It might be thought that the countries of the Middle and Far East were economically stronger than the Roman world. Considering, however, the natural difficulties of transportation in ancient times, especially for bulky commodities and over wide distances, it is difficult to believe that exchanges between the two areas were large enough to provoke serious disturbances in the weaker economy. The two areas were moreover in direct contact only along the relatively short borders in the Mesopotamian region. Surely trade between the two areas increased when the regularity of the monsoons was discovered at the beginning of our era; for now it became possible to sail from one area to the other and back within one and the same year.[3] Yet because of the enormous distances and the difficulties of transportation, trade was limited to the most expensive luxury products, such as silk, spices, unguents, perfumes, ivory, ebony, exotic animals, *objets d'art*. It moved mainly in the direction east-west.[4] The imported articles were paid for in gold. Actually, a considerable amount of Roman coins has been found in India and even in faraway China. According to some scholars this fact caused

[1] Strabo 4, 3, 2.

[2] On the problem see R. Etienne, 'Rome eut-elle une politique douanière?', in *Annales Econ. Soc. Civ.* 7 (1952), 371 ff. For the customs in the history of Rome, see the basic work of J. S. de Laet, *Portorium*, 1949: on the detailed question see chap. V, 309 ff. and 366 ff.

[3] Plin. *N. H.* 6, 26, 5–11. Cfr. R. E. Mortimer Wheeler, op. cit., 126–30.

[4] Strabo 16, 93. Indian products were sold in Rome at a hundred times their original price: Plin. *N. H.* 6, 24. On the trade with Far East see B. H. Warmington, *The commerce between the Roman Empire and India*, 1928; J. Filliozat, *Les Echanges de l'Inde et de l'Empire Romain*, in *Rev. Histor.* 102 (1949), 1–29; E. Lamotte, 'Les premières relations entre l'Inde et l'Occident', in *Nouvelle Clio*, 5 (1953), 83–118; J. Schwartz, 'L'Empire Romain et le commerce oriental', in *Annales Econ. Soc. Civ.* 15 (1959), 18 ff.

a gradual drainage of the Empire's gold resources and thus threw the whole monetary system into a crisis.[1] Data on the amount of gold that left the Roman territory in this way has come to us for the Early Empire only: one hundred million sesterces per annum. If the figures mentioned by Pliny in this connection are authentic,[2] this amount would have corresponded to about 15,000 pounds of gold.[3] At that time the annual budget of the Roman State amounted to about four milliards sesterces.[4] One might suppose that average annual national income could not possibly be less than forty milliards sesterces.[5] If these dangerous and hypothetical figures are correct, the value of the outflow of gold represented the fortieth part of the State's budget and certainly much less than the four-hundredth part of the total income of the Empire. Moreover, the very high customs duties levied on the value of the imported commodities (25 per cent) and the precautions undertaken to favour exportations of Roman products to the East, show the intention of the State to limit as far

[1] See G. J. Bratianu, 'La distribution de l'or et les raisons économiques de la division de l'Empire Romain', in *Etudes Byzantines d'Histoire Econ. et Soc.* 1938; A. Piganiol, 'Le problème de l'or au IVe siècle', in *Annales Hist. Econ. Soc.*, I (1945), 47–53; J. S. de Laet, *Portorium* cit. 309–11; 366 ff. Against see G. Mickwitz, 'Le problème de l'or dans le monde antique', in *Annales Hist. Econ. Soc.* 6 (1934), 235–47, Cf. also T. Frank, *Econ. Survey*, cit. 5, 298.

[2] Plin. *N. H.* 12, 84; cfr. Tacit. *Ann.* 3, 53.

[3] The weight is so obtained: 100,000,000 of sesterces (HS) = 25,000,000 denarii (1 denarius = 4 sesterces) = 1,000,000 aurei (1 aureus = 25 denar.) = g. 7,000,000 of gold (1 aureus = g. 7 of gold in the time of Neron). On the equivalence 1 aureus = 25 denarius see: Plut. *Galba* 20; Dio Cass. 55, 12, 4.

[4] Sueton. *Vespas.* 16. S. Mazzarino, *Trattato di Storia Romana*, 1956, 246 corrects the cipher with 400 million HS, but this sum was hardly sufficient for cost of the army: T. Frank, *Econ. Survey* cit. 5, 4 ff.

[5] This approximate sum is calculated on a population of 50–60 million inhabitants for the whole Empire, with an average annual income of 200 denarii a year which is deduced from: the cost of maintenance of a slave, 120 denarii per year (see below p. 33, n. 1); the pay of a worker, 240 denarii (see also p. 33, n. 1); the stipend of a soldier, 225 denarii (before the increase at the time of Domitian). There were certainly the great revenues of the landlords, of the State officers, of the higher middle classes; a lower revenue was on the other hand earned by the great majority and very many people in the country and towns had a base minimum. For the population of the Empire see J. Beloch, *Bevölkerung*, 506 ff. but other scholars estimate 100 millions of inhabitants: L. Pareti, *Storia di Roma*, 5, 1960, 703. Our calculation of the total revenue of the Empire, if wrong, is on the low side.

as possible the negative effects on the balance of trade of the importations of luxury products. These importations, however, declined very much in the third century and did not regain strength until the fourth.[1]

I do not believe that an outflow of gold could have caused by itself the fall of the Roman Empire. Such a mercantilistic view could hardly resist criticism nowadays. Moreover, it seems clear that the outflow of gold did not assume dramatic proportions.

For the Late Empire we do not possess any exact data. It is not even possible to figure out indirectly the quantity of gold which at that time flowed from the Roman area to pay for the imports. Trade with the Orient was still a trade in luxuries, practised mainly by oriental merchants, Syrians and Jews. Considering the relatively small circles for which it was destined, the whole quantity could not even then have cut perceptibly into the economy in general, the more so as at the very close of the fourth century gold was circulating in an abundance to which hardly anything equal can be found in previous centuries (see below p. 78, n. 5). This shows that the so-called drainage resulting from the oriental trade was in no way ruinous.

3. THE UNEXPECTED FALL OF THE EMPIRE IN THE FIRST HALF OF THE FIFTH CENTURY AFTER A PERIOD OF ECONOMIC EXPANSION

The breakdown of the Empire occurs in the first half of the fifth century, but one gets there all of a sudden, so to speak. There were, it is true, in the fourth century, invasions of barbarians (threatening were those of the Alemans in Gaul, who were later repelled by Julian in the victorious battle of Strasbourg in 357, and likewise those of the Goths, who after the defeat of the Emperor Valens at Hadrianople in 378 spread over the Balkan Peninsula, but settled down there as allies of the Empire). There were also internal struggles for the succession (among the sons of Constantine) or wars

[1] See H. Seyrig, *Syria*, 22 (1941), 233–70; cf. J. S. de Laet, *Portorium*, cit. 306; J. Schwartz, *L'Empire Romain et le commerce oriental*, cit. 43. On the export of products favoured in some cases by the Roman Government in East see R. E. Mortimer Wheeler, op. cit., 137 ff.; E. Lepore, *La parola del passato*, 10 (1955), 148, 150.

against usurpers (especially bad were the revolts both of Mag-
nentius, which, about the middle of the century, involved Gaul,
Britain, Spain and Africa and of the *princips maurus* Firmus around
372–4).[1] Yet similar or even graver revolts had not been lacking in the
past either, especially in the third century. It is difficult to agree with
Professor Piganiol when, attributing the fall of the Empire to revolts
and invasions, he concludes with the famous sentence: 'La civilisation
romaine n'est pas morte de sa belle mort. Elle a été assassinée.'[2] The
barbarians, it is true, did 'finish' the Western Empire, but the
Empire did not react, at that time, as it reacted in the preceding
centuries. In the fourth century, after the restoration of the State's
authority brought about by the Illyrian Emperors, we still see
Emperors who have the State firmly under control, courageously
take initiatives, issue laws, and co-ordinate public life. In 363 Julian's
Roman armies battled against the Parthians under the walls of
Ctesiphon near the Persian Gulf, in a region they had rarely reached
before. Towards the close of the century, under the reign of
Theodosius, the last Emperor to rule the entire territory of the
Empire, the State still constituted an immense political unit, still
encompassing all the old provinces with the exception only of the
Agri Decumates between the Rhine and the Danube, and of Dacia,
today's Romania. These had been lost or rather abandoned already
in the second half of the third century. Cultural life, although with
new orientations, was alive in every domain: in literature, the arts,
where an attempt at renovation is noticeable, in philosophy, where
the spreading of Christianity acted as a new ferment. Instruction
was extended to classes of the population that had been excluded
before.[3] At that time Ammianus wrote that 'as long as there are

[1] For the fourth century see general works: O. Seeck, *Geschichte des Untergangs der antiken Welt*, 6 vol. cit.; J. B. Bury, *History of the later Roman Empire*,
vol. 2, 1923; E. Stein, *Geschichte des spätrömischen Reiches*, 1928, trad. franç,
1959; A. Solari, *L'impero Romano*, vols. 4 and 5, 1947; A. Piganiol, *L'Empire
Chrétien*, cit.; F. Lot, *La fin du monde antique et le début du moyen âge*[2], 1951;
S. Mazzarino, *Trattato di Storia Romana* cit. 421 ff.
[2] A. Piganiol, *L'Empire Chrétien*, cit. 422. See also N. B. Baynes, 'The decline
of the Roman Power in Western Europe', in *Journ. Roman Studies*, 33 (1943),
29 ff.
[3] H. I. Marrou, *Histoire de l'Éducation dans l'Antiquité*[4], 1958, 410 ff.; and *Saint
Augustin et la Fin de la Culture Antique*, 1938, 105 ff.; cf. A. Piganiol, *L'Empire*

men Rome will be victorious and will increase with lofty growth'.
And yet only a few years later the catastrophe, unexpectedly, came –
a dramatic, irreparable catastrophe. Indeed, in 410, Alaric, leading
a host of Goths who were overrunning Italy from the Balkans,
reached and sacked Rome. In the course of a few years other
massive eruptions occurred: Burgundians, Alans, Visigoths, Suevians,
Vandals penetrated into the western provinces of the Empire. The
Burgundians occupied the eastern part of Gaul, while the Visigoths
founded a kingdom in its south-west in 416–18. The Vandals after
traversing Spain established in 429 their rule over Africa. Around
the middle of the century comes the onset of the Huns, who
wreck the whole edifice of the State, preparing in the West the
advent of the barbaro-Roman kings, in the East the definitive
separation of the Byzantine Empire. In 455 the Vandals under
Genseric sacked Rome again and even more savagely. The official
date of the end of the Empire is fixed at a few years later when
Odoacer, the barbarian king of the Heruli, after dethroning the last
emperor, yielded the imperial *insignia* to Constantinople, keeping
for himself those of the patriciate.[1]

Thus the fall of an immense State that had lasted a thousand years
was completed in the course of not much more than half a century.
What is then the economic reality of the Empire in the period that
precedes and follows its dramatic collapse? An economic decline
doubtless took place in the third century, when the State, as will be
seen later, was for political and military reasons on the verge of ruin.
It took place likewise in the fifth century, when a general disorder
that nearly brought about the gradual disintegration of the structure
of the State – attacked by barbarians from all sides – had interrupted the routes of communication, made transportation difficult,
caused crises in the cities and shrunk the markets. Although some
works have thrown light upon the various positive aspects of the

Chrétien, cit. 385–401; Guyer,' Untergang der Antike?', in *Museum Helve-
ticum*, 8 (1951), 271–8. On the opposition of the aristocratic culture towards
the new *élites* see M. Pavan, *La crisi della scuola nel IV sec. d. C.*, 1952. The
work of K. Pfister, *Der Untergang der antiken Welt*, 1940, is constructed on the
prejudice of corruption in the upper classes.

[1] For the fifth century see general works cit. above p. 24, n. 1; see also E.
Demougeot, *De l'unité à la division de l'Empire Romain*, 1951, 395–410.

epoch,[1] the majority see also in the fourth century a period in which continues – with some interruptions or indications of recovery – the economic crisis that had caught the Empire towards the end of the second century, immediately after the great prosperity it enjoyed in the Age of the Antonines. Still recently in two important studies on the Late Empire, undertaken from an economic angle, F. W. Wallbank and A. E. R. Boak have maintained that the progressive, inexorable decadence of the Roman economy was the prerequisite for the collapse of the Empire.[2]

However, on close examination it appears that this negative judgement was the product of two circumstances:

(1) The fourth century is inserted between two dramatic periods in the history of the Roman world – one dominated by a very grave crisis in every field, the other by the complete disintegration of the State.

(2) The influence of the religious polemic and of the Christian sources, favoured a negative interpretation of the economic reality of the period.

The first factor has caused historical critics to concentrate their attention more on the negative than on the positive aspects of the economic reality of the fourth century. As a result they make the three centuries from the third to the fifth appear as one long phase of economic decline. The other factor has made it extremely difficult to apprehend the social and economic reality of the time, because of the polemic distortions with which the facts were interpreted and presented. To illustrate this point it will suffice to

[1] On the continuity of the Roman economy to the fall of the empire see the fundamental work of G. Mickwitz, *Geld und Wirtschaft im römisch. Reiche des IV. Jahrhunderts n. C.*, 1932. For a favourable opinion on the economy of the fourth century see A. Piganiol, *L'Empire Chrétien*, cit.; S. Mazzarino, *Aspetti Sociali del IV secolo*, cit.; E. Demougeot, *De l'unité à la division de l'Empire Romain*, cit. 58 ff. See also L. Ruggini, *Economia e società nell'Italia Annonaria. I rapporti fra agricoltura e commercio dal IV al VI sec.*, 1961; my article 'Tendenze di fondo nell'economia del tardo Impero Romano', in *Studia Ghisleriana*, Ser. I, vol. III, 1962, 257–321.

[2] F. W. Wallbank, op. cit.; A. E. R. Boak, op. cit. See also S. I. Kovaliov, *Storia di Roma* (trad. ital.) 1953, 2, 249 ff.

cite the significant episode of the petition submitted, in 383, by Symmachus to the Emperor Valentinian II, to restore the Altar of Victory in Rome. According to the famous senator, only in this way would it be possible to ward off a recurrence of the famine that had hit the whole Empire in his time and ought to be interpreted as a vengenance on the part of the gods; for they had been angered by the impiety of the Emperor Gratian, who before his death had imposed limitations on pagan cults.[1] Saint Ambrose, rejecting the generalizations of Symmachus, maintained instead that not only had Gaul, Pannonia and Rhaetia harvested such abundant crops that the barbarians were induced to invade these provinces to lay their hands on this blessing of the Lord, but that also in Liguria and Venezia the crops, though they came late, were copious. As to the revenge of the offended gods, the Saint added maliciously, the very abundant crops of the following year showed how fast they had become reconciled.[2] This episode occurred in 383. The end of the fourth century is near; only a few years later the Empire was to be gripped by a political crisis defying remedy. If we did not have the counterstatement of Saint Ambrose one would be tempted to accept Symmachus' statement and generalize it for the whole Empire. This shows how much caution is necessary in using the sources of either party. In this case we have the Christian source to correct the distortions of the pagan one. But how many distortions occur also, for polemic reasons, in the Christian authors, for instance in Lactantius, Salvianus and even in Saint Ambrose himself. This, of course, does not mean that the information – particularly the incidental information – supplied by such partisan authors, cannot be put to good use. Moreover, the data offered by them are of special value when they come from men rich in experience, who like Saint Ambrose had participated in the active life of their time before they joined the clergy. However, the most informative texts are doubtless the pagan ones – collections of biographies and letters, panegyrics, manuals of agronomy, of military art, geographical studies, legislative compilations, such as the *Codex Theodosianus*, and historical writings such as those of Ammianus Marcellinus, whose work often reflects

[1] Symmachus, *Relat.* 3, 15–17.
[2] Ambros. *Epist.* 18, 17–21. On this episode see J. R. Palanque, 'Famine à Rome à la fin du IVe siècle', in *Rev. Et. Anc.* 33 (1931), 346 ff.

his personal experience as a high officer on the staff of the Emperor Julian and is marked by great objectivity and by his wide vision of the whole life of the Empire.[1]

If the data furnished by the historical and documentary sources are examined critically, with a mind unencumbered by inveterate prejudices, the overall impression for the fourth century is that of a prosperous and developing economy. At the base of the monetary system was a firm coin, the gold *solidus* (4·55 gr.) the introduction of which by Constantine had put an end to the monetary confusion of the third century. Trade was active, communications well organized, travelling and pleasure trips in vogue. The spreading of more rational production techniques and the cultivation of new lands – due partly to the new labour forces, brought into the Empire with the organized settlement of barbarians – had in many regions increased rural income. The State's factories integrated the activities of the craftsmen, that would have been inadequate to satisfy the sustained demand for goods, a demand the welfare policy of the Emperor of the time strongly stimulated. The cities were again peopled. There are no objective proofs of a demographic decline as most scholars have maintained. Building activites were vigorous, city life everywhere again expanded, public instruction was developing, new social classes were emerging from the lower strata. The capacity, appearing in the whole Empire, to produce returns, is well summarized in the *Expositio Totius Mundi*, a survey of the economic activities, compiled around the middle of the fourth century. It is implied in the preamble to Diocletian's edict on prices, in 301, and in the long list of goods and manufactured products of widespread consumption that the edict itself enumerates. Their variety attests advanced luxury and refined levels of living.[2]

[1]W. Ensslin, 'Zur Geschichtschreibung und Weltanschaung des Amm. Marcellinus', in *Klio* Beiheft 17, 1923, 1–9; M. L. V. Laistner, *The Great Roman Historians*, 1947, 141–61; E. A. Thompson, *The historical work of Ammianus Marcellinus*, 1947. For a critical list of the sources on the Late Empire see A. Piganiol, *L'Empire Chrétien*, cit. introd.

[2] For the economic trend of the fourth century see the work cited above p. 26, n. 1. Against the prejudice of the general decay of south Italy in the imperial age, see the recent work of U. Kahrstedt, 'Die wirtschaftliche Lage Grossgriechenlands in der Kaiserzeit', in *Historia*, Einzelschrift 4, 1960.

Economic disaster had shaken the Roman world during the third century. Yet just when this crisis had reached its peak, the Empire – thanks to the measures vigorously carried out by the Emperors of the Illyrian dynasty – had once more succeeded in recovering and a new similar phase of economic expansion took place showing the continued vitality of economic forces.

4. THE ANTECEDENTS: THE GOLDEN AGE OF THE ANTONINES

Now the question arises why the Roman State, which successfully recovered after the economic decline of the third century, disintegrated hardly more than a century later.

To answer this question it is necessary to go back to the antecedents of the crisis of the third century and to outline the course of the Roman economy from the Early to the Late Empire. The antecedents have to be sought, as Gibbon already saw,[1] in the Age of the Antonines, the golden epoch of the Empire, in which mankind enjoyed one of its rare times of universal long peace and widespread well-being. The great development of urban life at that time, also, in the western part of the Empire, and especially in the Po Valley, in Gaul, in Spain and in North Africa, the improvements in transportation, with the development of an imposing network of roads[2] and the opening of the maritime routes freed from piracy, had created an integrated system with intensive trade relations over an immense area. This system stretched from the Baltic Sea to the Euphrates, from the Carpathians to the Sahara and was governed by one political-economic system. The spirit of enterprise and the vitality of the provincial middle class, a solid currency whose circulation increased through the inflow of the precious metals Trajan carried back from his victorious war against the Daci[3] – all

[1] E. Gibbon, *The History of the decline of the Roman Empire*, Preface.
[2] See M. P. Charlesworth, *Trade Routes and Commerce of the Roman Empire*, 1924; C. A. Yes, 'Land and sea transportation in imperial Italy', in *Transactions and Proceedings Amer. Philol. Assoc.* 76 (1946), 221–44; Pflaum, *Essai sur le cursus publicus sous le Haut-Empire*, 1940; J. van Osteghem, 'Le service postal de Rome', in *Etud. Class.* 27 (1959), 187 ff.
[3] J. Carcopino, 'L'or des Daces', in *Point de vue sur l'impérialisme romain*, 1934, 73–86; G. Mickwitz, *Geld und Wirtschaft*, cit. 32 ff.; G. Biraghi, 'Il problema economico del regno di Nerva', in *La Parola del passato*, 6 (1951), 257–73.

these factors contributed to stimulate economic activity. Consumption expanded, also in large sections of the lower urban classes. The backward region of the Occident experienced then what had happened already in the past in various periods in the Middle East, in Greece, in Southern Italy, and in many seaboard regions of the Mediterranean; that is to say, with the emergence of organized urban centres the traditional agrarian economy, poor and simple, rapidly developed into an economy which, although still mainly based on agriculture, was vitalized by intense commercial exchange. Expansion was also experienced by the artisan sector where in certain fields activity developed into forms of organized manufacture, although within the limits allowed by the restricted technical knowledge of the ancient world.

Throughout the first and second centuries in many regions and particularly in Italy, agriculture became more and more specialized: a phenomenon which was favoured by the development of trade and communications, particularly along the whole coastal strip of the Mediterranean, but also in peripheral zones, in the marginal parts of the Empire.

The development and opulence of life in the cities are documented by our sources and, to a great extent, by archaeological remains. Cities even in the most peripheral zone were enriched with splendid buildings, forums, temples, public squares, triumphal arches, amphitheatres, thermae and basilicas. Many of these works were financed also by members of the wealthy local bourgeoisie who aimed at transmitting in this way their own name to posterity. There were productive investments in works of irrigation, draining of swamps, aqueducts, bridges, roads, means of transportation. The network of paved roads was highly developed in Italy, Gaul and Africa. Modern times had to wait for the railways, to recover the velocity of the *cisium*, the postal vehicle of the Romans, and only with the coming of the railways have some countries like Germany and Russia known public ways comparable to what the Roman roads had been. In addition to public works the intervention of the State took place also in various other forms. To promote agriculture and meet the needs of the small landowners burdened with families, the State established a kind of rural credit granting public loans to farmers; the interest was to be used for the sustenance of poor children.[1] Furthermore, it founded and supported public schools so that education was extended to groups that before had been excluded. The state of well-being that almost every part of the Empire enjoyed at that time is well described in the following passage by Aelius Aristides, a Greek rhetor of the second century:

> The whole world seems to be in a festive mood; people have discarded their old garb, which was of iron, to give themselves in full liberty to the beauties and the joy of living. All the cities have renounced their old rivalries, or rather they are all animated by the same emulation: to present themselves as the most beautiful, the most delectable. Everywhere we see gymnasia, fountains, propylaea, temples, workshops, schools.[2]

The long period of peace and the widespread prosperity were factors that promoted the process of unification on the political, economic and social levels and created the preconditions for the issue, in 212, of the *Constitutio Antoniniana* which extended Roman citizenship to all inhabitants of the Empire.[3]

[1] *C.I.L.* 9, 1147; 11, 1455. On the *tabulae alimentariae* see H. U. Justinsky, 'Zur Interpretation der Tabula Traiana', in *Wiener Jahresh.* 35 (1943), Beibl. cc. 33–8; P. Veyne, 'La table des Ligures Baebiani et l'institution alimentaire de Trajan', in *Mel. Ecol. Franç. Rome*, 69 (1957), 81–135.
[2] Ael. Aristid. 26 k 97: cfr. M. Pavan, 'Sul significato storico dell'encomio di Roma di Elio Aristide', in *La Parola del passato*, 17 (1962), 81–96. For detailed treatments of economic conditions in the early Empire see: M. Rostovtzeff, *Social and economic history* cit. chap. 5, 6, 7, 8 with quoted bibliography: see also *passim* L. Homo, *Le Haut Empire Romain*, 1933, and *Le siècle d'or de l'Empire Romain*, 1946; *Cambr. Ancient History* vol. 10 and 11, 1936; E. Kornemann. *Weltgesch. d. Mittelmeeraumes*, 2, 1949; M. Hammond, *The Antonine Monarchy*, 1959; L. Pareti, *Storia di Roma*, 5, 1960; A. Garzetti. *L'impero da Tiberio agli Antonini*, 1960. On the cultural problems see U. Kahrstedt, *Kulturgeschichte der röm. Kaiserzeit*, 2, 1944. On the government see: A. R. Burn, *The government of the Roman Empire from Augustus to the Antonines*, 1952.
[3] *Pap. Giessem* 1, 40; Dio Cass. 77, 9, 5. The bibliography on the *Constitutio Antoniniana* is abundant: see a reasoned review in S. Mazzarino, *Trattato di Storia Romana*, cit. 397 ff.

5. ECONOMIC INVOLUTION AFTER THE AGE OF THE ANTONINES

However, behind the splendid façade hidden diseases were breeding. The economic expansion eventually came to an end. Already at the end of the second century signs of economic stagnation were becoming manifest. The complex of causes cannot easily be analysed, but it is not altogether impossible to discover what were the main depressive elements. In the past, the Roman economy had periodically received considerable impulse from outside, when great treasures looted in the wars of conquest were pumped into it. The fabulous treasures that were taken from the Hellenistic world in the last two centuries B.C.[1] recall, with certain qualifications, those which modern Europe absorbed from the New World. The inflow of these treasures gave strong impulses of an inflationistic nature to the Roman economy. The last imposing treasures brought in were those of the Daci. On that occasion a veritable stream of gold flowed from the Orient to the Occident. The greater part of these treasures was used to provide money for the state's needs. But with Hadrian, whose inspection tour through all the provinces can be taken almost as symbolizing the final balance of this expanding phase of the Roman world, the Empire put itself on a defensive plane. From now on it was to count solely on its own economic resources. On the other hand, in the Age of the Antonines, either through the influence of humanitarianism, which the Stoic philosophy preached, or because of the cessation of the wars of conquest, the sources for the recruiting of slaves dwindled and became exhausted unless replacements were brought in from abroad.[2] Slave labour had always been more convenient than free labour (work done by slaves cost half as

[1] See for instance Plut. *Lucull.* 37; Plin. *N. H.* 37, 16; Cicer. *Epist. Fam.* 5, 20. On the treasures plundered by Caesar see J. Carcopino, *César*, 1938, 923. Because of the immense treasures imported from Egypt by Augustus the rate of interest fell from twelve to four per cent and in consequence there developed an impulse to purchase land: Sueton. *Aug.* 41; Dio Cass. 50, 21. For the effects on the Roman economy see A. Piettre, *Les trois âges de l'Economie*, 1955, p. 115 with some polemic exaggeration.

[2] Columella, *De re rust.* 1, 8, 9, recommended slave breeding in order to preserve and increase the servile patrimony.

much as that of free men)[1] and always played a strategic role in the cases of economic growth of the ancient world. The Roman economy, too, had taken advantage of it in the last stages of the republic and in the Early Empire. Now the gradual vanishing of these contributors of energy at low price could not fail to have, in the long run, heavy repercussions.[2]

Some difficulties, too, arose from the excessive levels reached by total consumption. Given high levels of private consumption, which could not be lowered easily, State consumption proved to be too high. The State engaged itself in a policy of welfare which was out of proportion to available resources: generous donations to the urban plebs spurred on opposite forces. The distributions of grain had begun in the era of the Gracchi, first with the *lex Sempronia frumentaria* at a controlled price, then with the *lex Clodia* of 58 B.C. completely free. To the grain were added gradually oil, pork, wine and gifts in money.[3] The expansion of public expenditure at a time when inflows of treasures from occupied territories were dwindling added to the financial difficulties of the State. Hadrian at the peak

---

[1] The pay of a worker at the time of Cicer. *Pro Roscio Comoedo* 10, 28, was 12 as, with a total, for a year of about 320 working days, of 3840 as, that is about 240 denarii (1 denarius=16 as). Seneca, *Epist.* 80, 7, 1, testifies that a slave received monthly 5 moggi of wheat and 5 denarii. A moggio was worth about half a denarius, then the total wheat and pay for a year was 90 denarii, to which would be added about 30 denarii for wine, greens, oil delivered to the slaves in addition to the wheat, according to Cato, *De agricult.* 56, 57, 58: the total cost of a slave was just 120 denarii, half that of a free worker. That servile labour was considered more profitable than that of free workers, is proved by the decree of Caesar that the landlords should employ one-third of free labour: Suet. *Caes.* 42. On the price of wheat see: A. H. M. Jones, 'Inflation under the Roman Empire', in *Economic Hist. Review*, 5 (1953), 295 f.

[2] Slave labour in some respects can be considered for times of high prosperity the ancient world's substitute for the machine; Varron. *De re. rust.* 1, 17 calls the slave *instrumentum vocale*, an animal of labour *instrumentum semivocale* and an agricultural instrument *instrumentum mutum*. The ancient economy was not however supported simply by slavery: on the problem see objective considerations in C. G. Starr, 'An overdose of slavery', in *Journ. of Econ. History* 1958, 16 ff. On slavery in general see also W. Westermann, *The Slave Systems of Greek and Roman Antiquity*, 1955.

[3] D. Van Berchem, *Les distributions de blé et d'argent à la plèbe romaine sous l'Empire*, 1939.

of prosperity was forced to resort to tax waivers that amounted to almost one-fourth of the annual expenses of the State's budget.[1] But even before that, under Trajan, some cities had shown signs of financial difficulties, so much so that the government had to intervene by appointing commissioners (*curatores*), to control the budget.[2] The locally produced income was not high enough to yield a surplus sufficient to satisfy the needs of the State's budget. The rapid development of urban life during the second century obviously stimulated the flow of population from country to city. Already since the time of Augustus the government had tried to obviate the consequence of such migration through the distribution of land to veterans and farmers.[3] Trajan too acted with great energy in this field.[4] The drive towards the city was stimulated by the fact that after the extensive use of slaves on the large Roman estates in the last two centuries of the republic[5] agrarian labour suffered from the contempt the ancients felt for any servile activity.[6] Even after the stabilization of the urban centres the flow continued although at a slower rate.

Evidence pointing to a shortage of farm labour in the Early Empire is not lacking.[7] Thus there was, on the one hand, a decrease

[1] *C.I.L.* 6, 697. Dessau *I.L.S.* 309; Hist. Aug. *Vita Hadr.* 7, 6; Dio. Cass. 69, 8: the fiscus remitted 900 million sestertii, a fourth part of the state budget: Suet. *Vesp.* 16. Frequent remittances of *aurum coronarium*: Hist. Aug. *Vita Hadr.* 6, 5; *Vita Anton.* 4, 10; Plin *Paneg.* 55; *C.I.L.* 6, 8686.

[2] Plin. *Epist.* 10, 103: *qui inviti fiunt decuriones*. Before the conquest of Dacia Trajan sold imperial property for the needs of the budget: Plin. *Paneg.* 50, 2; 51. 1. Marcus Aurelius did the same: Hist. Aug. *Vita Aur. Phil.* 17, as did his successors.

[3] S. Riccobono J., 'La politica agraria di Augusto', in *Atti Accad. Peloritana*, 40 (1938), 24 ff.

[4] V. Sirago, *La politica agraria di Traiano*, 1958. Analogous measures were taken by Hadrian in Africa; *C.I.L.* 8, 10570; 14428; 14451; 25943; 26416 and by Perthinax who conceded the propriety after ten years, of land occupied and tilled: *C.I.L.* 6, 26416; Herodian. 2, 4, 6.

[5] Appian. *B.C.* 1, 7, 31; Cicer. *de rep.* 1, 61.

[6] Varro, *De re. rust.* 1, 16, 17; Suet. *Caes.* 41. But all paid work was held in contempt: Cicer. *De off.* 1, 150; *Pro Sestio* 106; Varro, *De re. rust.* 1, 17, 2; Ovid. *Fasti* 3, 779–83. On this subject see F. M. De Robertis, 'I lavoratori liberi nelle "familiae" aziendali romane', in *Stud. Doc. Hist. Iuris*, 24 (1958), 268 ff.

[7] Strabo, 7, 327; 8, 362; 9, 403; Plut. *De defect. orac.* S; Dio Chryost. *Or.* 33,

in productive forces in the country, on the other an increase in consumption in the city – two forces that moved in contrary directions. Here may be found also the explanation for the rising prices that can be observed in the second half of the second century.[1]

Through the crisis, one of the basic evils of the ancient economy became more and more evident, namely the concentration of wealth in the hands of a few. This phenomenon grew more marked in the period of expanding economy.[2] Investment in land responded to a

---

25 ff.; 31, 157 ff.; *Eub.* 34–40. The rural classes were not everywhere declining but labour was no longer able to produce enough to meet the increased demands of the overcrowded towns. Oil was a rarity in the third century: Hist. Aug. *Vita Sever.* 23. On the demographic problems of the Empire see, but with caution, A. Landry, 'La dépopulation dans l'antiquité gréco-romaine', in *Rev. Hist.* 77 (1936), 1 ff.: see also A. E. R. Boak, *Manpower Shortage*, cit. 1 ff. Sure proofs of a noticeable decline in the population of the Empire are lacking.

[1] The devaluation and the rise of prices did not have a precipitous course as F. M. Heichelheim thought: 'Zur Wachrungskrisis des röm. Imperium', in *Klio* 26 (1933), 105 ff. followed by G. Mickwitz, *Geld und Wirtschaft*, cit. 48 f., 56 f. and by A. Ch. Johnson, *Roman Egypt, Economic Survey of Rome.* cit. 2, 436. Against this opinion see A. Passerini, 'Sulla pretesa rivoluzione dei prezzi durante il regno di Commodo', in *Studi G. Luzzatto*, 1949, 2 ff. and Th. Pekary, 'Studien zur römisch. Währungs- und Finanzgeschichte von 161 bis 235 n. chr.', in *Historia*, 8 (1959), 443–89.

[2] The tendency of wealth to concentrate in the hands of a few can be seen also within the framework of the social structures of the ancient world, for differences in social conditions nearly always coincided with economic ones and remained at all times quite distinct. A significant piece of evidence is the difference between the pay of a high official and the pay of the legionaries. In the second century the annual pay of officials of equestrian rank ranged from a minimum of 60,000 sesterces (*sexagenari* = 15,000 denari) to a maximum of 300,000 (*tricenari* = 75,000 denarii): this is known from a number of inscriptions. The pay of the African proconsul was up to 1,000,000 sestertii (= 250,000 denarii): Dio Cass. 78, 22, 5: cf. Tac. *Agr.* 42. The pay of a legionary was then 300 denarii, that is about 833 times less than the salary of the proconsul of Africa. Such a great gap between the two salaries would be unthinkable in our age. The vast disproportion reflects the extent of the fundamental social differences existing in the ancient world, even in time of economic prosperity. All this becomes even clearer if one considers the amount of land that the highest official was able to buy after a year of office. At about the end of the first century a jugerum of cultivable land was valued at 250 denarii: Colum. *De re. r.* 3, 3, 8. Supposing that a fifth of the wage went on

profound instinct of ancient man.[1] It was an irreplaceable condition of personal prestige.[2] And the large estates, once they were established, tended to absorb those at their borders. The *cupido agros continuandi*[3] exercised an irresistible attraction on the man who was enriching himself and often found his limit only when he in *alterum divitem inciderit*.[4] His ambition was favoured by the difficulties which the small landowners encountered for various causes: indebtedness because of insufficient income in the years with adverse seasonal conditions, slump of market prices because of critical overproduction in the years of abundant crops, heavy taxation, competition, and the drive towards the city.[5] In the course of time production on the large estates tended to decline because of extensive cultures, of which since ancient times pasturage had been considered the most profitable.[6] Pasturages were most easily adapted to the administration of the *latifundia* and to slave labour.[7] The

personal and official expenses, the proconsul of Africa could buy, in one year, with 200,000 denarii, 800 jugera, that is about 200 hectares of land.

[1] According to M. Knight, *Histoire économique de l'Europe jusqu'à la fin du M. A.*, 1930, the capital engaged for loan and commercial activity of the publicans was one per cent of the capital invested in land.

[2] Plin. *N.H.* 18, 17 tells of one Rufus who once bought land for 100 million HS *ad gloriam*, that is for ostentation. Such a sum might buy 100,000 jugera of cultivated land = about 25,000 ha.: a jugerum cost, as it is said, about 1000 HS for Columell. *De re. rust.* 3. 3, 8.

[3] Liv. 34. 4. 9: cfr. Plin *Epist.* 3, 19: *pulchritudo iungendi*; Cicer. *ad Rullum* 3, 4; *de leg. agr.* 2, 21; Frontin. 44.

[4] Quintil. *Decl.* 13.

[5] Evidence of large estates is abundant: Appian. *B.C.* 1, 7; Cicero, *De off.* 2, 73; Columell. *De re. rust. praef.*; Senec. *Controv.* 5, 5; Seneca Phil. *Epist.* 90, 38–39; Plin. *N.H.* 18, 35; Plin. *Epist.* 33; 135; Hist. Aug. *Vita Aurelian.* 10, 2. On the problems of *latifundia* see: T. Frank, *Econom. Survey* cit. 1, 313 ff.; G. Tibiletti, 'Il latifondo dall'epoca graccana al principio dell'Impero', in *Relaz. X Congr. Internaz. Science Storiche*, 2, 237–292.

[6] On this problem see A. Aymard, 'Les capitalistes romains et la viticulture italienne', in *Annales Econ. Soc. Civil.* 2 (1947), 257 ff.

[7] That the slaves were in greater proportion in the pastoral estates is testified by the fact that according to a decree of Caesar the obligatory regulation of labour involving the employment of one-third of free labourers applied only to sheep farmers and not to all farmers: see above p. 33, n. 4. On the abandonment of cultivation for pasture in Italy see now C. A. Yes, 'The overgrazing of ranchlands in ancient Italy', in *Trans. Proc. Amer. Phil. Assoc.* 79 (1948),

process of the concentration of wealth resulting in the establishment of large estates was already about to extend from Italy to the provinces that had only recently been Romanized, to Gaul, Spain and Africa.[1] It gained even more strength by the fact that to the large private estates were added those of the public domain and the Emperor's *res privata* which was then already developing under an analogous form of administration.[2]

To sum up: the most relevant causes of the economic recession after the Age of the Antonines seem to have been: the end of external contributions to the national wealth; the concentration of wealth and the expansion of conspicuous waste; the crisis of agriculture; the disturbed balance between production and consumption, the latter having risen too fast in comparison with the former. Similarly it seems that public expenditure grew out of proportion because of the enlargement of the bureaucratic apparatus to which many new tasks were assigned that now rested upon the State; because of the welfare policy carried on more and more strongly; finally because of the enlargement of the cadres of the army, which was necessary, since the incursions of the barbarians became more frequent and their advance along the Rhine and Danube more and more menacing.[3]

275-309. On the general problems of ancient agriculture see W. E. Heitland, *Agricola, a study of agriculture and rustic life in the graeco-roman world from the point of view of labour*, 1921; R. Scalais, 'Les revenues que les Romains attendaient de l'agriculture', in *Musée Belge*, 31 (1927), 93 ff.

[1] See the famous statement of Plin. *N.H.* 18, 6, 35: *latifundia perdidere Italiam, iam et provincias*: on the significance see Th. Mommsen, 'Die italische Boden-theilung und die Alimentartafeln', in *Hermes*, 1884, 415 (= *Ges. Schr.* 5, 268–285). The larger estates were in the possession of the ancient local nobility or *nouveau-riches* or Italiots transferred to the provinces: L. Pareti, *Storia di Roma* cit. 5, 713.

[2] The emperor had become the greatest holder of real estates, *saltus*, *praedia*, mines which derived from conquests (the most important was Egypt), confiscations, legacies and, after the time of the convention of Constantine, of temple property. On the administration of the imperial patrimony see G. R. Monks, 'The administration of the privy purse', in *Speculum*, 32 (1957), 753 ff.

[3] On the barbarian invasions of the third and fourth centuries see now R. Latouche, *Les grandes invasions et la crise de l'Occident un Ve siècle*, 1946.

In the past the State had met public expenses with the spoils won in the wars, with the normal fiscal revenue consisting of the tributes of the provinces, the five per cent tax levied on inheritance and manumission of slaves, the one per cent or one-half per cent tax on commercial transactions, the internal and external customs, the income derived from the working of the mines, and the rents on public lands.[1] After the wars with the Daci spoils diminished. To compensate for this, the rate of taxation of the normal fiscal revenue could have been raised. Yet this measure was not taken. The tax waivers granted by Hadrian clearly indicate that a greater pressure would have been unbearable. Some parts of the fiscal revenue, for instance the levy on business transactions or the customs duties, must actually have shrunk with the stagnation at the end of the second century.

6. POLITICAL, SOCIAL, AND ECONOMIC DISORDER IN THE THIRD CENTURY

To overcome the difficulties the State proceeded to a debasement of the currency. The debasement, consisting in the gradual reduction of the fineness of the silver denarius,[2] started under Commodus and was practised to a greater extent under Septimius Severus

---

[1] On the revenue systems of Rome see: R. Cagnat, *Etude historique sur les impots indirectes chez les Romains*, 1882; J. Marquardt, *De l'organisation financière chez les Romains* (trad.) 1888; Ch. Cullen, 'The Roman revenue systems', in *Washington University Studies*, 1921, 201–242; J. S. De Laet, *Portorium* cit.; E. F. Di Renzo, *Il sistema tributario romano*, 1950; A. H. M. Jones, *Inflation under the Roman Empire* cit. 293 ff. On the origin of fiscus with relation to the *aerarium* see: A. Garzetti, '"Aerarium" e "fiscus" sotto Augusto', in *Athenaeum*, 31 (1953), 298 ff.

[2] For more than half a millennium, that is from the third century B.C. to the third century A.D., the Roman monetary system was based on the silver denarius, with its fractions *quinarius*$=\frac{1}{2}$ denarius, and sestertius$=\frac{1}{4}$ denarius becoming in fact, in imperial times, the official monetary unit (*nummus*). To have an idea of the purchasing power of such money, one should consider that, in time of normal commerce, with one denarius it was possible to buy, in the Early Empire, two moggi=l. 17.50 of corn and that the pay of a day labourer fluctuated, in Ciceronian times, round about $\frac{3}{4}$ of a denarius. The denarius, originally weighing 4.55 g., was reduced to 3.90 g. during

and Caracalla, during whose reign a new coin was struck, the *Antoninianus*, slightly above the denarius in weight, but corresponding to two denarii in value.[1] The peak was reached on the eve of Diocletian's coming into power, when the silver content was no more than 5 per cent of the weight.[2] Nevertheless, it was no ruinous debasement. In the course of eighty years the loss averaged 1 per cent a year. Commerce continued, although with a narrower scope because of the persisting economic stagnation. The latter was aggravated by the frequent military and political crises that made communication difficult. Yet there was no such general retrogressive trend towards the forms of a barter economy as the followers of the materialistic school headed by K. Bucher thought.[3]

At the beginning the debasement proved undoubtedly profitable for the state. Nevertheless, in the course of years, this expedient was abused and the century of inflation which had been thus brought about was greatly to the disadvantage of the State's finances. Prices were rising too rapidly and it became impossible to count on an immediate proportional increase in the fiscal revenue, because of the rigidity of the apparatus of tax collection. Raising the rate of taxation met with insurmountable difficulties.[4] The taxes on succession and manumission, for instance, which had been doubled by Caracalla, were very soon brought back to their former rate by his

the war with Hannibal (when the change with asses was raised from an original 10 to 16) and to 3.40 g. two centuries later, in the time of Nero; the fact that it was maintained in almost unaltered form and purity until the end of the second century, was an important factor for the stability of the Roman economy. The state also struck a gold coin, the *aureus*, originally 8 g. which was gradually reduced to 7 g.; this coin, which was equal to 25 denarii, was current exchange bullion. Copper money had only a fractional function.
[1] Dio Cass. 77, 14, 4.
[2] On the monetary system of Rome see H. Mattingly, *Roman coins from the earliest times to the fall of the Roman Empire*, 1927; S. Bolin, *State and currency in the Roman Empire to 300 A.D.*, 1958. On the inflation of the third century see also A. H. M. Jones, *Inflation*, cit. 308 ff.
[3] K. Bucher, 'Die Diocletianische Taxordnung vom Jahre 301', in *Zeitschrift für ges. Staatswissenschaft*, 50 (1894), 188–219. Against the theory of natural economy in the third and fourth centuries see G. Mickwitz, *Geld und Wirtschaft*, cit.
[4] Ostraka and papyri in Egypt testify steady taxation in spite of inflation: J. L. Wallace, *Taxation in Egypt*, 1938.

successor Macinus.[1] The earnings of the bureaucracy and the military were gradually losing their purchasing power. This created widespread uneasiness and dissatisfaction. As a remedy the government resorted to extraordinary donations and to supplements in kind.[2] The means for both were procured through extraordinary fiscal assessments as well as periodical requisitions, which gave rise to grave abuses and odious arbitrariness on the part of the bureaucracy and the army. For many public services burdensome liturgies (service in the public interest without pay) were imposed upon the well-to-do, forced labour upon the lower classes. The era of the liberal Empire came to an end; there followed rigid control of economic life by the State. The resulting conflict between the State's apparatus and the taxpayers in a short time involved also the Emperor, for he was now forced to find the legitimation and source of his power in the army, whose importance became predominant as its tasks increased in the wars against the barbarians. Thus the balance of power turned in favour of the army, for the Senate and the urban nobility were no longer able to secure, as in the Antonine Age, the continuity and incontestability of the imperial power. A steadily decreasing number of men from the old, thoroughly Romanized provinces entered the army. Their place was taken by soldiers from the new, not yet assimilated provinces and a considerable part came even from barbarian tribes.[3] Thus the army grew more heterogeneous while retaining consciousness of its indispensability in the defence of the State, which was threatened from all sides. The Emperor had to satisfy all its demands; if he refused, he was killed and replaced by others who were more flexible. Hence interminable struggles among the various divisions of the army ensued. Private citizens too were involved in the

[1] Dio Cass. 79, 12, 2.

[2] For these problems, see D. van Berchem, 'L'annone militaire sous l'Empire Romain au IIIe siècle', in *Mém. de la Soc. Nationale des Antiquaries de France*, 80 (1937), 117–202. Echoes of the State's economic difficulties are to be found in the works of Dio Cassius; see E. Gabba. 'Progetti di riforme economiche e fiscali in uno storico dell'età dei Severi', in *Studi in onore di A. Fanfani*, 1962, 5–32 (extr.).

[3] On the changes in the conscription of Roman army see G. Forni, *Il reclutamento delle legioni da Augusto a Diocleziano*, 1953.

struggles, for they were often forced to side with one or the other candidate. In the middle of the third century, in a period of fifty years, we count 37 legitimate, and twice as many illegitimate Emperors. The defeated faction were subjected to reprisals including massacres, robberies, confiscation of goods;[1] these were used to enlarge the imperial estate. Transfer from a private owner to the State, the anonymous owner, rarely proved beneficial to production. Commerce, already affected, suffered a new setback: long-range commerce was greatly hampered by the insecurity of the routes of transport. Where fighting took place agrarian production declined and the decline consequently extended to the handicraft activities in the cities; urban life was thrown into a crisis. Building also suffered from the depression: we know of no great construction in the third century between the Severi and Diocletian. Furthermore, the barbarians pressed nearer and nearer and became an ever greater menace until they finally reached the very heart of the Empire. Only a few years after the Emperor Philip celebrated with great splendour Rome's millennium, Aurelianus, in 272–3 surrounded the city with strong walls – the immediate threat to its material eternity was realized.

It was the provincial nobility that had in great part to defray the costs of such great political as well as economical disorder, the same nobility that had been favoured so much by the early Emperors. In fact, the flourishing of the Early Empire had been based on their prosperity; they had been its strong support.[2] Now they were called instead to pay heavy taxes in gold to a State that had lost confidence in its own currency.[3] It was they who were harmed by the land confiscations, which, from Septimius Severus on were executed with increasing frequency for the benefit of the imperial domain.[4] Thus a considerable part of the wealth that had been concentrated in their hands was scattered to satisfy the greed of undisciplined

[1] For an idea of what occurred in ancient world on the transit of an army in revolt see Tacit. *Histor.* 1, 64–9; 2 12–13.
[2] For the attitude of the provincial *élites* towards the Roman Empire see F. Gabra, 'Storici Greci dell'Impero Romano da Augusto ai Severi', in *Riv. Stor. Ital.* 71 (1959), 361–381.
[3] Hist. Aug. *Vita Alex. Sever.* 39; Dio Cass. 78, 14, 3–4.
[4] Hist Aug. *Vita Sever.* 12–13.

D

armies and urban plebs, whose favour the Emperors, succeeding each other in a steady rhythm, had to court.[1]

7. THE STATE BUREAUCRACY AND ECONOMIC RECOVERY IN THE FOURTH CENTURY

The old nobility was first joined and then replaced by new ruling classes, coming mostly from the army and the bureaucracy. When the Senate became their representative, the powers of the State found a new equilibrium and the Emperor a new incontestable legitimation of his authority. The time was now ripe for a general reorganization of the State; this task was accomplished by the Emperors of Illyrian origin who reigned during the last decades of the third century. The reorganization turned on two pivots, the military and the fiscal. The Army, whose cadres were enlarged and made more efficient,[2] was divided into two large sections; the one, the *limitanei*, was stationed along the borders for the normal tasks of defence, the other, the *comitatenses*, was concentrated at the place of the Emperor's residence for the defence of his power, but ready to be rushed as a strategic task force wherever the pressure of the barbarians became most violent and menacing.

After the Emperor had found reliable support in a personal army, his power at last attained stability. The development towards the type of a military monarchy thus reached its apex. Immense and dependable means were, of course, needed to keep the huge

[1] On the political and military events of the third century see A. Alföldi, 'La grande crise du IIIe siècle', in *Ant. Class.* 7 (1937), 5–18; M. Besnier, *L'Empire Romain de l'avènement des Sévères au Concile de Nicée*, 1937; W. Ensslin, 'The End of the Principate', in *Camb. Anc. Hist.* vol. 12, 352–82; G. Gigli, *La crisi dell'Impero Romano*, 1947; A. Calderini, *I Severi, La Crisi dell'Impero nel III secolo*, 1949; L. Pareti, *Storia di Roma* cit. 5, 375 ff. On the economic conditions see M. Rostovtzeff, *Social and Economic History* cit. chap. 9–11.

[2] On the reforms of the army under Diocletian see Th. Mommsen, 'Das römische Militarwesen seit Diocletian', in *Hermes*, 24 (1889), 257 ff. (=*Ges. Schrift*, 6, 206 ff.); R. Grosse, *Römische Militargeschichte*, 1920, 23 ff.; N. H. Baynes, 'Three Notes on the Reforms of Diocletian and Constantine', in *Journ. Rom. Stud.* 15 (1925), 201 ff.; H. M. D. Parker, 'The Legions of Diocletian and Constantine', in *Journ. Rom. Stud.* 23 (1935), 174 ff.; A. Passerini, 'Legio', in *Dizionario Epigrafico di Antichità Romane*, 4, 622 f.; D. van Berchem, *L'armée de Dioclétien et la réforme Constantinienne*, 1952.

military machine efficient; hence the fiscal reform to procure them. For this purpose the whole territory of the Empire was divided into parcels of equal taxable value. These were called *juga* or *capita*, according to whether the reference was to the unit of land, probably corresponding to an area necessary for the maintenance of a family, or to the amount of human labour necessary to make it bear fruit.[1] The taxes that had to be paid on each land unit, either in kind or in money or in both, were fixed by the Emperor for set periods (*indicationes*) according to the needs of the State's budget. It was the intention of the reform, which codified and regulated procedures and methods already in use in the preceding period, that the burdens should from then on be distributed more fairly among the tax-payers of the Empire by removing the arbitrariness of the unforeseen and uncontrolled requisitions.

The military and fiscal reforms were only the most conspicuous ones among the many Diocletian introduced or perfected. They concerned the currency, a new political and administrative sub-division of the Empire, the bureaucratic organization, the transport system, the economic structures, etc. The edicts issued by Dio-cletian amounted to 1200. A certain scholar speaks of an inflation of laws,[2] but the inherited situation was one of bankruptcy; everything had to be re-ordered.

Thus internal security was re-established, new confidence in the State arose, and the pressure from the barbarians was abated either immediately or within a short time, partly through receiving and settling large groups of them within the Empire.[3] All

[1] On the problems of fiscal reform in the Late Empire see A. Piganiol, *L'impôt de capitation sous le Bas-Empire*, 1916, and 'La Capitation de Dio-clétien', in *Rev. Hist.* 176 (1935), 1 ff.; A. Déléage, *La Capitation du Bas Empire*, 1945; A. H. M. Jones, 'Jugation and Capitation', in *Journ. Roman Stud.* 47 (1957), 88–95; F. Lot, *Nouvelles recherches sur l'impôt foncier et la capitation du Bas-Empire*, 1955; W. Seston, *Dioclétien et la Tetrarchie*, 1946, 261–94. For the review of different opinions, also on the denomination, see E. Stein, *Histoire du Bas-Empire*, cit. 441, n. 44.

[2] A. Piettre, *Les trois âges de l'Economie* cit. 143.

[3] After the settlements of Marcomanni organized by Marcus Aurelius in the second century: Dio. Cass. 71, 2, 4; Hist. Aug. *Vita Anton. Phil.* 22, 2, new settlements were made in the third century in large numbers in Britain, Gaul, Italy, Moesia, Thrace by Aurelian and Probus: Hist. Aug. *Vita Aurelian.* 48, 2; *Vita Prob.* 15, 2; 18; 21; Zosim. 1, 68, 3; 71, 1, 2.

these facts resulted in a general recovery of the economy and of commerce along with an increase in agrarian as well as industrial production.[1] A significant proof of the new wealth they produced is the large-scale renewal of public works subsidized with part of the yield from intense taxation.[2]

8. CONCENTRATION OF WEALTH AND INVESTMENT IN THE LAND

Income soon tended to become concentrated in the hands of a few, as had already happened in the Age of the Antonines. Indirect proofs for such development can be found for instance in the public burdens the State imposed on private citizens. In 321 Constantine imposed, for a period of three years, on the owners of large estates the transport of foodstuffs belonging to the fiscus, evidently because they alone with their means and equipment were able to bear such a

[1] See my research on the subject: 'Tendenze di fondo nell'economia del tardo impero romano', in *Studia Ghisleriana*, Ser. I, vol. 3, 1962, 257–321 cit.

[2] One thinks above all of the imposing constructions of Diocletian at Split, Rome, Nicomedia (C. E. Van Sickle, 'Diocletian and the decline of the Roman municipalities', in *Journ. Rom. Stud.* 28 [1938], 9–18), of those of Constantine at Rome and Constaninople, the new capital of the eastern part of the Empire, and then in the course of the fourth century, of those of various emperors at Milan, Trèves, Antioch, etc. Many cities in Gaul, were newly fortified with walls, new roads were built, and old ones repaired, the frontiers on the Rhine and the Danube, in Syria and Mesopotamia were strengthened. For love of popularity, there was almost a competition between the provincial governors in the construction of buildings at state expense, the works were sometimes undertaken without even waiting for the official authorization, and the State was obliged to intervene to stop new constructions being started before those being built had been completed: Cod. Th. 15, 1, 3; 15; 16; 20; 21; 27; 28; 29; 30; 31; (from 326 to 394). Under Constantine building activity in Africa was such that it was difficult to find enough architects for the undertakings: Cod. Th. 13, 4, 1 (334). On the building activity in Africa to the end of the fourth century see P. Romanelli, *Storia delle Province Romane dell'Africa*, 1959, 497 ff. The building construction in Antioch during the whole of the fourth century was impressive. Libanius *Or.* 11, 193–5 liked to think it a sign of grandeur and glory, but Theodosius protested against the building mania of the governors: Liban. *Or.* 10, 18, 23; cfr. P. Petit, *Libanius et la vie municipale à Antioche au IVᵉ siècle ap. J.C.*, 1955, 314 ff. On the intense building activity of the emperor Gratian see M. Fortina, *L'imperatore Graziano*, 1953, 139 ff.

burden.[1] Also many corporations of the Late Empire, as for instance the *navicularii*, probably originated from associations of the very rich.[2] Such associations must have known times of great prosperity, as can be seen from the practice of vast banking operations, the appearance of the draft, and the acquaintance with the procedure of endorsement.[3] Ranking first among these wealthy people were the representatives of the senatorial class, all of them great landlords.[4] They were forbidden to lend money at interest. The prohibition, which was in accordance with ancient custom, was renewed in 397[5] but was abrogated in 405, provided the rate of interest did not exceed 6 per cent.[6] Thus as far as the senators were concerned power and wealth tended to unite in the same hands. From this situation a great menace to the autonomy of the State threatened. The public functionaries too, especially those to whom the fiscal collections were assigned, amassed enormous wealth. In the legislation of the Late Empire provisions are directed continuously against the malversations of the tax collectors; but the repetition of such provisions that were as severe in form as they were inefficient in substance indicates the gravity of the evil.[7]

[1] Cod. Th. 4, 13, 1: cfr. 13, 5, 18 (390). The *navicularii* were frequently landlords in Africa: Cod. Th. 13, 5, 3 (315); 14 (371).

[2] A. Piganiol, *L'Empire Chrétien* cit. 302. The aristocrats of Rome assumed the tutelage of corporations: V. Waltzing, *Etude historique sur les corporations professionnelles des Romains*, 1895–1900, I, 425–46.

[3] E. Heichelheim, *Wirtschaftsgeschichte*, 1938, 782. On the immense fortunes amassed see Anon. *De rebus bellicis* 2, 1: *ex auri copia privatae potentium repletae domus in perniciem pauperum clariores effectae*. On the importance of the monetary reform of Constantine with the introduction of the gold solidus see S. Mazzarino, *Aspetti Sociali* cit. 114; 165 ff.

[4] The great proprietors, *potiores*, in many cases were *negotiatores*, and sold the produce of their *praedia* directly: Cod. Th. 13, 1, 5 (364); 13, 1, 10 (374). For the fifth century see: Cassiod. *Var.* 2, 26 and 28: 4, 7; 12, 23; cfr. Ambros. *De Off.* 3, 37–41.

[5] Cod. Th. 2, 33, 3. On the usury practised, however, by the senators see: Chrysost. *Homil. in Matth.* 57; Greg. Nat. *Or.* 16, 18; Ambros. *Hexaem.* 5, 10. For the usury practised by others: Ambros. *De Tobia* 36–37.

[6] Cod. Th. 2, 33, 4. On usury in the ancient world see A. Segre, 'Il mutuo e il lasso d'interesse nell'Egitto greco-romano', in *Atene e Roma*, 5 (1924), 119–38.

[7] Cod. Th. 11, 26, 1 (369); 2 (400); 13, 11, 11 (406); 8, 8, 9 (409); Nov. Val. 7, 1 (440); Nov. Major. 2, 2 (458); 6 (458). Ammian. Marcell. 27, 9, 2, tells of a proconsul of Africa who *superare hostes in vastandis provinciis festinabat*.

Wealth generally took the form of land possession. Evidence of the existence of large estates is abundant. That great *praedia* existed in Africa is attested by the representations on the mosaics found among the remains of villas of that time. Symmachus writes in his letters, in the second half of the fourth century, about his three residences in Rome; the three villas he possessed in the environs of the city, furthermore villas at Laurentum, at Tivoli, at Praeneste, others on the Bay of Naples, at Cumae, at Baiae, at Puteoli; real estate in Samnium, in Sicily and in Mauretania.[1] Olympiodorus says that in the beginning of the fifth century many Roman families obtained from their property an annual income of 4,000 pounds of gold in addition to produce amounting to one-third of this sum, that is, a total of about 5,300 pounds.[2] If we figure the returns at the rate of 4 per cent of the value of the land and assume that land had still the same value as in the Early Empire, a property of about 149,562 hectares must have corresponded to the annual 5,300 pounds of gold.[3] Moreover, one and the same family could have real estate in distant provinces. For instance, as late as the sixth century the Anici possessed wealth and influence extending from Gaul to Palestine.[4]

For the use of false weight and measures in the collection of species: Cod. Th. 11, 8, 3 (409): cf. 12, 6, 21 (386).

[1] J. A. MacGeachy, *Quintus Aurelius Symmachus*, 57 f.: for the praetura of his son, Symmachus spent 2,000 pounds of gold.

[2] Olympiod. in Migne, *P.G.* 103, 280; F. H. G. 4, 67, fr. 44; on this passage see J. Sundwall, *Weström, Studien*, 1915, 153.

[3] The approximate figure is thus arrived at: 5,300 gold pounds, at a rate of 4 per cent, correspond to the revenue on a capital of 132,500 pounds, with which it was possible to coin, in the first century, 5,962,500 *aurei* (1 *libbra* = 45 *aurei*), which could be changed for 149,062,500 denarii (1 *aureus* = 25 *denarii*). With such a sum, on the evidence of Colum. 3, 3, 8, who valued an iugerum of cultivable land at 250 denarii, one could buy 596,250 jugera, that is about 149,062 hectares. The income, in such a calculation, has been valued, for cereal cultivation, on a lower mean than that of the Early Empire, that was 6 per cent: Colum. 3, 3, 9. (Vallon. *De r.r.* 3, 2, 8 gives a still higher revenue), but then the rate of interest was 4 per cent which however rose to 6 per cent in the Late Empire (Cod. Th. 1, 38, 4 of 405) and the fact must have had as a consequence a change in the value of land: cfr. A. Segré, *Circolazione monetaria e prezzi nel mondo antico*, 1922, 95.

[4] A. Momigliano, 'Gli Anici e la storiografia latina del VI secolo', in *Rendiconti Lineci Class. Scienze Morali*, Ser. 8, vol. 11, 1956–7, 279–97. On the estates of Probes placed everywhere see Ammian. 27, 11, 1.

The great number of domestic slaves owned by some families was likewise a sign of their ample financial means. Melania enfranchised 8,000 slaves on one occasion.[1] The very wealthy were escorted by large numbers of slaves;[2] the wealthy people of Antioch owned between 1,000 and 2,000.[3] In Palladio's treatise on agriculture, written at the close of the fourth century, the recommendation is made to put to use on the estates specialized artisans, such as carpenters, smiths, brickmakers, and coopers, in order to deprive the peasant of all pretexts to move to the city.[4] The passage in itself is an indication of a new economic system developing on the large estates, namely self-sufficiency, independence of the city. Not much later the Church and the monasteries, with their immense possessions worked by tenant farmers and slaves, were to strengthen this autarchic system.[5] The manorial economy of the Middle Ages was around the corner.

Large estates were by no means an exception; this is proved by the survival of place names, ending in *-anus* in Italy, *-acus* in Gaul. They are derived from the name of the owner of the *fundus*. The territory of the villages which still bear his name corresponds frequently to the original *latifundium*.[6] Also the remains of many villas show how widely diffused large real estate was. Although maps were rarely compiled during the Late Empire, an idea of the partition of the soil in this epoch can be derived from the law of the ancient barbarians, the formulas of fiscal declarations, the mortgage tablets, and, of course, the information in the literary sources as well as the evidence furnished by toponymy and archaeology.[7]

[1] P. Allard, 'Une grande fortune romaine au Ve siècle', in *Revue de Questions Historiques*, 41 (1907), 1, 5–30 cfr. A. Piganiol, *L'Empire Chrétien*, cit. 404.
[2] Amm. Marcell. 14, 6, 17.
[3] Chrysost. *Homil.* in *Matth.* 43, 4 Clem. Alex. *Paedagogium* testify the greatest division in servile labour.
[4] Pallad. 1, 6, 7, 8.
[5] See the interminable enumeration in the *Liber Pontificalis* of the donations with which Constantine endowed the churches of Rome and Italy: *Vita Silvestri*, ed. Duchesne 1, 170 ff.
[6] M. Roblin, 'Les grands domaines de l'artistocratie gallo-romaine et la toponymic', in *Revue Anthropologique*, 1956, 139–148.
[7] On these problems see: E. Beaudoin, *Les grands domaines dans l'Empire Romain*, 1899.

As has been shown, the formation of the great *praedia* took place at the expense of the smallholdings that were ruined by the excessive fiscal burden. The desire to increase one's land more and more had become an obsession. St Ambrose stigmatizes the abuses of the rich landowners to the ruin of the modest and small ones.[1] To form an idea of the gravity of this almost irresistible tendency, it suffices to recall what happened in Antioch when the Emperor Julian arrived there in 361. He wished to meet the needs of the lower classes and to restore the group of small farmers, a wish that was constantly present in the minds of those Emperors who were most aware of the inexorable evil threatening the roots of ancient economy in periodical return. Julian therefore had 3,000 lots of land distributed: within a short time they were in the hands of the richest citizens. Julian stigmatized the episode in the Misopogon, the bitter satire he wrote against the Antiochians.[2] The event recalls the precaution taken half a millennium earlier by Tiberius Gracchus, who when proclaiming his agrarian reform announced that the lots of land assigned to the farmers were inalienable. Also the great numbers of laws Julian issued in the social and economic fields – waivers and reduction of taxes in favour of the lower classes, distribution of lands, fixing of prices for foodstuffs, abolition of fiscal privileges which the *potentiores* were enjoying, etc. – imply that this Emperor fully recognized the danger that would arise for the whole structure of the State from the formation of great properties.[3] Obviously his provisions did not find favour among the wealthy, who interpreted them as dictated by demagogic intentions.[4] The grave problem of the accumulation of wealth with all its inherent consequences was well understood too by some of the Fathers of the Church. St Basil recommended that the rich man let his

[1] Ambros. *De Nabuthae* I: *Quis opulentissimorum non exturbare contendit agellulo suo pauperem atque inopem aviti ruris eliminare finibus. . . . Hoc metu percitum humanum genus cedit iam suis terris, migrat cum parvulis pauper onustus pignore suo.*

[2] Julian. *Misop.* 370 D. See Gl. Downer, 'The economic crisis at Antioch under Julian the Apostate', in *Stud. in honour of A. C. Johnson*, 1951, 311–21.

[3] On the legislation of Julian see I. W. Ensslin, 'Kaiser Julians Gesetzgebungswerk', in *Klio*, 18 (1922), 103 ff.; R. Andreotti, 'L'opera legislativa ed amministrativa dell'imperatore Giuliano', in *Nuova Riv. Storica*, 14 (1930), 352 ff.

[4] Ammian. Marcell. 22, 14.

wealth circulate, and St Ambrose sketched the theory of the just price.[1]

There was no lack of legislative rules intended to prevent the great estates from expanding at the expense of the free peasants. A *constitutio* of unknown date gave the *consortes* (free inhabitants of a village) priority in the acquisition of local lands. Its abrogation which was sanctioned by Theodosius in 391[2] profited the most affluent who bought up holdings everywhere. The measure was taken to further the cultivation of abandoned lands, but it resulted in the enlargement of the great estates with the ensuing diffusion of the system of tenant farmers. In 368 Valens declared it illegal to renounce one's liberty in order to place oneself under the patronage of a great landlord.[3] The small landholder who had no protection against the fiscus was led to such renouncement and it was the great landlord who profited by the situation. In 372 a prohibition – in force since the Early Empire and repeated on several occasions[4] – was renewed, by which the decurions, administrators of the cities, were not allowed to lease out municipal lands on their own account; it was likewise prohibited to lease them to nonnatives.[5] The repetition of such provisions indicates that in practice they did not function for the most part because a way to elude them was always found.

The expansion of the great *praedia* could also take place at the expense of the public land every city owned. It originated either from the land that had at the very foundation of the city remained undivided for communal use or from later donations. In 319 Constantine enlarged such public patrimony with confiscated lands.[6] Around the middle of the fourth century, however, these lands were absorbed by the imperial domain. Julian restored them later to the cities to draw from them the rents that were indispensable to balance their budget.[7] But very soon the cities were again robbed of them, until in 374 and likewise in 395 their right was acknowledged to

---

[1] Ambros. *De Off.* 3, 6, 37. On the social thought of Ambrose see L. Orabona, *L'usurpatio in un passo di S. Ambrogio (De off. 1, 28) parallelo a Cicerone (Se off. 1, 7) su ius-commune e ius privatum*, in *Aevum*, 33 (1959), 495–504.
[2] Cod. Th. 3, 1, 6.   [3] Cod. Th. 11, 24, 2.
[4] Cod. Th. 7, 7, 2 (365); 10, 3, 4 (384).   [5] Cod. Th. 10, 3, 2.
[6] Cod. Th. 12, 1, 6.   [7] Ammian. Marcell. 25, 4, 15.

reserve to themselves one-third of the rent on the public lands to be used for reinforcing their surrounding walls.[1] Great changes in the allotment of municipal lands and of the relative incomes testify that they were endangered by the usurpations of the *potentiores*, both the municipal administrators and provincial governors.[2]

Since the time of the Early Empire the State had favoured all those who made unproductive lands bear fruit by granting them in the *lex Manciana*[3] the right of quasi-ownership. Hadrian's *lex de rudibus agris* extended this privilege to include lands of the crown's domain.[4] In the Late Empire the concession could also be granted for lands that had been cultivated for some time. In order to get an immediate income the Emperors were very generous in granting public lands, renouncing in fact the State's right of ownership. The short-term lease that had to be renewed every five years changed to a lease of long duration, *ius emphyteuticum*, for the lands which the leaseholder pledged himself to ameliorate. Thus a form of *ius privatum ac perpetuum* gained ground, a hereditary contract without termination, with immutable rent, even without an obligation to carry out ameliorations. It is easy to understand that this right too, which was sanctioned by a *constitutio* of Theodosius in 386.[5] furthered the development of large estates, for it was precisely the great *conductores* who in the end benefited the most from it; they succeeded somehow in finding their way into the holdings of the small farmers, who had no protection against the fiscus.[6]

A contributing factor was the generosity of some Emperors, particularly of Constantine who distributed public goods among

[1] Cod. Th. 4, 13, 7; 15, 1, 32.

[2] In the Early Empire it was forbidden to lease municipal land by long term. In the Later Empire perpetual lease of which the *decuriones* were the contractors was usual and resulted in grave abuses: Cod. Th. 7, 7, 2 (365); 10, 3, 4 (384); see above p. 49, n. 4.

[3] *C.I.L.* 8, 25902; 25943. On the *lex Manciana* see J. Toutain, 'Culturae Manciange', in *Mél. Martroye*, 1940, 93–100; Ch. Saumagne, *Tablettes Albertini*, 1952, 136–42: cfr. G. Tibiletti, *Lex*, in *Diz. Epigr.* 4, 1957, 768 f.

[4] See above p. 34, n. 4 the same measures taken by Perthinax at the end of the second century.

[5] Cod. Th. 5, 13, 30: *sibi habeat suis relinquat.*

[6] On these problems: L. Mitteis, *Abhandl. der Sacch. Ges. der Wiss. Phil. Hist. Kl.* 20, 4, 1901, 50–66; E. Kornemann, *R. E.* Suppl. 4, c. 266 ff.; cfr. E. Stein, *Histoire du Bas-Empire* cit. p. 278.

his favourites. The largess of the distributions was lamented by contemporaries.[1] The distribution of *beneficia* was only one of the duties of the *comes sacrarum largitionum*, the superintendent of the imperial fiscus.[2]

Another force that worked in the long run in the same direction was the institution of the *épibolé* or *adiectio*. It consisted in assigning to the local landowner other lands of little value – either not cultivated or abandoned by fugitive peasants – with the obligation to cultivate, and to pay taxes on them. The institution, already in use in ancient Egypt, found wide application in the late Empire.[3] Since it concerned mostly uncultivated lands ample equipment was needed to make them productive. Such equipment was at the disposal of the great landlords alone. Hence the *épibolé* was one more cause of ruin for the smallholdings.[4] In any case even the great landlords must have suffered damage from it when the fiscal collections hit everyone and everywhere; but after a time when ways were found – as will be shown later – to evade the fiscus, the *épibolé* to them became a new means to aggrandize further their *praedia*, from which they obtained ample gains thanks to the easy sale of their products in the densely populated cities.[5]

The *épibolé* was also applied with regard to the tenant farmers on the lands of the State and of the Emperor's private domain, which had enormously increased through the indiscriminate confiscations of the third century. The farmers who were there at the time of the confiscation continued for a while to cultivate them, but later were not able to sustain the oppression of the fiscus, and then, little by little, the big leaseholders moved in. In this connection the famous

[1] Julian. *Caesares* 336 B.; Ammian. Marcell. 16, 8: *proximorum fauces aperuit primus omnium Constantinus*: cfr. 22, 4, 4; 30, 4, 2; Zosim. 2, 38. The liberality takes place at the expense of the crownlands with which was now united the *res privata*; on the abuses of the administration see G. R. Monks, *The administration of the privy purse*, cit. 753 ff. On the usurpations of crownlands see Cod. Th. 5, 15, 19 (365).

[2] *Not. Dignit. Occ.* 12, 32.

[3] See O. Seeck, *R.E.* s.v. '*épibolé*'; M. Rostovtzeff, *Studien zur Gesch. des roem. Kolonates*, 1910, 368–99.

[4] Cod. Th. 11, 24, 1 (360) fixed that the peasants formed a *consortium* and were responsible for fugitives: 13, 10, 7 (371) established that the *capitatio* of fugitives shall be paid for by what remained.

[5] M. Rostovtzeff, op. cit.

constitutio issued by Constantine in 332 was of capital importance: it further developed previous norms about the inseparability of the rural labourers from the land to which they were assigned and created the juridical basis for mediaeval serfdom.[1]

Thus a great number of circumstances contributed to the gigantic growth of large private property. Each war could become a new opportunity to augment the private fortunes of the *potentiores*.[2] This explains in part why the barbarians were sometimes greeted as liberators from the invasions of the rich.[3] The huge estates of the Middle Ages did not spring up all of a sudden; the antecedents are to be sought far back. Already in the Late Empire complex and powerful forces were working in that direction.[4]

9. VAST INCREASE IN PUBLIC EXPENDITURE

Meanwhile, the expenditure of the State increased more and more. The bureaucratic apparatus, required by the application of Diocletian's fiscal reforms, was enormous. Lactantius states that the beneficiaries of the public expenditure, officials and soldiers, had become more numerous than the taxpayers.[5] The statement is certainly paradoxical, but it indicates an alarming reality. The bureaucracy of the court too had enlarged its apparatus because of the establishment of the tetrarchy with the ensuing multiplication of imperial residences. The number of provinces had doubled. Libanius mentions a *praefectus praetorio* who seems to have decided to let nobody practice a free occupation thereafter, so numerous were the appointments he made to posts in the various offices, which seemed to descend with the density of snowflakes.[6] The red tape of the Late Empire is likewise criticized at some points of the *Historia Augusta*. The policy of

[1] Cod. Th. 5, 17, 1.

[2] Ammian. Marcell. 18, 1, 1: *hi quorum patrimonia publicae clades augebant*.

[3] Themist. *Or.* 8, 115 C.

[4] F. Lot, *La fin du monde antique* cit. 62; J. Brissaud, *Le régime de la terre dans la société étatiste du Bas-Empire*, 1927, 127–50.

[5] Lactant. *De mort. pers.* 7, 2. Approximate figures on the State budget at the time of Diocletian see Costa, '*Diocleziano*', in *Diz. Epigr.* 1862.

[6] Cfr. J. Bury, *History of the later Roman Empire*, 1923, I, 33 n. 1, who from figures inferred by Cod. Th. 1, 12, 6 (398); 6, 30, 15 (399) affirms that the number of civil servants in the Prefectures of the East and of Illyricum cannot have been much less than 10,000. A calculation of the offices of the provincial

public welfare, of largess and of the splendour of the court also required the availability of large funds. The distributions, either free or at a reduced price,[1] which had once been restricted to the Roman plebs, were extended to the inhabitants of the other imperial residences,[2] and there too splendid buildings and monuments were erected in competition with Rome. In addition the transportation service performed by the State caused a higher expenditure. Each year almost a quarter of the horses had to be replaced.[3] The consumption was due to the officials, who were always moving about, and after peace with the Church was made, also to the bishops who attended the various councils.[4]

The greatest expenditure, however, was due to the army, whose cadres had been almost doubled by Diocletian's reorganizations; there were now approximately half a million men.[5] The army's place of operations was almost always in Northern Europe, along the line of the Rhine and Danube, hence deep in the hinterland. Communications required great expenditure for transportation and services. Frontier incidents, though not grave, were frequent, the consumption of the cadres never stopping. It must be added that the chances of war spoils had become almost zero because of the econ-

Governors in Illyricum for the dioceses and provinces of the Orient and Illyricum as enumerated in *Not. Dignit.* would give about 8,000, to which we must add probably more than 1,000 for the offices of the Prefect. The pay was indeed individually lower than in the Early Empire, as is the opinion of A. H. M. Jones, *Inflation under the Roman Empire* cit. 305 ff., but the expense was on the whole greater owing to a tremendous increase in numbers.

[1] Valentinian fixed in 365 that wine was to be sold for a quarter less than the current price, a law which incited the opposition of the possessores: Cod. Th. 11, 2, 2. Ammian. Marcell. 27, 3, 4. On the provisions of the fourth century see now A. Chastagnol, *La préfecture urbaine à Rome sous le Bas-Empire*, 1960, 296–334.

[2] For Constantinople see Cod. Th. 14, 16, 2 (416); Socrat. 2, 13; *Chron. Pasch.* 531 B. The so called *panis aedium*, that is the right of the builders or proprietors of buildings in Constantinople to receive free distributions of bread, was in 369 still in force in Rome: Cod. Th. 14, 17, 5.

[3] Cod. Th. 8, 5, 34 (377).

[4] Julian tried to restrict the *evectiones*, that is the permissions of free passage: Cod. Th. 8, 5, 12; 5, 14 (362).

[5] R. Grosse, *Röm. Militärgesch.* cit. 253; A. Piganiol, *L'Empire Chrétien*, cit. 331. On the higher expense than in the Early Empire see A. Segré, 'Annona civica' and 'Annona militaris', in *Byzantion*, 16 (1942–3), 433.

omic backwardness of the barbarians. On the contrary, appeasement of some tribe was often paid for in gold; such a measure evidently cost the treasury less than a victory in battle.

The means to sustain such great expenditure were furnished mainly by the tax on landed property and the rent on the lands of the immense imperial domain and, in the second place, by the other fiscal revenues: the exploitation of the mines, the contribution of the State's factories that had greatly developed in the fourth century and integrated the production of private manufacturing.[1] The internal customs dues, on the other hand, had disappeared because of the uniformity that had developed within the Empire in all spheres of life.[2] After Diocletian's fiscal reform it was thus primarily the land that was called on to defray the costs of the State's imposing apparatus. The taxes, as has been stated, were not fixed but regulated according to the needs of the State. The higher the expenses grew the more onerous became the tax collections. At the time the reform was introduced, the burden could not have been intolerable. The picture Lactantius gives of the first application is certainly dramatic,[3] but it is well known that any fiscal innovation, even the most equitable one, strikes against some psychological resistance which may be inflexible. The burden of taxation was in any case bearable for the great landlords; but it must have been unbearable for the small landholders, mainly because they had no way of defending themselves as the great landlords had[4] against the abuses

[1] On the Government factories see A. Persson, *Staat und Manifaktur im röm. Reiche*, 1923. On the cloth industry see now A. H. M. Jones, 'The cloth industry under the Roman Empire', in *Econ. Hist. Rev.* 13 (1960), 187 ff.
[2] J. S. de Laet, *Portorium* cit. 455 ff.
[3] Lactant. *De mort. pers.* 7, 2. More objective Aurel. Vict. *Caes.* 39, 32 who affirms that at the beginning, the taxes were bearable. Aurelius Vict. was writing towards the middle of the fourth century, more than half a century after the introduction of the reform: to one paying higher taxes, the taxes of a half century earlier must naturally have seemed low, not to mention the rise in revenue in the meantime. The contributor relates taxes and income with difficulty when both are rising at the same rate: he worries more about the increase of the former, hence his complaints.
[4] On the abuses and arbitrary acts of tax collectors see: S. Mazzarino, *Aspetti sociali del IV secolo* cit., 137 ff.; A. H. M. Jones, 'The Roman civil service', in *Journ. Rom. Studies*, 39 (1949), 50 ff. See also the article cit. above n. 113 of G. R. Monks, pp. 772 ff.

and the arbitrariness of the tax collectors. Statements about the heavy hand of the treasury are numerous.[1] An impressive confirmation is found in the decree of 392 in which the Church's right of granting asylum was abolished with regard to the debtors of the treasury.[2] The consequence of this state of affairs was, as has been said, the gradual reduction of small landed property and the expansion of the large holdings.

10. FROM TAX SYSTEM TO TAX EVASION

The fiscal pressure reached its climax around the middle of the fourth century; this is confirmed by both direct and indirect evidence. According to information which can with good reason be taken as well founded, taxation was doubled within not much more than half a century after the time of Diocletian.[3] When Julian, still a Caesar, left the territories of Gaul in 355, the tax he had imposed on the province was 7 *solidi per caput* instead of the 25 he had found there.[4] We have no reliable data on the value of a *caput*, for it varied according to the kind of soil, the quality of cultivation, and the location.[5] However, the fact that an Emperor like Julian, who was well aware of the economic reality of his time and its inherent dangers, so greatly reduced the rate of taxation, indicates that taxation had now reached a level intolerable even for the great landowners. It absorbed perhaps one-third or one-quarter of the income while in the past it had in the provinces absorbed not more than one-tenth.[6] If the little anonymous treatise *De rebus bellicis* was actually composed around the years of Julian's reign, the fiscal truce it advocates re-echoes this very situation.[7] Also the *Historia Augusta*,

[1] Ammian. Marcell. 16, 6, 6–9; 17; 27, 7, 8; 29, 1, 19; 21; 43; 30, 5, 5; 8, 8; 34, 14, 5. Zosim. 4, 3, 2; 16, 1; *Pap. Columbia* inv. 181–2 published by C. J. Kraemer and N. Lewis in *Trans. of the Amer. Philog. Ass.* 68 (1937), 357 ff.
[2] Cod. Th. 9, 45, 1.   [3] Themist. *Orat.* 8, 133.
[4] Ammian. Marcell. 16, 5, 14: on the significance of these figures see O. Seeck, 'Die Gallischen Steuern bei Ammian', in *Rhein. Museum*, 49 (1894), 630–2.
[5] F. Lot, 'De l'étendue et de la valeur du caput fiscal au Bas-Empire', in *Revue Hist. de Droit*, 4 (1925), 5 and 177; see also A. Déléage, *La capitation du Bas-Empire* cit.
[6] A. H. M. Jones, 'Over-taxation and the decline of the Roman Empire', cit. 39.
[7] On the Anon. *De rebus bellicis* see E. A. Thompson, *A Roman Reformer and Inventor, a New Text of the Treatise de rebus bellicis*, 1952; S. Mazzarino, *Aspetti Sociali* cit., 72 ff.

which notoriously reflects the interests of the great taxpayers, is probably under the influence of the same climate of fiscal alarmism. This collection of biographies of the Emperors of the second and third centuries had perhaps already been compiled in the age of Constantine, but revised in a later epoch. One catches in it an echo of the fiscal preoccupations of the time; for of the Emperors whose lives are narrated only those are shown in a favourable light who respected the interests of the great landowners.[1]

The situation was further aggravated by the legislation that enforced the cultivation of the greatest possible surface of land, because this meant for the State an increase in the quotas of the fiscal revenue. Constantine had already decreed that the public lands which nobody wanted should be placed under the care of the nearest proprietors.[2] In 337, it was sanctioned that, when good lands of the domain were sold, uncultivated lots were to be added.[3] On the basis of the already mentioned institution of *adiectio* or *épibolé*, the State imposed the taxes for abandoned lands on the local landowners, small and great, collectively.[4] But those who abandoned them were, of course, the small landowners. A *constitutio* of 371 forbade the heirs to retain only the cultivated lands of their inheritance under penalty of the confiscation of the whole.[5] This policy of full cultivation, however, did not always have a sound economic foundation. The forced investments in submarginal lands along with the heavy tax payments reduced the income of the landowners. In other cases, the taxpayers were induced to destroy the cultures in order not to exceed the limit of land beyond which a higher rate of taxation

[1] On the problems of *Historia Augusta* see A. Momigliano, 'An unsolved problem of Historical Forgery: The '*Scriptores Historiae Augustae*', in *Journal Warbury Courtauld Institutes*, 17 (1954), 22–46; see also 'Atti del colloquio patavino sulla Historia Augusta', in *Pubblicazioni dell'Ist. di Storia Antica, Univ. di Padova*, 4, 1963.

[2] Cod. Just. 11, 59, 1.   [3] Cod. Th. 11, 1, 4.

[4] Cod. Theod. 11, 24, 1 (360). This decree recalls another of half a century later fixing that in selling State property to peasants, groups of *consortes* should be preferred evidently because the State wanted a security on the group of tax which the little farmer often was not able to pay: also this fact favoured the collective ownership: Cod. Th. 5, 14, 9 (425).

[5] Cod. Th. 11, 1, 17.

would apply. The *iugatio* was especially high for ground planted with grape-vines. It was based on the number of vines; beyond a certain number the income gained was exceeded by the additive tax, and then the owners resorted to destruction. The State, that was bound to have them obtain the maximum yield, intervened in 381 by establishing the death penalty and confiscation of their possessions for those who carried out such destruction.[1]

The landowners then, not to succumb, were induced to seek help in the unfortunate association that was developing; that is to say, they made every effort to escape the fiscus or obtain exemptions and immunity through the sympathetic condescension of the high functionaries, who were themselves often owners of estates. The coincidence of interests – conspicuous instances of it are not lacking – ended with the alliance of the two parties.[2] Such evasion and immunity naturally caused an even worse fiscal burden for the others who found no way to defend themselves. Thus a new blow was dealt to the categories of the modest and small landowners. Consequently the revenue of the State shrivelled because the big men resorted to evasion or enjoyed immunity, which is legalized evasion, while the small men in many cases had nothing with which to pay, or sometimes, when they were able, placed themselves under the protection of some influential person, and not even then did they pay. Thus the State found itself financially impoverished and could no longer meet its obligations.

For this reconstructed picture of the last act of the drama of the Empire corroborating circumstances must now be shown. Constantine had already, in a *constitutio* of 313, tried to remedy a fraud perpetrated by the *honestiores* who acted in agreement with the tax

[1] Cod. Th. 13, 11, 1. Fraud was already punished in the second century: Ulpian. Dig. 50, 15, 4.
[2] Evidence of public servants who are proprietors are given by imperial rescripts which grant immunity of confirm tax to them: Cod. Th. 12, 1, 42 (354); 8, 4, 7 (361); 6, 26, 3 (382); 11, 16, 15 (382); 1, 5, 13 (400); 6, 26, 15 (401); 6, 35, 4 (421); 6, 23, 2 (423): see L. Ruggini, 'Ebrei e Orientali nell'Italia Settentrionale fra il IV e VI secolo d. Cr.', in *Stud. Doc. Hist. Iuris.* 25 (1959), 273 n. 271. After his prefecture Symmachus, *Epist.* 2, 55, censured his successor Plinianus because he, blocking up a large quantity of wheat in the granaries, foreseeing scarcity, had provoked the rise of prices favourable only to the landlords.

B

collectors, to put the burden of their taxes upon the *humiliores*.[1]
This legislative document is fundamental for the understanding of a
current that was destined to have dramatic consequences. It confirms the validity of the analogous assertion which Salvianus makes
a century later; in them lies the key to the understanding of the
paralysis which little by little laid hold of the State. Salvianus is
certainly an exponent of the social tradition of primitive Christianity, and the copious accounts he gives of the diverse classes of the
Empire's population and their behaviour at its dawn may well be
influenced by his ethical principles; but ample confirmation of his
assertions in regard to tax evasion is also found in official documents
and legislative acts of the time. His affirmations cannot be discarded.
'It is mean and blameworthy', he complains, 'that not all sustain a
burden which to bear is everyone's duty, that, on the contrary,
the tributes of the wealthy weigh on the poor and the weakest are
burdened with the taxes of the most affluent.'[2] How this could
happen is easy to imagine.

When the process of the census took place, the fiscal agents fixed
the total number of *capita* for each district and left the individual
assessments to the local authorities. These, in turn, acted in accord
with the *potentiores*. The same happened when additional taxes were
imposed and the assessment was entrusted to the most affluent of the
district: with these taxes too the lesser taxpayers were burdened.
'What a despicable crime,' exclaims Salvianus, 'two or three persons
make a decision that will be the ruin of many.'[3] When the wealthiest,
in order to provide for the fiscus the revenue it demanded, deliber-
ated on surtaxes on their estates among which the smaller holdings
were situated, they were not too much concerned to keep the
volume within limits, for, as Salvianus again confirms, 'they raise
them because they do not raise them for themselves'. If the State,
paying attention to the complaints of the taxpayers, granted tax

[1] Cod. Th. 13, 10, 1: *Quoniam tabularii civitatum per conlusionem potentiorum
sarcinam ad inferiores transferunt, ut, quisquis se gravatum probaverit, suam tantum
pristinam professionem agnoscat.*
[2] Salvian. *De Gubern. Dei* 5, 7, 28. On the work of Salvian see R. Thouvenet,
'Salvien et la ruine de l'Empire Romain', in *Mél. Ecol. Franç. Rome*, 38 (1920),
145 ff.; P. Schaefer, *Römer und Germanen bei Salvian*, 1930; P. Courcelle,
Histoire littéraire des invasions germaniques, 1948, 119 ff.
[3] Salvian. *De Gubern. Dei.* 5, 8, 33.

reliefs or abolished some fiscal units, the wealthy knew how to take the whole advantage, leaving the burden of the poor unchanged, if they did not increase it outright. 'Thus' – the speaker is still Salvianus in a famous passage – 'what else have the reliefs that were granted to some cities achieved but to give immunity to the wealthy and burden the poor even more?' In the light of these admissions the assertion that the small taxpayers were more and more reduced in number wins full validity. They were strangled, as Salvianus puts it, by the fiscus as if by the hands of brigands.[1] When the Emperor Julian, who was alert to the defects of the system and pledged to remedy them, granted reliefs, he did it, as we have seen, by reducing the rate of taxation, not, as Constantine had done in the case of the Aedui, by deducting a certain number of tax units, lest the wealthy alone should profit from the deduction.[2] The unfair procedure must have been quite common around the middle of the fifth century. Marcianus tried in vain to take vigorous measures against the tax evasions on the part of the owners of estates to the damage of the State and of the cities.[3]

Neither was there lack of legal expedients to evade taxes. One consisted in paying the taxes for property that was situated in diverse provinces in the lump in the district of one's own choosing, obviously in that district in which an obliging collector was in office. In 346 and later too, in 385, sanctions were established against the abuse.[4] In 387, however, it became codified.[5] On the other hand, behind the frequent transferring of the authorities who were supervising the tax collections was the concern to break off collusion of interests. When Julian was Caesar, he prevailed on the Emperor to have the taxes of the province Belgica Secunda collected by his trusted men instead of by the corrupt fiscal agents.[6] Later on he delegated the tax collection in general to the *decuriones*, but Valentinian still entrusted it to organs of the State.[7] In 383, other innovations in this field took place: the taxes of the *possessores*

[1] Salvian. *De Gubern. Dei*, 4, 6, 30.
[2] *Panegyr.* 5, 5, 4–5; 6, 1–5; 11, 1–4; 13, 1: see A. Grenier, 'La Gaule Romaine', in T. Frank, *An Economic Survey of Ancient Rome* cit. III, 602–6.
[3] Nov. Marcian. 2, 5 (450); 3 (451).
[4] Cod. Th. 11, 22, 1; 2.   [5] Cod. Th. 11, 22, 3.
[6] Ammian. Marcell. 16, 5, 14; 17, 3; 18, 1.
[7] Cod. Th. 12, 6, 6; 7 (365).

potentiores were to be collected by the governor of the province, those of the *minores* by the *defensor civitatis* (a magistracy which had already been established in the age of Constantine to protect the people from the iniquities of the powerful and to denounce the officials who tried to enrich themselves with acquisitions and sales) and those of *curiales* by the *decuriones*.[1] These changes show the gravity of the abuses and the collusion of the *potentiores* with the high officials to load the tax burden upon the *minores*.[2]

However, one can easily imagine that the big men succeeded in having the high officials on their side because of the identity of interests that united them. A famous case is that of the *proefectus praetorio* Petronius Probus, head of the powerful Anici, one of the most conspicuous families in the fourth, fifth and sixth centuries. He enriched himself enormously at the cost of his subjects during his administration, between 367 and 387, in Illyria, Italy and Africa and also allowed those persons who placed themselves under his protection to commit the worst robberies. Ammianus, who mentions it, says that it was easy for him to act in this manner since other officials did even worse things.[3] 'What else is the prefecture of certain men whom I am not going to name', exclaims Salvianus, 'but brigandage?'[4] 'Once the magistrates were poor', adds the author, 'but they made the republic prosperous.'[5] In the same way the author of *De rebus bellicis* treats judges and governors of provinces as merchants.[6]

The *capitatio* of farmers working on the great *praedia* was paid

[1] Cod. Th. 11, 7, 12. But from 409 the defensor was nominated by the *principales* and lost all power to control: Cod. Inst. 1, 55, 8.

[2] Frequently officials left office before having collected all the tribute in their dependant territories: a constitution of 381, prohibits the leaving of the province before having put all the finances in order: Cod. Th. 1, 10, 1. A constitution of 379 prohibits the *apparitor* of the provincial governor from excusing a public debtor his obligations to the treasury: Cod. Th. 6, 30, 4, evidently because such a prerogative was enforced arbitrarily, certainly not to the advantage of minor contributors.

[3] Ammian. Marcell. 26, 1, 6; 28, 1, 12; 30, 2, 10; 5, 10: see J. R. Palanque, *Essai sur la préfecture du Prétoire*, 1933, 109–18. The prefects of Rome owned large estates in Italy, Africa and elsewhere: A. Chastagnol, *La préfecture urbaine à Rome sous le Bas-Empire*, cit. 452.

[4] Salvian. *De Gubern. Dei*, 6, 21.   [5] Salvian. op cit. 1, 10.

[6] Anon. *De rebus bellicis*, 4.

directly by the farmers themselves; the proprietors were charged only to pay for the *juga* they managed directly and for the slaves who cultivated them. Yet from 371 on the collection of the *capitatio* of the farmers was generally entrusted to the owners themselves.[1] The measure was probably dictated by the intention to simplify the public service of tax collection, to economize in personnel, and to charge the great taxpayers with the guarantee for the revenue, which, because of the precarious conditions of the tenant farmers, was not always certain or regular. In reality, however, the great taxpayers soon found a way to evade their new obligations as well. And so the harm done to the treasury of the State increased. The owners of the great *praedia* gradually obtained *autopragia* also, the right to pay their taxes directly, bypassing the provincial or municipal fiscal agents. This practice, which was already known in the fourth century, became general in the course of the fifth, despite the attempts of the State to oppose it. Particularly vigorous were those of the Emperor Antemius in 408.[2] The *autopragia*, which was a severe attack upon the State's authority, put its finances at the mercy of the good – or not so good – intentions of the great taxpayers towards the treasury.

Along with the evasions went tax relief, exemptions, and immunities. As the official texts show, they were granted with great generosity. In 361 the senators expressed their gratitude to Constantius II, who exempted them from the *coemptio*, that is from the delivery of the products from their estates at legally fixed prices, and from other extraordinary duties.[3] In 376, when Gratianus assumed power, all tax arrears were waived in the framework of a general amnesty.[4] These were certainly generous provisions, but they were not favourable to the treasury. The *Codex Theodosianus* lists, in ch. 28 of book XI, 17 provisions for tax relief for the time between 363 and 436. A general relief was granted in 434; others followed in 445, 450 and 458.[5] In 384 the senators of Macedonia and

[1] Cod. Th. 11, 1, 14.

[2] Cod. Th. 11, 22, 4: see N. Gelzer, *Studien zur byzant. Verwaltung Aegyptens*, 1909, 89; G. Rouillard, *L'administration civile de l'Egypte Byzantine*, 2, 1928, 13 ff.

[3] S. Mazzarino, *Aspetti sociali*, cit. 55, 161.

[4] Thermist. *Or.* pp. 171, 174, 179.   [5] Nov. Valent. 13; Nov. Marcian. 2.

Thrace were exempted from the payment of the *collatio glebalis*, the surtax that weighed heavily upon their properties.[1] In 397 the taxes owed by the senators were in arrears in many provinces.[2] Other exemptions were granted in 417, again to the senators, who were all great landowners.[3] One would think that relief and exemptions were obtained because of accidental difficulties. This actually happened in some cases: the invasion of the Goths into the Danube peninsula and Italy had wrought destruction and thinned the labour force. Other cases, however, must be considered as mere pretexts.[4] It is significant that the tendency to enlarge one's *praedia* still existed and even in the frontier areas which were most exposed to barbarian incursions and which the State would have wished to reserve for the formations of the *limitanei*.[5] This proves that, with the prospect of fiscal evasion, the interest in cultivating as much ground as possible had, at end of the fourth and at beginning of the fifth century, greatly increased. The tax privileges, conceded or extorted, became so great and so numerous that in 441 Valentinian III abolished them in a lump upon the request of the very persons who were benefiting from them.[6] Evidently, the situation of the treasury had become serious. But there is reason to believe that the law remained in great part a dead letter, because a few years later, in 458, Maiorianus in a *constitutio* assailed the *potentes* who shirked their obligation to the State and fixed for each year for which the tax had been evaded a fine of twice its amount. Yet before taking this measure he too had waived all tax arrears.[7] Some years before, Marcianus had likewise abolished the tax imposed by Constantine upon the senatorial class after he too had, upon his assumption to power, waived the tax arrears.[8]

With evasions there was immunity. The surtaxes, *superindicta*, had meanwhile assumed an ever-increasing importance. The normal

[1] Cod. Th. 6, 2, 14. On the *Collatio glebalis* see O. Seeck, *R.E.* IV, 1 c. 365–7.
[2] Cod. Th. 6, 3, 4.   [3] Cod. Th. 6, 2, 24.
[4] Cod. Th. 11, 36, 32 (396) reprove the *calidae artes* with which the taxpayers evade the fiscal duties.
[5] The legislation of Honorius corrected in Africa the usurpation of the possessors in the frontier land: Cod. Th. 7, 15, 1 (409). On the usurpation of crownland which occurred after the harm done by the fiscus see Cod. Th. 5, 15, 19 (365).
[6] Nov. Valent. 10.   [7] Nov. Major. 2.
[8] Cod. Iust. 1, 39, 2; Marcell. *Chron. com. ad a.* 452, 1.

revenue had dwindled through evasions and because of the many reductions of fiscal units while the great landowners with their influence profited or bribed the fiscal agents. The state had therefore to compensate for the loss of such revenue by resorting to the *super-indicta*.[1] These, however, could not amount to much because of the many immunities that had been granted especially to the lessees of the domain and of the holdings with hereditary lease.[2] In addition the Church claimed it for its *juga* and it is well known that at that time ecclesiastical property was rapidly developing and increasing.[3]

In the course of time the principle of immunity had as corollary, sooner or later, the institution of the *patrocinium* and then of exter-ritoriality. When the small landowners did not allow themselves to be swallowed up by the big ones, they tried to place themselves under the protection of some powerful person, often a military chief, to be defended against the odious tax collectors. 'Thus', remarks Salvianus, 'the parents obtained security at the price of their sons' misery.'[4]

The first indication of the *patrocinium* appeared in 360.[5] Libanius presents in his courageous oration on the *patrocinia* an eloquent picture of how the tax collectors were received in areas which had placed themselves under the protection of a military chief.[6] From a constitution of 399, one may ascertain that to appeal to the protection of a powerful patron not to pay taxes had become a general rule.[7] The patron was wont to consider these farmers as his own men; he also usurped the right of jurisdiction and was authorized by

[1] On the frequency of *superindicta* see O. Seeck, *Geschichte des Untergangs des antiken Welt.*, cit. 6, 422.

[2] Cod. Th. 5, 15, 15 (364); 7, 7, 1 (368); 2 (365); 10, 3, 3 (380); 11, 16 1, (319); 2 (323); 5 (343); 9 (359); 12 (380); 17 (385); 20 (395).

[3] Cod. Th. 11, 1, 1 (315) but see 16, 2, 15 (360). A rescript of 412 fixed that the Church was subject to normal charge but not to extraordinary tax: Cod. Th. 16, 2, 40: see on the problem A. H. M. Jones, 'Church finance in the fifth and sixth centuries,' in *The Journal of Theological Studies*, 11 (1960), 84–94.

[4] Salvian *De Gub. Dei* 5, 8; *tuitio parentum mendicitate pignorum comparatur.*

[5] Cod. Th. 11, 24, 1. On the *patrocinium* see F. Martroye, 'Les patronages d'agriculteurs et de "vici" aux IVᵉ siècle', in *Rev. Hist. Droit Franç. et Etranger*, 7 (1928), 201–48.

[6] Liban. *Or*, 47, 13.

[7] Cod. Th. 11, 24, 4. Salvian *De Gub. Dei* 5, 38–45 describes with sombre colours the *patrocinium*.

Valentinian to punish, personally, the fugitive farmer. Things went so far in this respect that in 388 Theodosius had to intervene to forbid private prisons.[1] A *constitutio* of Honorius forbids in 415 the great landowners to give asylum to the fugitive *convicani*, the small peasants of the *vici*.[2] However, the State tried in vain to combat the new institution that encroached on some of its fundamental prerogatives. In 370 corporal punishment was decreed for the peasant who placed himself under the protection of some powerful person and for the patron a fine of 25 pounds of gold in addition to one-half of what he had received for granting the *patrocinium*.[3] A cited *constitutio* of Honorius took new repressive measures: it forbade new *patrocinia* for the future and ordered with regard to those already existing, the payment of the tax arrears owed by the protected. Yet by the same *constitutio* those protected were, along with their holdings, assigned as serfs to the patrons.[4] Evidently, the objective of the *constitutio* was primarily to recover the unpaid tax quotas; but to attain this end the State had necessarily to compensate the patrons. This was done in a dangerous act of renouncing the State's rights. The evil must have been deep-seated. In fact, the *patrocinium* spread in spite of so many peremptory prohibitions and was aggravated by that other institution, the *bucellari* (*bucella* was the name for the bread distributed), private soldiers, mostly barbarians, organized in cadres and by ranks, in the following of powerful persons. They played an important part in the military vicissitudes of the last phase of the Empire.[5]

In the patron the manorial lord of the Middle Ages is already foreshadowed. Palladio recommends that the residence of the great landowner, the *practorium*, be built on elevated terrain, with a tower as a dovecote.[6] It is the prototype of the feudal manor house. A kind of exterritoriality for the large estates already begins to gain

[1] Cod. Th. 9, 11, 1. Esmein, *Quelques renseignements sur les origines des justices privées*, in *Mél. Ec. Franç. Rome*, 6 (1886), 416: cfr. A. Piganiol, *L'Empire Chrétien*, cit. 363.

[2] Cod. Th. 11, 24, 6.   [3] Cod. Th. 11, 24, 2: see n. 102.

[4] Cod. Th. 11, 24, 6: on the interpretation see M. Gelzer, *Studien zur byzantin. Verwaltung Aegyptens*, 1909, 73–9.

[5] On the *bucellari* see R. Grosse, *Röm. Militaergeschichte* cit. 287; O. Seeck, *Geschichte des Untergangs der antiken Welt*, cit. 6, 101; 412.

[6] Pallad. 1, 6 and 16.

ground.[1] One can understand how the collection of taxes gradually lost every objective validity. The evolution of this system was at its peak when at the time of the Empire's agony Cassiodorus states that only small contributions, *exiguae illationes*, were demanded from the senatorial families, but not even these were paid.[2]

Also with regard to the personal *munera* immunity spread like a blot of oil. The *munus* was an unpaid service which the State could exact according to its needs in the fields of transportation, public works, fortifications, maintenance of roads, etc. The assets represented by these services were an important complement to the fiscal revenue. The more urgent the demands of the State became in the Late Empire, the hotter the race for exemptions for classes and professions grew. Senators obtained them, State officials, soldiers, veterans, pensioners, members of certain corporations, especially of Rome, priests, artists, artisans, physicians, teachers, etc.[3] The services were considered '*munera sordida*'. The class of the privileged grew more and more and with it the evasions.

II. CONTRACTION OF FISCAL YIELD AND GRADUAL PARALYSIS OF THE BUREAUCRACY-STATE

The effects of the exhaustions of the fiscal sources on the State's efficiency were the more severe the more inordinately large the bureaucratic apparatus and the public services had become. Moreover the situation of the public finances became increasingly precarious because of the frequent grave malversations of the officials to whom the tax collections were assigned. In this way they robbed the treasury of indispensable items of revenue.[4] The first alarming signs of heavy difficulties in the treasury had already appeared at the

[1] M. Rostovtzeff, *Studien zur Geschichte des röm. Kolonates*, cit. 377; E. Beaudoin, *Les grands domaines dans l'Empire Romain*, cit. 543 ff.

[2] Cassiod. *Var*. 2, 24. The great landlords could not be compelled to pay the tax by force within the given terms: Ammian. Narcell. 16, 5, 15; Julian. *Epist*. 73.

[3] W. Liebenam, *Städteverwaltung im röm. Keiserreiche*, 1900, 417–30; A. Piganiol, *L'Empire Chrétien*, cit. 342 ff. Cod. Th. 6, 35 catalogues a long series of privileges in favour of *palatini*.

[4] Cod. Th. 10, 1, 10 (397); 10, 1, 16 (399); 13, 11, 11 (406); 6, 29, 11 (414).

time of Julian, who, when he was proclaimed Augustus in 360, complained in a letter addressed to Constantius that during his Caesarship his troops had not received their *annuum stipendium*.[1] Earlier, in one of his speeches, he referred to the disastrous condition of the treasury, *direptum acrarium*, to persuade his soldiers not to ask for extra gratuities.[2] On the eve of the Empire's fall, when the Huns were about to invade, Salvaianus asks himself: 'Where are the riches of Rome? The imperial finances are in a state of indigence and the treasury reduced to misery.'[3]

The policy of tax relief which Julian pursued by reducing the rate of taxation, by return to the voluntary *aurum coronarium*, reduced to a minimum rate,[4] etc. may seem to be in contrast with the urgent needs of the treasury. It was, in fact, misunderstood by his contemporaries, who blamed the Emperor for not taking enough care of the State's finances.[5] But this policy, which aimed primarily at giving new strength to small property, entered on a programme of general reorganization. To the reduction of the revenue ought to correspond a return to fiscal equity and an adequate reduction of public expenses. Therefore Julian abolished exemptions[6] and firmly resisted requests for waiving arrears, from which only the wealthy benefited.[7] Accordingly, the Emperor took measures appropriate to this goal. He proceeded to mass discharges of court personnel, to reduce the number of State employees to a minimum, to reorder the postal service, abolishing it where it was of no use,[8] to further productive investments,[9] to reorganize the system of provisioning the army, applying every possible economy[10] along with the principle

[1] Ammian. Marcell. 20, 8, 8: cfr. Mamertin. *Paneg.* 3, 1.

[2] Ammian. Marcell. 23, 3, 5.   [3] Salvian. *De Gub. Dei* 6, 43.

[4] Cod. Th. 12, 13, 1 (362); Liban. *Or.* 18, 193; Ammian. Marcell. 25, 4, 15; Mamertin. *Paneg.* 3, 9, 1.

[5] Eutrop. 10, 16: *mediocrem habens aerarii curam*.

[6] Cod. Th. 11, 19, 2 (362).

[7] Ammian. Marcell. 16, 5, 15; Julian. *Epist.* 73.

[8] Ammian. Marcell. 17, 3, 4; 22, 4, 1; 10: Lisban. *Or.* 18, 130; Socrat. 3, 1; see J. Bidez, *La vie de l'Empereur Julien*, 1930, 213 ff.

[9] He constructed a large part of Constantinople: see W. Ensslin, 'Kaiser Julians Gesetzgebungswerk,' cit., in *Klio*, 18 (1923), 164: 170–72; rebuilt the roadway system: Cod. Th. 15, 3, 2 (362): many milestones with his name have been found everywhere.

[10] Ammian, Marcell. 17, 3, 4; 22, 4, 9; cfr. Cod. Th. 7, 4, 8 (362).

of highest efficiency, and to pay the soldiers punctually.[1] The sources mention a lost work of his, bearing the significant title μηχανικά.[2] The necessity of new machines and tools of war seemed very urgent during the expedition against the Barthians which required an enormous amount of ships and baggage.[3] Such innovations were dictated by his anxious desire to obtain greater efficiency at lesser cost. This can likewise be concluded from the suggestions the anonymous author of *De rebus bellicis* – probably written, as has been said, in the climate of the era of Julian – submits to the Emperor concerning the most suitable means to reduce public expenditures. He insists on the practicability of reducing the cadres of the army by shortening the duration of service but compensating this with an increase of its efficiency through recruiting young men and using appropriate machines. These, the working of which he illustrates, were: *ballistae*, catapults, vehicles armed with scythes, dismountable bridges on hoses of leather, ships driven by animal energy, etc. They could all obtain striking results without much personnel.[4] The concern did certainly not originate from any scarcity of the labour force, which in antiquity was nearly always superabundant, but from a financial computation. The State had no longer great means at its disposal and the expense had to be contained within the limits of what was available.

Julian's plans would have needed time to be successful. His premature death interrupted their realization. Yet the new spirit he had injected into the fiscal policy survived him. In fact, the attempts to keep the demands of the fiscus within tolerable limits appears frequently in the legislation of his successors, especially of Valentinian and Valens. They carried out economic measures and safeguarded the *commoda provincialium* against the vexations and abuses of the officials.[5] Theodosius went so far as to invite the taxpayers to submit to him formal accusations.[6] In the past this would have been con-

[1] W. Ensslin, 'Kaiser Julians,' cit. 125 ff. But Julian was opposed to *extraordinaria donativa* even at the expense of unpopularity among the soldiers.
[2] Lydus, *De magistr.* 1, 47.   [3] Ammian. Marcell. 23, 4.
[4] Anonym. *De rebus bellicis*, chap. 5–20: on the argument see S. Reinach, 'Un homme à projet du Bas-Empire,' in *Rev. Archéol.* 16 (1922), 205 ff.
[5] Ammian. Marcell. 27, 7, 8, 30, 9, 1; 31, 14, 2: Themist. *Or.* 8, 10, pp. 112–15; 129 C; Symm. *Or.* 2, 31; Aur. Viet. *Epit.* 46, 3; Zosim 4, 10, 4; 13, 1.
[6] Cod. Th. 9, 27, 6 (386).

sidered rebellion against the authority of the State.[1] It was the same Emperor who authorized the provincial governors to flog with lead-tipped lashes the *curiales* who had probably tried to protect their own fortunes against the fiscal burdens imposed upon them (the *aurum coronarium* had again become obligatory immediately after Julian's death[2] and was charged to them) and, who therefore, recouped their own losses at the expense of the taxpayers – that is to say of the lesser owners.[3]

To put an end to the high *adaerationes*, that is the excessive amount demanded by the officials when money was to be paid in place of goods in kind, and to equalize with this rate that for which the goods themselves could be bought at the same time on the market, Theodosius peremptorily ordered in 384 that the grain tax should be collected in kind without leaving the taxpayers the choice to redeem it in money.[4] Yet this plan, which was meant to reconcile the interests of the State with those of the taxpayers, turned out to be expensive in practice, because it required a compact corps of officials and a whole system of costly services, not to speak of the fact that the abuses of the officials were to worm their way into it with greater vigour. These very officials were later, in a *constitutio* of 424, presented as those who for greed and voracity 'tore the entrails out of the provincials'.[5]

Moreover, the fiscal truce would have been effective only if the public expenditure had been kept within the limits of Julian's programme. In fact, laudable attempts in this direction were made by Valentinian and Valens. However, less than twenty years after Julian's death, the number of imperial *notarii*, secretaries of high rank, and of *agentes in cebus*, spying informers whom he had reduced to four and seventeen respectively, again rose to hundreds and thousands respectively.[6] Furthermore, when after the death of

---

[1] Ammian Marcell. 27, 7, 5; 8; 30, 4, 2; 8, 13; cfr. Cod. Th. 1, 6, 2 (364).
[2] Cod. Th. 12, 13, 2 (364).   [3] Cod. Th. 12, 1, 117.
[4] Cod. Th. 11, 2, 4: on the interpretation see S. Mazzarino, *Aspetti sociali* cit. 141 ff. No contradiction to Cod. Th. 11, 1, 19 of the same year, which confirms payments which before were made only with gold. For the earlier substitution on the delivery of *species* with money see Cod. Th. 11, 1, 6 (354).
[5] Cod. Th. 7, 4, 35: cfr. Nov. Major 2, 2 (458). Cod. Th. 8, 8, 9 (409) name of the *discussor*, the tax recoverer, as *visceribus praedator insidens*.
[6] Liban. *Or.* 2, 58; 18, 131–42; Socrat. 3, 1.

Theodosius the Empire remained definitely divided into two parts, in the Western half the high officials obtained designations superior to their rank. The *clarissimi*, for instance, became *spectabiles*, the highest designation, and were, of course, economically also treated accordingly.[1] Besides, the wealthy aristocracy got hold of more and more high official posts, which they exploited in favour of their own interests, hence to the disadvantage of the State.[2]

12. THE EFFECT ON MILITARY EFFICIENCY AND THE DEFENCE OF A LARGE EMPIRE

Thus, while on the one hand the *potentiores* complained of the measures of the tax truce, taken in favour of the weak, on the other, the fortunes of the members of the high bureaucracy were fattened, while the treasury of the State was in a pitiable state. The funds for meeting the massive expenditure for the military machine began to fail. Already in the victorious battle of Strasbourg against the Alemanni in 357, Julian had at his disposal an army of barely 13,000 men. Nor was the army of Valens, which was defeated by the Goths at Hadrianopolis in 378, more numerous.[3] Although the cadres of the army had, as has been stated above, been augmented by Diocletian, the number of effectives no longer corresponded to them, that is to say they remained merely on paper.[4] It would be impossible to explain otherwise the continuously diminishing resistance to the bands of barbarians who were by no means irrepressible. They had at their disposal an insidious cavalry, but Roman tactics had gradually been adapted to this.[5] The military forces were losing their

[1] The provincial governors appear *spectabiles* in the West: O. Hirschfeld, *Kl. Schr.* 670 ff., but still *clarissimi* in the East; Joch, *Die byzant. Beamtentitel*, 1903, 14; cfr. E. Stein, *Histoire du Bas-Empire*, cit. 223.

[2] K. F. Stroheker, 'Die Senatoren bei Gregor von Tours,' in *Klio*, 34 (1941), 283 ff. *Der Senatorische Adel im spätantiken Gallien*, 1948; W. Ensslin, *Das neue Bild der Antike*, 2, 1942, 412–32; see also J. A. Geachy, *Q. A. Symmachus*, cit. chap. III: 'L'aristocratie dans la vie économique de l'Empire'.

[3] H. Delbrück, *Geschichte der Kriegs Kunst*, 1902, 2, 294.

[4] Veget. I, 5.

[5] Veget. I. 20: see H. Delbrück, op. cit. 270; 300 ff. According to A. Segré, 'Annona civica and annona militaris', in *Byzantion*, 16 (1942–3), 433, the effective force of the Roman army in the fifth century comprised about 200,000 soldiers.

efficiency because they were now composed of inferior soldiers –
requisitioned tenant farmers and barbarian mercenaries only.[1] In

[1] The system of recruiting the army was now very different from the old one.
It is known that in the era of the ancient republic the core of the army had been
formed by the peasant class, consisting of small and medium landowners.
From Augustus on the army had become professional and the service of very
long duration. Recruiting little by little shifted from Italy first to the oldest
Romanized provinces, then to the more peripheral. The inclusion of barbarian
elements, in the beginning gradual and limited, became little by little the
rule. But in the late Empire recruiting became increasingly difficult, not
because of scarcity of men, but because of the reluctance of the great *prosses-
sores* to hand over their own tenant farmers as recruits. This is explicitly stated
by Vegetius, *Epit. Rei Milit*, 1, 28, around the close of the fourth century; the
implicit confirmation is found in Symmachus, *Epist*. 6, 64, who showed
reluctance to hand over some tenant farmers, as he was obliged to. Enlisting
was organized in such a way that for each cluster of *iuga* or *capita* one soldier
had to be provided. For the small landowners on whom the lot fell no escape
existed. For the great proprietors, however, the burden was less grave because
they, as Vegetius testifies, l.c., found a way to hand over inferior tenant
farmers. The system could even offer new means to evade the tax. Each
recruit who was handed over implied the deduction of one fiscal unit, provided he was of local origin: Cod. Th. 7, 13, 6 (370). One can easily imagine
that the proprietor in order to obtain the deduction by all means, passed off
a farmer brought in from outside as a local man and retained his own on the
estate. Or that he handed over the farmer who had been required and replaced
him with one he had hired from another estate. The flight of farmers which
the sources occasionally mention is partly the effect of this contest among the
proprietors. In fact Cod. Th. 11, 1, 12 (365) forbids the landlords to accept
rustic serfs coming from *desertis agris* without paying the *capitatio* for the
abandoned land; 5, 17, 2 (366) establishes the fine of one gold pound for
whoever engages or conceals another's farmer; 4, 23, 1 (400) fixes rules for
disputes on the belonging of farmers to the different land tenements; 11,
24, 6 (415) prohibit the landlords from receiving the fugitive *convicani*. In
the contest the big men in the end defeated the medium and small men
because the farmers found with the former a better protection against the
agents of the government. What happened in regard to the recruits repeated
itself in regard to the horses: those handed over were the most inferior so
that the State preferred to substitute for the service in kind the payment of
the corresponding amount in money. For such buying back the highest prices
were demanded by the officials. In this matter too Julian intervened to aid
the taxpayers: Mamertin, *Paneg*. 3, 9, 1; Cod. Th. 8, 5, 16 (363) in favour of
rustica plebs. (On the high prices asked by officers see my article 'La equorum
adaeratio nel Basso Impero', in *Studia Ghisleriana*, Ser. 1, vol 2 [1954], 191 ff.).
In the *Vita Probi* in *Historia Augusta* which reflects, as has been said, the
interests of the great landed proprietors, one finds, in chap. 20, symptomatic

367 the required stature for the recruits of Italy was reduced in order to fill up the cadres.[1] 'Military service', Saint Ambrose later observed, 'is no longer common obligation but servitude; to avoid it is therefore the only concern.'[2] Hence desertions were frequent.[3] To obviate such difficulties, which were created by the callous resistance of the great taxpayers, the State made the same concession as that concerning the horses,[4] that is to say it permitted to be bought back with money the farmer who ought to be handed over. For this procedure the so-called *aurum tironicum* was introduced, which became a true and real capitation tax. In 376 a recruit was valued at 36 *solidi*, of which 30 went to the State and six to the recruit.[5] It was not a high price if compared with that current for slaves, which at that time varied from 15 to 20 *solidi*.[6] With the money received to give the farmers back, the State planned to recruit soldiers directly. Yet here the usual frauds insinuated themselves. There were even officials who kept false lists of soldiers in order to pocket the *annonae*.[7] Neither were exemptions from the obligation to deliver recruits or horses lacking, especially in favour of public functionaries.[8]

opinions on the advantages there would be if there were no longer need of soldiers, or of supplies, that all would be well, no more weapons would be manufactured, that oxen would be used for ploughing and horses for peaceful activities. It was an ideal situation longed for by a ruling class, in whose minds the state was less real than in fact it was.

[1] Cod. Th. 7, 13, 3; Veget. 1, 5. The height of the recruit was reduced to 5 feet and 7 inches=about m. 1·63.

[2] Ambros. *Exaemeron* 5, 15 cfr. Veget. 2, 5.

[3] Cod. Th. 7, 18 (363–413) with many measures against *desertores* and *occultatores*.

[4] See above p. 70, n. 1.

[5] Cod. Th. 7, 13, 7: cfr. 7, 13, 20 (410); 25 *solidi* in Cod. Th. 7, 13, 13; 14 (397). The burden of the cost of food and equipment was on the contributors. The figure of 80 *solidi* in Socrat. 4, 34, is a textual error.

[6] For a slave Cod. Iust. 6, 1, 4 (317) gives the figure of 20 *solidi*; *Pap. B.G.U.* 1, 316 (359) 18 *solidi*. The prices are still the same in the Byzantine period: Cod. Iust. 6, 43, 3 (531): cfr. G. Ostrogorsky, 'Lohne und Preise in Byzanz', in *Byzant. Zeitschrift*, 32 (1932), 300. On the price of slaves in the ancient world generally see W. Westermann, op. cit., 99 ff.

[7] Cod. Th. 7, 1, 10 (367). For *tironum comparatio* with *equorum vel frumenti coemptio* as opportunity for abuse and profit by officers, see Anon. *De rebus bellicis*, 4.

[8] Cod. Th. 6, 27, 13 (403) with advantage: of *agentes in rebus*; 6, 26, 15 (410); of *in sacris scriniis militantes*; 6, 30, 20 (413); of *palatini*; 6 , 23, 2 and 3 (423–32) of *decuriones* and *silentiarii*.

The imperial estates too were exempted to such an extent that a special provision to limit the exemptions became necessary.[1] It must be added that the division of the army into two parts, the *exercitus comitatensis* and the *exercitus limitaneus* though it had furthered political stability, had, on the other hand, weakened the defence of the frontiers. The better units were those of the *comitatenses*.[2] They were to act as task forces, ready to hasten to danger spots. Yet they were stationed mostly at the imperial residence and thus became gradually used to the amenities of city life. Their fighting spirit weakened. 'Knowing how much they cost, one felt depressed', observes an author, 'to see them fighting without any vigour.'[3] Julian, whose view was right also in this respect, paid particular attention to the divisions of the *limitanei*, reinforcing and reorganizing the frontier garrisons.

As a consequence of the system and criteria of recruiting, however, the fateful barbarization of the military cadres continued. Constantine had begun to enlist compact groups of barbarians for the army, and his example found followers. First under Gratian and then under Theodosius entire barbarian corps were stationed within the Empire, serving under the command of their chieftains. The term *foederati*, by which they were called, appears first in 406.[4] The contemporaries were well aware of the danger to the State of this situation. In reality, the barbarian formations paved the way for the advent of the Roman-barbarian kingdoms on the soil of the Empire.

After the death of Theodosius, Sinesius exhorted Arcadius to restore compulsory military service for the native inhabitants of the Empire, lest the State let itself be protected by armies composed of men who belonged to the race of slaves.[5] The exhortation was out of touch with reality but it testifies the anxiety of the times. Actually, recourse to slaves – after liberty had been bestowed on them – was already in practice in order to fill up the cadres. However, even into this kind of recruiting the frauds of the great taxpayers sometimes

[1] Cod. Th. 7, 13, 12 (397).
[2] Cod. Th. 7, 22, 8 (372) assigns recruits of low stature and bad complexion to the frontier. The *comitatenses* were better sold: Cod. Th. 7, 22, 8 (372).
[3] Ammian. Marcell. 20, 11, 5.
[4] Cod. Th. 7, 13, 16. The term *barbari* was to become synonymous with soldiers.
[5] A. Piganiol, *L'Empire Chrétien*, cit. 421.

found their way; instead of their own they handed over other people's slaves of low value, whom they had procured to this end. Accordingly a provision of 382 threatened a fine of one pound of gold to those who committed such fraud.[1] In 406, Honorius proceeded also to enlist slaves.[2] It was an extreme measure, against all tradition which based recruiting on the principle of preventive personal liberty.[3] Four years later the Goths, headed by Alaric, sacked Rome.

To sum up, in the last analysis the military problem of the Late Empire can be reduced to a financial problem. This had been the case too in the Early Empire. Then, to obviate the scarcity of means that did not allow a satisfactory treatment of the men in military service, the area of recruiting was enlarged just in time to prevent the legions being filled with the poor and desperate. For these alone were induced to enlist in order to obtain a livelihood.[4] In this way, for budgetary reasons the sword passed in the Early Empire from the hands of the Italici into those of the provincials and from them, in the late Empire, into the hands of the barbarians. Theodosius resorted to the system of heavily subsidizing barbarians to make them defenders of the Empire. After the fatal day of Hadrianopolis he concluded a peace treaty with the Goths, who were spreading over the Balkan regions, granted them high pay, and exempted them from all taxes; in return they served in autonomous military formations under their own chieftains.[5] In this way they considerably augmented the cadres of the Roman army.[6] This system must evidently have turned out to be less costly than to equip anew, and to maintain, regular troops.

The interdependence of military and financial problems became more evident in the fifth century when it assumed dramatic aspects. The barbarian groups, becoming more and more compact, settled down on the lands yielded to them at the rate of one-half or one-third, and little by little transformed themselves into working and

[1] Cod. Th. 7, 13, 11 (382).   [2] Cod. Th. 7, 13, 16.

[3] Cod. Th. 7, 13, 8 (380); see R. Grosse, *Röm. Militärgeschichte*, cit. 198–9.

[4] *Vagi et inopes* in Tacit. *Annal.* 4, 4, 2: see G. Forni, *Il reclutamento delle legioni* cit. 130.

[5] Zosim. 4, 40.

[6] How does one explain Themist., *Or.* 18, 222 A, who affirms that the Roman army was never before so great.

F

productive forces. Yet on the lands granted them the collection of
taxes ceased because the barbarians considered them incompatible
with their notion of personal liberty.[1] Even where the barbarians
after a first settlement again withdrew, the fiscal income suffered a
collapse. A *constitutio* of 445 fixed the taxes for the provinces the
Vandals had returned to the Empire at an eighth of the previous
quotas with the former contributions in kind now to be paid in
money. The total was 9,600 *solidi* for Numidia and 5,150 for
Mauretania Sitifensis instead of 77,000 and 41,000 respectively at the
time before the invasion of the Vandals.[2] On the basis of such – and
of other indirect – data one is tempted to establish for the Late
Empire the volume of revenue in the entire State,[3] Such revenue
seems to have been notably inferior to that of the Early Empire.
But in this field calculations hardly indicate anything because it is
not possible to state precisely the contributions of the rents from the
estates of the domain, which were particularly extensive in Africa,
Egypt and Cappadocia, nor for the various other taxes or goods the
State manufactured. Neither is the relation between income in
money and contributions in kind or in services known. The latter
two, as has been mentioned, from the third century on played an
important part in the total of the fiscal revenue, though it must be
taken into account that in the fourth and fifth centuries the government gradually returned to tax collection in money. In any case, a
considerable diminution is beyond any doubt.

The financial situation rapidly deteriorated when the barbarian
infiltrations of the fifth century multiplied. An imperial rescript

[1] On the *hospitalitas* see F. Lot, *Revue Belge Phil. Hist.* 7, (1928), 975–1011.
Before the violent invasions of the fifth century, pacific settlements of barbarians within the Empire, especially in Italy, had occurred in the fourth
century and even in the third: Ammin. Marcell. 28, 4, 15; 31, 9, 4; *Not.
Dignit. Occ.* 42, 56, 59. On the different conditions of the barbarians within
the Empire, *inquilini, laeti, gentiles* see A. Piganiol, *L'Empire Chrétien*, cit.
278–328.
[2] Nov. Valent. 13 pr. 3–5: cfr. E. Stein, *Histoire du Bas-Empire*, cit. 342, n.
132.
[3] See E. Stein, op. cit. 343 and n. 133: against see A. Segré, *Annona civica*
and *annona militaris'*, cit. 436 n. 87. Higher figures were given by J. Sundwall,
Weströmisch. Studien, 1915, 150 and R. Grosse, *Röm. Militärgeschichte*, cit. 208.
These calculations should be accepted with caution.

explicitly speaks of the time of the *locupletioris adhuc reipublicae*.[1]
The large tax waivers have already been mentioned. The revenue
had contracted in Gaul and Spain, where Burgundians and Visigoths
had established themselves. A considerable contraction had likewise
taken place in the Danube region, first because of the invasion of the
Goths,[2] then because of that of the Huns. To the Huns contributions
had to be paid which gradually grew in the same proportion as their
power increased.[3] To raise an army of native recruits under these
conditions became a hopeless enterprise. For each recruit 30 *solidi*
were needed, hence for a contingent of 10,000 men 300,000 *solidi*
would have been necessary. Now the two provinces Numidia and
Mauretania Sitifensis paid at the most 15,000 *solidi* per annum into
the treasury. In 440 and 443 conscriptions were levied under the title
of a contribution.[4] In 444 an ordinance imposed upon the members
of the senatorial class, to buy themselves free from the conscription,
a unique, extraordinary payment of 90, 30 or 10 *solidi* according to
the category; 30 *solidi* was estimated for each soldier.[5] In the same
year the former tax of 1 per cent on business transactions was raised
all at once to $4\frac{1}{6}$ per cent.[6] Thus the State tried to draw from the still
active commerce the necessary means which the land, of which more
and more was acquired by the great proprietors, could no longer
supply.

The poor condition of the treasury can help to explain the scheme
to institute a kind of military colonate along the frontiers of the
Empire. Such an institution can already be found in the third century
when the soldiers obtained permission to marry. By assigning them
lands for cultivation as an hereditary, inalienable property with
special privileges and tax exemptions, the attempt was made to
create a class of small landowners, hereditarily forced to military

[1] *C.I.L.* 6, 1783 l. 23.
[2] Allowances of taxes in Cod. Th. 13, 11, 2 (386); 13, 11, 13 (412); 11, 28,
7 (413); 11, 28, 12 (418); Cod. Iust. 11, 52 (393).
[3] 350 Pounds of gold from 430; 700 from 434; 2100 from 443: see Priscian.
fr. 1 and 5=F.H.G. 71, 72, 74; Theophan. A.M. 5942.
[4] Nov. Valent. 5, 4; 6, 1; 6, 2.   [5] Nov. valent. 6, 3.
[6] Nov. Valent. 15. This tax was still in force during the reign of the Osthro-
goths: Cassiod. *Var.* 2, 4; 12; 26, 4; 30, 3; 3, 25, 1; 26; 4, 19; 5, 31, 1. For the
survival into the fourth century of ancient commercial taxes on sales see
Cod. Th. 7, 20, 2 (320): cfr. 6, 26, 14 (407).

service, self-sufficient, without weighing upon the public budget.[1] Later, in the seventh century, the system found widespread application in the Byzantine Empire, where it was successful. But it was not so in the Late Empire, when after the division of the military forces into two great armies the better formations were, especially by Constantine, made part of the army of the *comitatenses*. That of the frontier, on the other hand, was reduced to a rural militia of little military value.

In view of these difficulties one can well understand that for having an army no other alternative was left but the widest possible utilization of the military formations of the barbarians. The last great battle of the Roman State, fought on the Catalonian Plains near Châlons in 451 against Attila's Huns, was won by an army consisting almost entirely of barbarians under the command of Aetius, a general of barbarian origin. The barbarians had now become the masters of the Empire. In 455 the Vandals of Genseric sacked Rome, for the second time in less than half a century. The attack had come from Africa by sea. The quiet that had reigned over the Mediterranean since the third century had led to the neglect of the fleet. The naval tradition had weakened – the awakening was grim. From then on the Mediterranean was no longer a Roman lake.[2]

13. DISINTEGRATION OF THE STATE

These negative consequences of the shrinking fiscal revenue on the efficiency of the army existed also in regard to other fundamental services of the State – provisioning of the great cities, gratuitous distributions to the urban plebs, transportation, maintenance of roads, public games, etc. Upon those who were assigned to these services and upon those who worked in the State's factories or in the mines duties were imposed that became more and more oppressive. At their cost the State tried to recover its diminishing fiscal means in

[1] H. Delbruck, *Geschichte der Kriegskunst*, cit. 2, 227–40; R. Grosse, *Röm. Militärgesch.*, cit. 65–7; O. Seeck, *s.v.* 'Riparienses Milites', in *R.E.* I[2] c. 916–18; W. Seston, *Dioclétien et la tétrarchie*, 1946, 300 ff.

[2] G. Gigli, 'La flotta e la difesa del Basso Impero', in *Memorie Accademia Lincei*, Classe Lettere 8 Ser. 1, 1948, 3–43.

order to keep its costly apparatus working; it balked their attempts to flee by imposing the obligation to stay at the job.[1]

Financial anaemia had led to the gradual paralysis of the State. Yet on the eve of its fall, in any case in the fourth century, the economic conditions viewed in general do not appear to have been in a stage of general depression. Commerce was lively (a proof of this is also the heavy increase in the rate of taxation on business transactions), the production of manufactured goods satisfactory, the cities densely populated.[2] On the large *praedia* a certain organized distribution of cultures had augmented the crops, and much new land had been made productive. The residents of Carthage were taken by surprise in the amphitheatre, when the Vandals attacked. The patricians of Cologne were sitting peacefully at a banquet, when the barbarians were already near their walls.[3] Those of Trier demanded from the Emperor circus games to assist them after the misfortunes and ruins caused by the pillaging of their city by the barbarians.[4]

The villas of the great landowners like the cities contained hippodromes and temples.[5] They were adorned with precious tapestry from Sidon and feather cushions wrapped in the most exquisite

[1] The hereditary engagement to the charges and employees fixed for the *curiales* in 313 and 325 and for the peasants in 332, was extended in 335 to the employment of transport, in 364 to bakers, 380 to soldiers, 408 to butchers, 398 to other professions: see in order: Cod. Th. 12, 1, 1; 12; 5, 17, 1; 13, 6, 2; 7, 22, 10; 14, 3, 3; 14, 4, 8; 14, 7, 1. Nov. Major. (458) forbids employees of public services to go away from their cities; Cod. Th. 14, 3, 21 (463) prohibits a baker to contract marriage outside his own corporation; see F. M. De Robertis, *Il diritto associativo romano*, 1938, 418 ff. On the problem of *dirigisme* in the late Empire, see A. Piganiol, 'L'économie dirigée dans l'Empire Romain, au IVe siècle ap. J.C.', in *Scientia*, 81 (1947), 95–100; P. Lambrecht, 'Le problème du dirigisme d'état au IVe siècle', in *Ant. Class.* 18 (1949), 109–26.
[2] R. Von Pohlmann, *Die Übervölkerung der antiken Grossstädte*, 1884; A. H. M. Jones, *Ancient Econom. History*, 1948, 14 f.; S. Mazzarino, *Aspetti Sociali* cit. 243 ff. See with reservations A. Degrassi, 'Dati demografici in iscrizioni cristiane di Roma', in *Rend. Lincei Class. Scienze Morali*, 18 (1963), 20–8.
[3] Salvian. *De Gub. Dei* 6, 77; 80; 84.   [4] Salvian. *De Gub. Dei* 6, 84.
[5] Olympiod. in Migne, *P.G.* 103, 278=F.H.G. 4, 67: see R. Paribeni, 'Le dimore dei "potentiores" nel Basso Impero', in *Röm. Mitteilung.* 1940, 131–148. M. Rostovtzeff, *Social and economic history*, cit. Plates LXII, LXXVII, LXXX. For the villas of the upper Adriatic in the sixth century see Cassiod. *Var.* 17, 22, 24.

silks: they were perfumed with clouds of incense, and gold shone everywhere, *auro ardens tota domus*.[1] The life that was lived there is well described in the works of Ausonius, Paulinus of Pella, Sidonius Apollinaris and Salvianus.[2] In a world pictured as disturbed and agitated the *potentiores* moved in relative security, at least as far as can be concluded from collections of letters and from biographical documents in the period between Symmachus and Cassiodorus.[3]

The effect of the barbarian migrations has certainly been exaggerated by the authors of the fifth century, particularly by the Christian writers. Living with this nightmare and under the menace of the barbarians, they thought to see in them the harbingers of the end of the world as an atonement for the sins of the Empire. Actually, the political organization broke down, but not the framework of rural life, the forms of property and the methods of exploitation.[4] Even in the political disorder the economy was able to recover when the causes of disorder ceased.[5] The *possessores* lastly found a way to come

[1] Zeno, 1, 9. The villa of Probus was considered one of the marvels of Italy: Paulinus *Vita Ambrosii* 25: cf. Secundini Manichaei *Epist. ad Augustinum*, Migne, *P.L.* 4, 42, 574.

[2] For social life see: G. Dill, *Roman Society in the last century of the Western Empire*, 1899; see also P. Charanis, 'On the social structure of the later Roman Empire', in *Byzantion*, 17 (1944-5), 38-57. On Sidon. Apoll. see C. E. Stevens, *Sidonius Apollinaris*, 1933. On the culture of the aristocratic class see J. A. Geachy, *Q.A. Simmachus*, cit. chap. VI.

[3] A. Momigliano, *Riv. Stor. Ital.* 69 (1957), 232 (review to A. E. R. Boak, *Manpower Shortage*, cit.). On the rapid transport between Rome and Milan in the fourth century see Symmach. *Epist.* 1, 102; 3, 52; 4, 20; 31, 36; between Pavia and Ravenna by water in the fifth century see Sidon. Apoll. *Epist.* 1, 5, 8, 2: see generally D. Gorge, *Les voyages, l'hospitalité et le port des lettres dans le monde chrétien du IVᵉ et Vᵉ siècle*. 1925; G. Bardy, 'Pélérinages à Rome vers la fin du IVᵉ siècle', in *Mélanges P. Peeters*, 1 (*Analecta Bollandiana*, 67) 1949, 224-35.

[4] On the problems of the survival of ancient institutions and of the changes caused by barbarian invasions see P. Courcelle, *Histoire littéraire des grandes invasions germaniques*, 1948; H. Moss, 'The economic consequences of the barbarian invasions', in *The Economic Review*, 7 (1936-7), 209-16; B. Paradisi, 'Pace e impero alla fine del mondo antico', in *Stud. Doc. Hist. Iuris*, 24 (1958), 278 ff. A. Pirenne's well-known thesis that there was no hiatus in the economic life of the Roman West after the fall of the Empire has some validity, though with certain qualifications.

[5] The substitution of gold money by payment in kind due to fiscus becomes

to an agreement for mutual aid with the barbarian chiefs.[1] Other labour forces joined the *coloni* and the slaves, who appear not to have been included when the lands were ceded to the new *hospitales*.[2] The Roman Senate seems to have found support in the reign of Odoacre and drew large benefits from it.[3]

14. CONCLUSION

At this point an attempt should be made at recapitulation. The crisis of the third century followed an over-expansion of global consumption that took place in the Antonine Age and that exceeded the possibilities of the economy. The prevalence of the idea of the Welfare State little by little imposed upon the State great charges and tasks, that were out of proportion to the possibilities of its income especially when, after the end of wars of conquest, the contribution of extra treasures failed. Moreover, the expenditure made at the time when revenue had been abundant had not always been the result of a careful choice but was for the most part made with no precise plan as to its productivity.

From this situation the State saved itself, first at the expense of the old urban nobility, whose wealth was confiscated – a sacrifice imposed upon them by rival groups forming in the army and bureaucracy – then with the revenue drawn from both the small and the large property, a revenue rendered regular by Diocletian's

predominant in the fifth century not only in the East: Cod. Th. 11, 1, 37 (436) but also in the West: in Africa: Cod. Th. 11, 1, 32 (412); 11, 1, 34 (429); Nov. Valent. 3 (445); in Italy: Nov. Valent. 13 (445); Nov. Major 2, 3; 7, 14 and 16 (458). The *solidus* and franctions tremissis are current money; G. Mickwitz, *Geld und Wirtschaft*. cit. 156 ff. Chrysargyrium, the trade tax to be paid in coin, gold and silver, and not in kind, established by Constantine, is paid only in gold: Cod. Th. 13, 1, 9 (372); 11 (379); 15 (386); 17 (399); 18 (400); 19 (403); 20 (410); 21 (418) with exception of 1, 5, 14 (415) also in silver. The salaries of the employers and soldiers are paid in gold coin: Cod. Th. 7, 4, 35 (423): Cod. Inst. 1, 52 (439). All loans in Egypt are contracted after Julian in gold: C. Segré, *Il mutuo e il tasso d'interesse nell'Egitto Greco-Romano*, cit. 122.

[1] K. F. Stroheker, 'Zur Rolle der Heermeisterfränkischer Abstammung im Späten vierten Jahrhundert', in *Historia*, 4 (1944), 314–30.
[2] *Lex Burgund.* 54 Extr. 21, 12.
[3] J. Sundwall, *Abhdl. zur Gesch. des ausgeh. Roemertums*, 1919, 180–3.

reform. A little more than a century later, at the close of another cycle of economic expansion, the State lacked the means to carry on. The State had given itself closed organization, doubtless its most modern feature in the period of the Late Empire. But the cost soon turned out to be beyond the tax-yielding possibilities of an economy that was essentially agrarian.[1] The bureaucratic organization, advantageous in the beginning, developed, in fact, structures that exceeded their tasks. To procure the means to keep it going, fiscal

[1] To meet the expenditure needed for such bureaucratic organization without endangering the state's basic economic equilibrium, a drastic expansion of the national product would have been needed. This in turn could be procured only by an adequate progress in labour techniques which would have allowed increased production with less energy. But such progress was lacking.

On the problems of technique in the ancient world see A. Rehm, 'Zur Rolle der Technik in der griechisch. römisch. Antike', in *Archiv für Kulturgesch*. 38 (1938), 158 ff.; R. J. Forbes, 'The Ancients and the machine', in *Archiv. Intern. d'Histoire des Sciences*, 2 (1949), 919–33; A. Crombic, 'Augustine to Galileo', in *The History of Science (A. D. 400–1650)*, 1952, chap. IV, 2–3; F. Klemm, *Technik, Eine Geschichte ihrer Probleme*, 1954, chap. 5; Kretschmer, *Technik und Handwerk im Imperium Romanum*, 1958.

It is our duty here to refer to the theses of other modern scholars which have some analogy with that maintained in this work. Mazzarino ends his work, *Aspetti sociali* cit., with the statement that the final crisis of the Western Empire, economically, would have been avoidable only with a greater output of necessary goods to balance the decline in prices started, in the second half of the fourth century, in favour of the working classes; the Empire of the East was probably saved, in fact, because a greater production was possible with the system of peasant soldiers which assured, through better demographic conditions, as well more hands to work in the fields. But it may be objected that it was not only in the West that output diminished in respect to the East, but that the world revenue produced was not enough to meet the expenditure necessary to maintain the tentacles of the bureaucracy, the doubled army, and the city plebs. Public expenditure had started on a course from which there was no escape except at the expense of the ruin of the great estates. But the great landowners knew how to defend themselves and, in order not to pay too much ended up by not even paying their official due, and the state found itself with meagre finances. The only way to meet the excessive taxation would have been to bring about an adequate increase in production, but this, as has been said, would have been possible only with mechanization process that would have lowered costs.

A. H. Jones, 'Overtaxation,' cit., sees in the high taxation an important cause of the fall of the Empire, in as much as the peasants ruined by the treasury

pressure had to grow beyond reasonable limits. Immediate victims of its pressure were the medium and the small property owners, little by little absorbed by the large ones. The large proprietors, in turn, when the pressure grew unbearable, defended themselves with evasion and immunity which became ever more frequent.

A dangerous vicious circle comes into action. Increased state expenditure on the army, the bureaucracy, in welfare state commitments brought about a continual unbearable tax pressure. Tax pressure grew heavier and the tendency to evasion – illegal or legitimate – on the part of high officials and large landowners, was increased. Evasion on the part of the *potentiores* was increased and the pressure of taxation came to be concentrated on the middle-classes, automatically bringing about a redistribution of wealth distinctly in favour of those classes that in one way or another refused to pay tribute to the State. This vicious circle could lead to only one result, that which clearly shows itself in the course of the

deserted the land, especially the border lands, from which ensued the impoverishment of the Empire and hence its ruin. But also here it may be objected that there was not an effective impoverishment of the Empire on the eve of its fall: the harmful effect of taxation was rather that of increasing the bureaucracy in order to stop tax evasion, which owing to the anti-economic effect of the system, led to organized evasion and government corruption, and was the end of the state. In conclusion it is not only in the West that there was a decline in production, it even increased: the great landowners of North Italy, who stored crops in order to sell them at high prices, seemed more worried about fruitful years than bad ones: Ambros, *De Offic.* 3, 37, 41. There was rather a transformation, destined to take root even more in the traditional picture of the beneficiaries of agricultural revenue: the large estate, still made up of many small farms, run by colonials who must however hand over a large part of their income, once at the disposal of the smallholder, takes the place of the smallholding, of one farm. At the beginning of the transformation, the colonials are even the retainers of the landowners, who defend them and themselves from the treasury when the state declined, and as long as the fashionable time created by the supplies to the large cities lasted, even the condition of the colonials need not have been very bad. But when the cities declined, their conditions worsened, the amount of revenue for their use declined, while that due to the landowner remained still the same. Already towards the middle of the fifth century the colonate is called *vilissimus* in Nov. Valent. 27. The result was the gradual amassing of wealth in the hands of the *potiores* which ended in its crystallization. From this transformation came the static economy of the Middle Ages.

fifth century. The bankruptcy of the enormous State[1] at the same time as small privileged groups, while they evade taxation, heap up

[1] In considering the immediate and remote causes of the collapse, one should also take account of the fact that the Roman Empire had evidently grown beyond the possibilities that were granted any ancient State, that is to say a fundamentally agrarian one. The fears of the last historian of the republic who already in the days of Augustus was aware of the difficulties of a State that suffered from its own immensity, were well founded: Liv. *Praef.*: *ab exiguis profecta initiis co creverit ut iam magnitudine sua laborat*: see E. Gibbon, *The History of Decline*, cit. after chap. 38 on the general observation on the fall of the Roman Empire in the West: 'the stupendous fabric yielded to the pressure of its own weight . . . instead of enquiring why the Roman Empire was destroyed, we should rather be surprised that it had subsisted for so long.' The very fact of being restricted within limited boundaries explains most convincingly the survival of the eastern part of the Empire. Certainly, there were other circumstances that likewise favoured such survival. The Orient had remained outside the great currents of the barbarian invasions. Furthermore, the Anatolian peninsula, mountainous in its central part, constituted a reserve of vigorous men able to organize in homogeneous formations: M. N. Baynes, 'The Decline of Roman Power in the Western Empire', in *Journ. Rom. Studies*, 33 (1943), 29 ff. Financial means were abundant: the *pars Orientis* of the Empire had always been the richest: G. J. Bratianu, 'La distribution de l'or et les raisons économiques de la division de l'Empire Romain', in *Études Byzantines d'Histoire Economique et Sociale*, cit. Byzantium became soon the greatest commercial centre in the Christian world, thanks too to its position as an intermediary for the trade in luxuries with the Far East, luxuries that were destined for the great lords of the West. Unlike Rome it was not only a centre of consumption but of manufacturing too. The landowners of the East probably never became as wealthy and powerful as those of the agitated West: A. H. M. Jones, 'The decline and fall of the Roman Empire', in *History*, 1955, 224; id. 'Census records of the later Roman Empire', in *Journ. Rom. Stud.* 43 (1953), 49–64; P. Charanis, *On the social structure of the later Roman Empire*, cit. 48 ff. Though in the East too corruption was widespread and the transfer of tax burdens practised, they rarely succeeded in securing high administrative posts; these remained instead mostly a privilege of officials who came from subaltern positions and were therefore more inclined to serve the interests of the State: G. R. Monks, *The administration of the privy purse*, cit. 774. The designations of the public offices were not so easily inflated: Koch, *Die byzant. Beamtentitel*, 1903, 14. The social relation between city and country never weakened: urban life had deeper roots there than it did in the West because it had developed by virtue of natural economic forces in harmony with the environment. The agents of the State, operating in a more restricted area, could continue to co-ordinate, with the same principles of rigid control that were dominant in the Late Empire, social and

riches and create around their villas economic and social micro-cosms, completely cut off from the central authority. It was the end of the Roman world. It was the beginning of the Middle Ages.

economic forces without finding themselves confronted with insoluble problems: G. Bratianu, 'Les Études Byzantines d'Hist. Econ. et Sociale', in *Byzantion*, 14 (1939), 509 ff. The administrative structures, the attitude towards life, the inherited habits, could therefore be preserved more easily.

TWO

Manpower and the Fall of Rome[1]

M. I. FINLEY

The second half of the fourth century was not one of the more creative periods in western history, at least not outside the Church. One would be hard put to think of a dozen names which merit our attention, and the man who interests me here has no name known to us at all. He addressed a pamphlet to an emperor, probably Valentinian I, in which he put forward proposals for army reform and a number of ingenious, though perhaps not very practical, military inventions. In explaining his motives, which he did at some length and with much carefully self-protective language, he delivered a detailed and slashing attack on the costs of the almost perpetual warfare of his time, on the oppressive taxation and the corrupt and extortionate provincial administration of the empire.

One did not lightly criticize in that way in the fourth century; no wonder our man remained anonymous. There is no way of knowing whether the emperor ever received the document, but we need have no hesitation in asserting that the pamphlet, which was probably written shortly before the shameful disaster at Adrianople at the hands of the Goths in 378, had not the slightest effect on imperial behaviour or thinking.

Yet the pamphlet survived somehow in manuscript, under the title of *De rebus bellicis* ('On Military Affairs'). It was first printed in a book, with illustrations of the inventions, in Basle in 1552 and it was reprinted at least five times in the next two hundred years.[2] It was read by humanists and others who were fascinated by the machines, and by occasional writers on military history. It could have been read by Gibbon, who is known to have possessed two copies

[1] This article was first published as chapter XII of *Aspects of Antiquity: Discoveries and Controversies*, The Viking Press, 1966.
[2] Most recently by E. A. Thompson in a *A Roman Reformer and Inventor* (1952).

and who went through masses of rare and abstruse Latin and Greek texts in preparation for writing his *Decline and Fall of the Roman Empire*. But Gibbon did not read it so far as I can tell, and that is a fact of some significance. To be sure, by Gibbon's time interest in Anonymous's inventions had disappeared and there were better and fuller sources of information about imperial corruption and extortion. However, Anonymous also threw out strong hints about one factor which has impressed some modern students, and that is what we should call manpower shortage. The saving of manpower was one of his strong and explicit arguments in favour of his schemes, and this aspect of the later Roman Empire needs to be looked at with some care.

At its greatest extent, at the accession of Hadrian in 117, the territory of the Roman Empire embraced something like 2,000,000 square miles. If we deduct some very temporary acquisitions we get a more meaningful total of about 1,600,000 square miles. Such a figure may no longer leave us gasping by comparison, say, with the United States or the Soviet Union, but it was still impressive enough. The empire extended from the Euphrates river in Iraq all the way to the Atlantic, the whole of North Africa, Europe below the Rhine-Danube line (and a bit above), and most of Britain along the way. When the empire was functioning properly, furthermore, it was a unified State in fact and not just in name (unlike the Holy Roman Empire of mediaeval and early modern times). It included a large enough number of people, too, but there the figure bears no modern comparison. Actually we do not know the number, nor did any contemporary, not even the emperor himself or his bureau heads. That need not cause any surprise. Modern habits of counting and recording everybody and everything had not yet become sufficiently widespread or necessary (though they were not unknown). A fair guess would be that at its maximum, in the first two centuries of our era, the total population was something like 60,000,000, and that meant everybody – men, women and children, free men and slaves.

The precise numbers do not matter so much when they reach that level. What matters are trends and distribution. How was the population moving in the course of the history of the empire: up or down, or not at all? And how was the population distributed among the social classes and the necessary (or unnecessary) employments?

In particular, what proportion was in the army, which was now a wholly professional body, and was that enough?

In the heyday of the empire, say from Augustus to Marcus Aurelius, the army was a fairly modest one of about 300,000 men. Gibbon noticed that this figure was equalled by Louis XIV, 'whose kingdom', as he said, 'was confined within a single province of the Roman Empire'. But the army was sufficient for its purposes; it kept the peace within the empire; it could cope with rebellions, such as the Jewish revolt of 66–70, though that might require time; it protected the frontiers; it was even able to make a few further conquests, including Britain. Then one day it became inadequate, too small in number and sometimes unreliable in performance. The turning point was the reign of Marcus Aurelius (who died in the year 180). The Germanic tribes in central Europe, which had been fitfully troublesome for several centuries, now began a new and much heavier pressure on the frontiers which never stopped until the western empire finally came to an end as a political organism.

We must be careful here not to make too much use of our hindsight. Yet surely there were few Roman leaders, whether emperors or senators or field commanders, so stupid that they did not realize the enormity of Rome's difficulties and the need for effort on a greater scale than had been required before. They did make efforts, and they failed. It is astonishing that they did not fail earlier. In the third century the armies were busier with civil war and politics than with the frontier menace, as they had been once before after the assassination of Nero. For fifty years emperors and claimants to the throne came and went in an endless succession. Then Diocletian restored order, reorganized the administration and the defences, and doubled the army strength, at least on paper. And still the Germans came and the losing struggle against them went on, while civil wars and general disorganization kept recurring.

There was the open symptom of the coming fall of Rome. And this is how Gibbon saw it:

> The timid and luxurious inhabitants of a declining empire must be allured into the service by the hopes of profit, or compelled by the dread of punishment. . . . Such was the horror for the profession of a soldier, which had affected the minds of the de-

generate Romans, that many of the youth . . . chose to cut off the fingers of their right hand to escape from being pressed into service.

Note the language carefully: 'timid and luxurious', 'declining empire', 'degenerate Romans'. Even if one were to accept the characterization – and I am not concerned to argue that now – it does not explain. One would still have to give reasons why the Romans had become 'timid' and 'degenerate', if that is what they now were. Professor A. H. M. Jones does not use language of that kind in his great three-volume work on the later Roman Empire. That is not simply because he has a different set of values from Gibbon's, but because historians now put different questions to the past, and therefore come out with a different picture. Jones's *Later Roman Empire* covers the same ground as the first half of Gibbon's *Decline and Fall*. The chief actors are the same; so are the dates and the battles and the defeats. But the history somehow is not the same in the end; the focus has been changed, as is clear on this question of manpower.

The paper strength of the army after Diocletian was about 600,000 a very small figure by contrast with the armies which a modern state with the same total population can muster in wartime. Why, then, were Diocletian and his successors unable to put even their full paper strength into the field against the barbarians, let alone increase the levies? Certainly the stakes were high, the emergency critical. Patriotism in the Roman Empire may have been lukewarm at best: the ordinary man, regardless of class, felt no personal obligation to fight to defend it. That is true, but it is equally true that they wanted even less to have the empire ripped apart by invading Germans. The Roman Empire, despite all its troubles, its burdensome taxation and terrible poverty, its bitter conflicts between Christians and pagans and then among the orthodox Christians and the heretics, was nevertheless an integral part of the order of things, central and eternal. When a Visigothic army led by its king Alaric captured the city of Rome in the summer of 410, St Jerome, then living in Bethlehem, added these words to the preface of the *Commentaries on Ezekiel* he was writing: '. . . the brightest light of the whole world was extinguished . . . the Roman

Empire was deprived of its head . . . , to speak more correctly, the whole world perished in one city. . . .'

One reason for the astonishment was that Roman armies still fought well most of the time. In any straight fight they could, and they usually did, defeat superior numbers of Germans, because they were better trained, better equipped, better led. What they could not do was cope indefinitely with this kind of enemy. They were not warring with a neighbouring state like themselves, but with migratory tribes who wanted to loot or to settle in the richer world of the empire. As early as the reign of Marcus Aurelius groups of Germans were allowed to settle on the land and to join the Roman army themselves. That did not work either, though the attempt was repeated many times, partly because they would not be Romanized but chiefly because it simply encouraged more Germans on the outside to demand the same. It was physically impossible for 600,000 men to protect a frontier that ran from the mouth of the Rhine to the Black Sea and then on to the borders of the Persian kingdom in the east.

More men seemed the obvious answer – or a technological revolution, and that raises the critical point. It was in a sense misleading when I noted that we throw a far greater proportion of our manpower into battle in an emergency. When we do that, our whole civilian life is at once readjusted, not merely by austerity programmes and general belt-tightening, but also by increasing the *per capita* production of those (including women) who remain on the farms and in the factories. And that no ancient people could do because their technology was too primitive, resting almost entirely on the muscles of men and beasts; and because most of the population, the free as well as the half-free *coloni* and the slaves, had nothing to sacrifice to an austerity programme to begin with. Furthermore, the modern comparison fails for still another reason. Contemporary states have been able to make these extraordinary efforts for a limited time, on the assumption that the war will end soon enough. But this was not the Roman problem. They were not engaged in a war in that sense but were undergoing a persistent hammering, and it is pointless to talk about tightening the belt and working overtime seven days a week for a period of 200 years.

The Roman position can be presented in a simple model. With the stabilization of the empire and the establishment of the *pax Romana* under Augustus, a sort of social equilibrium was created. Most of the population, free or unfree, produced just enough for themselves to exist on, at a minimum standard of living, and enough to maintain a very rich and high-living aristocracy and urban upper class, the court with its palace and administrative staffs, and the modest army of some 300,000. Any change in any of the elements making up the equilibrium – for example, an increase in the army or other non-producing sectors of the population, or an increase in the bite taken out of the producers through increased rents and taxes – had to be balanced elsewhere if the equilibrium were to be maintained. Otherwise something was bound to break. Stated the other way round, if the boundaries of the Roman Empire had been at the ends of the earth, so that there were no frontiers to defend, and if the court and the aristocracy had been content to keep its numbers and its level of consumption unchanged, then there was no obvious reason why the Roman Empire should not have gone on indefinitely.

But of course none of the 'ifs' happened. The parasitic classes (and I use the word in its strictly economic sense with no moral judgements implied) kept growing larger, with the triumph of Christianity an important contributing factor after Constantine. So did the pressures on the frontier. A larger military establishment and more frequent battles in turn meant greater demands on the peasantry who made up the bulk of the population in this fundamentally agrarian world. With their primitive technology, there came a time when they could no longer respond, whatever their will may have been in the matter.

As the final insult in this tale of frustration, the population was apparently not even able to reproduce itself any longer. This is a difficult subject because we lack figures. Yet there are signs of some decline in the total population, at least from the time of Marcus Aurelius, the reign we keep returning to as the pivot. The surest sign is the increasing frequency of abandoned farmland, in Italy, North Africa, and elsewhere. In an age without technological advances, occupation of the soil is a gauge of the movement of population. When the population is going up, marginal lands have to be brought into cultivation, and then they are abandoned when the curve goes down. The documents of the period make it clear that manpower shortage was a problem, and a recognized problem, particularly in agriculture. The efforts of landed magnates to keep their peasants out of the army played a greater part in the military manpower difficulties than the occasional young man who chopped off his fingers. And the peasants, in their turn, showed a tendency to flee from the land into the cities or to become outlaws.

Decline in the birth-rate is a mysterious business. I know no satisfactory explanation for it in the Roman Empire. Some historians have tried to blame it on the low life-expectancy of the time, but an equally low life-expectancy was the rule everywhere until the nineteenth century, and still in in large parts of Asia, and we all know about the explosions in their population. I find the same difficulty with Professor Jones's suggestion that the peasantry had become too poor and too starved to rear children. I doubt if they were hungrier than the peasants of modern India or Egypt; and the upper classes, who ate far too much for their own good, did not seem to be breeding at a satisfactory rate either.

Whatever the explanation, the word 'depopulation' is too strong. It overstates the situation. Manpower shortage is a relative term. All resources – and manpower is another resource – are, or are not, sufficient not by some absolute measuring-stick but according to the demands made on them and the conditions of their employment. In the later Roman Empire manpower was part of an interrelated complex of social conditions, which, together with the barbarian invasions, brought an end to the empire in the west. The army could not be enlarged because the land could not stand further depletion of manpower; the situation on the land had deteriorated because taxes were too high; taxes were too high because the military demands were increasing; and for that the German pressures were mainly responsible. A vicious circle of evils was in full swing. Break into it at any point: the final answer will be the same provided one keeps all the factors in sight all the time.

I concede that this is neither a dramatic nor a romantic way to look at one of the great cataclysms of history. One could not make a film out of it. But it provides the necessary underpinning for the military and constitutional history and the magnificent moralizing of Gibbon. The Roman Empire was people and institutions, not just emperors, degenerate or otherwise. And it was the inflexible institutional underpinning, in the end, which failed: it could not support the perpetual strains of an empire of such magnitude within a hostile world.

THREE

The Economic Decay of Byzantium[1]

CHARLES DIEHL

The Byzantine Empire was rich and prosperous; yet even in its most golden days, the financial situation was often unstable and difficult. The burden of expenditure was heavy. War and diplomacy, the vast and intricate machinery of public administration, the splendour of the court and of public buildings, and the numbers of religious and hospitable foundations – in short, all the magnificence required by tradition not only to satisfy the people of Constantinople, but to impress foreigners, was extremely costly. Revenue already inadequate for so many requirements was further diminished by the greed and corruption of officials. Thus at every period of Byzantine history, taxation was a crushing burden on all citizens, and the budget was always exceedingly difficult to balance. The situation became even worse when the sources of revenue dwindled and at last dried up altogether.

I. THE DECAY OF AGRICULTURE

Agriculture was one of these sources. The causes of its decline increased with the centuries. The Turkish conquest at the end of the eleventh century deprived Byzantium of some of its richest provinces, in particular, the major part of Asia Minor, which was the Empire's strength. Even the territories that the emperors were able to hold were in a permanent state of insecurity and misery, owing to war and incessant raids by Ottomans, Serbs and Bulgars, to say nothing of the ravages of the Byzantine army itself – so much so, that at the beginning of the fourteenth century, Constantinople was reduced to relying for its very existence on cargoes

[1] This article was first published as chapter VI of *Byzantium: Greatness and Decline* (translated from the French by Naomi Walford), Rutgers University Press, 1957.

of grain and fish from the Black Sea, the fertile plains of Thrace and Macedonia having been devastated by Catalans and Turks. On the other hand, government measures to prevent the continuous growth of the large estates and to stop the usurpations of the strong fell more and more into oblivion; by the middle of the fourteenth century they were an antiquated notion to which no one paid any attention. The free peasant disappeared with the independent small-holding, and the commonest form of labour between the thirteenth and fifteenth centuries was that of the πάροικοι: men bound to their master's land and liable to him for numerous dues and duties.

During the Empire's final period, communities of free peasants became more and more rare. A great part of the land belonged to the Emperor or the treasury; they employed πάροικοι to work it or leased it to others. Churches and religious houses, too, owned great numbers of estates, which were cultivated by the monks and their πάροικοι, and although in theory these properties were liable to land tax, in fact they were often exempt; and in any case they were free of any supplementary charges. The remainder was private property. It consisted firstly of large estates belonging to the nobility, who cultivated them by the labour of their own πάροικοι or leased part of them; secondly of military fiefs, from whose owners only military service was required; and finally of rural communities and farms. These last were the fewest and most heavily burdened; for, besides countless taxes, they owed certain obligations to the local lord whose patronage they had willingly or unwillingly accepted. The occupiers of such holdings were known as 'the poor' – and so indeed they were.

The consequences of such a state of affairs may be imagined. The preponderance of large estates and the manner of their cultivation resulted in an inferior yield. The hardship to which the πάροικοι were subjected brought destitution and the abandonment of the countryside, aroused universal discontent among the lower classes. In the fourteenth century especially, a social situation of great and increasing tension arose. The many exemptions enjoyed by the big landowners diminished the revenue from land tax and, by causing the greater part of the burden to fall on the poor, added to the people's distress and goaded them to rebellion. This state of affairs was aggravated by increased exactions to meet the deficit and by the extortionate methods used, and peasants were made to pay six or even twelve times the amount they owed.

In the nation's agony, the rural population had nothing to look forward to but a change of masters; and it was natural that, as in the last days of the Roman Empire, the peasants regarded the coming of a new lord almost as a deliverance. As early as the eleventh century, provincials sometimes appealed to the enemy or joined forces with rebels; often, to escape the fiscal tyranny, they fled into the mountains or went abroad, and vast tracts of country lay deserted. In the fourteenth and fifteenth centuries the situation was far worse, and the disappearance of taxable property left the nation's finances in a desperate state.

2. DECAY OF TRADE

The Greek Empire had recovered without too much difficulty from the Arab conquest in the seventh century, which resulted in the loss of the rich provinces of Egypt and Syrian and their thriving ports. It bore less easily the eleventh-century Turkish occupation of some of its wealthiest regions. Yet in the twelfth century trade still flourished, as is shown by the prosperity of Constantinople and Thessalonica at that time. The primary causes of the subsequent decline in this prosperity must be sought elsewhere, and mainly in the mistaken economic policy of the Byzantines, who neglected their navy and allowed themselves to be ousted from eastern markets.

Merchants in the commercial cities of Italy soon perceived the profits to be made by exploiting the Byzantine Empire, and seized every opportunity of doing so. From the middle of the tenth century, Bari, Amalfi and, above all, Venice were foremost in maintaining close relations with the Empire, not only by lawful trade, but also in the smuggling of prohibited articles. The Venetians soon wanted more, and as the Greek government often needed their help and their shipping, it allowed them many exemptions and privileges. The treaty of 992, the first of a series that was to make Venice's fortune in the East, allowed Venetian merchants considerable reductions in import and export duty payable at the Dardanelles, as well as guarantees against molestation by Byzantine officials. The treaty of 1082, renewed, confirmed, and amplified during the twelfth century, increased these privileges. Thenceforth Venetian merchants could buy and sell in every part of the Empire, free of duty or customs examination. Many ports were opened and vast territories made accessible to them for free trade. These unheard-of concessions gave them a pre-eminent position in eastern waters. On the coasts of the Peloponnesus, the Archipelago and Thrace, and in the Sea of Marmara, they found all the ports they needed to establish communication with the distant East. In Constantinople they had their own quarter, situated at the finest point on the Golden Horn. Their vessels sailed into the Black Sea, to the Crimea, and to the end of the Sea of Azov, to fetch wheat from south Russia and the precious wares that came along the trade routes from Central Asia. The ports of Asia Minor lay open to them; Crete, Rhodes and Cyprus offered fine harbours for the Syrian eastern route. At last their activities extended into the interior, as far as Adrianople and Philippopolis in Europe, and in Asia as far as Philadelphia. Thus the Venetians found a foothold and enjoyed privileged treatment throughout the Greek Empire; they became the necessary intermediary for all traffic between East and West, and their Italian rivals of Bari, Amalfi and even Genoa, less privileged than they, had difficulty in competing. The decay of the Byzantine merchant navy helped them to keep the monopoly they had won.

Throughout the twelfth century their hold upon the East was strengthened. Being exempt from the taxes and dues imposed on others, the Venetians settled on Greek territory and founded thriving colonies; in 1171 that of Constantinople numbered over 10,000. Indeed, a Byzantine emperor wrote that he regarded them 'not as foreigners but as Greeks by birth', while Nicetas said of them that they had become 'the compatriots and best friends of the Romans'.[1] They wormed their way in everywhere – even the ships' companies of the imperial fleet were full of Venetian seamen – and were so intoxicated by their good fortune that they forgot they were not at home and behaved as if in a conquered country. They made no effort to disguise their mercenary greed or their arrogance and treated not only the lower classes with insolent disdain, but also those of high rank; even the Emperor himself was not spared their

[1] The Byzantines called themselves 'Romans', assuming that they were the only true inheritors of the Roman Empire. [*Ed.*]

insults. 'They treated citizens like slaves,' said a twelfth-century Greek chronicler. 'Their boldness and impudence increased with their wealth', wrote Nicetas, 'until they not only detested the Romans but even defied the threats and commands of the Emperor.' In time they became altogether insufferable.

The Greeks, justly uneasy at the rapid success of the Venetians and their ill-disguised ambitions, tried to hold them in check. In return for the privileges they enjoyed, Emperor Manuel Comnenus tried to impose upon the Latins some of the obligations of Greek citizens, such as military service and the payment of certain taxes. At other times, as in 1122, Byzantine sovereigns refused to renew the treaties or resorted to sterner measures, as in 1171, arresting all Venetians established in the East, confiscating their property, and seizing their ships. Or again, as in 1182, they allowed the population of the capital to storm the Latin quarter and massacre the inhabitants. Venice retaliated by war, and the goodwill of earlier times gave place to smouldering hostility. Gradually the idea was borne in upon the Republic that if it was to retain its monopoly of the eastern trade and continue to profit by the fine markets of the Greek Empire, one course alone lay open to it: to conquer Byzantium and lay the foundations of a Venetian colonial empire upon its ruins.

Pisans and Genoese had also settled in the East. 'Maritime Italy', said Nicetas, 'entered the imperial city under full sail.' It is true that the first treaties concluded with Pisa and Genoa were less advantageous than those with Venice; yet in the course of the twelfth century the Greek emperors sought to check the Venetians by favouring their competitors. These, too, had their own quarter and colony in Constantinople – in 1162 there were a thousand Pisans in the capital – and they were allowed customs concessions and free access to all the ports of the Empire. But they often caused anxiety to the government, which at times withdrew its permission for them to settle in Constantinople itself and made them move outside, or allowed the populace to attack and rob them. Nevertheless, their alliance was necessary to Greek policy, so that in the end they always received satisfaction, to the great annoyance of the Venetians – who were jealous of any competition – and to the detriment of the Empire, since the number of its exploiters was hereby increased.

The Fourth Crusade – born of Venetian ambitions and the Venetian desire to secure the monopoly of eastern trade against all comers – dealt a decisive blow to the economic prosperity of the Greek Empire. In the partitioning of the Empire, the Republic seized the best of the Byzantine possessions: fertile lands, coastal territory, the most useful ports, and the most important strategic points. Venetian patricians settled in the Archipelago, and for Venice their domains were so many friendly states, open to a profitable trade. And although the fall of the short-lived Latin empire and the return of the Greeks to Constantinople was for a time very damaging to this prosperity, it did not benefit the Byzantine Empire. To check the Venetians, the Palaeologi favoured the Genoese, giving them complete customs exemption, handing over to them the important site of Galata for their colony, and allowing them to settle on the coast of Asia Minor and at Caffa on the Black Sea, where they might claim the monopoly of all trade in those waters.

This was merely to change masters. The historian Pachymeres records, 'The Genoese closed all maritime trade routes to the Romans.' And as Venice was still mistress of the Archipelago and firmly entrenched in Euboea and Crete, Byzantium found itself even more at the mercy of exploiting foreigners than before, especially as Michael Palaeologus soon allowed Venetians and Pisans the concessions which at first he had reserved for the Genoese.

By the beginning of the fourteenth century, all the eastern seas were surrounded by Latin colonies. The Genoese were masters of Phocaea, Chios, Lesbos and Aenos on the Thracian coast; they colonized Caffa, Tana and Trebizond; they were lords of Galata, and in 1348 they made so bold as to build a naval station on the Bosphorus itself and denied entry into the Black Sea to any Venetian or even Greek ship without their express permission. The Venetians on their part held the islands of the Archipelago: Naxos, Andros, Paros, Tinos, Santorini, Cerigo, Coron and Modon in the Morea, also Negropont and Crete; while their colonists had quickly returned to Constantinople and Thessalonica, despite the hostility of the Greeks and the obstacles placed in their way by the imperial government. Rivalry between the two cities was very bitter; at the end of the thirteenth century and throughout the fourteenth it broke out periodically in open warfare, the Empire being the battlefield and the victim.

To protect his capital, Michael Palaeologus attempted to neu-
tralize the waters lying between the entry of the Dardanelles and
the outlet of the Bosphorus and here forbade any naval engagement.
In defiance of this, the fleets of Venice and Genoa joined battle in
the Bosphorus, before Constantinople, and in the Golden Horn
itself; colonists from both cities fought in the streets of the capital,
and the weak rulers of the house of the Palaeologi were toys in the
hands of the Latins. In 1292 Roger Morosini arrived before Constantinople with a fleet of seventy-five sail, in defiance of the
Emperor. In 1305 a Venetian fleet sacked the Princes' Islands and
forced the Emperor to renew his treaties with the Republic. In 1351
a Venetian squadron compelled the *Basileus* to abandon his neutrality
and side with Venice against Genoa. In 1375 Venice made the Byzantines cede the important position of Tenedos, which commanded
the Dardanelles; whereupon the Genoese retaliated by touching off
a palace revolution in Constantinople and overthrowing John V
Palaeologus. All was violence and insolence, in things great or small.
For instance, it was the custom for every Latin vessel passing
Constantinople to heave to before the imperial palace, in order to
salute and acclaim the Emperor. Genoese and Venetians constantly
omitted this courtesy, by which Byzantine vanity set great store. In
1348, when John Cantacuzenus was planning to refit the Byzantine
navy and, in order to restore activity in the port of Constantinople,
proposed to lower the customs duties collected there, the Genoese
expressed their disapproval of measures so damaging to their trade
by attacking Constantinople, destroying the vessels under construction and repair, and burning the merchantmen stationed in the
Golden Horn.

The Greek people protested loudly at 'Italian pride and arrogance', and at the disdain shown by the Latins for the *Basileus* of the
Romans. But the emperors put a good face upon it. They usually
received insults with a smile and confined themselves to making
courteous representations. Or, if they did venture upon any
gesture of resistance or reprisal, they gave in in the end, conscious
of the hopeless weakness of their position. 'The naval power of
Byzantium had long vanished,' said a Greek historian at the end of
the thirteenth century. Upkeep of the fleet seemed to the Greeks to
entail unnecessary expense, and apart from the few ships moored in

the Golden Horn, all the vessels that had once constituted the strength and wealth of Byzantium lay empty and unrigged, or rotted on the bottom. As Nicephorus Gregoras wrote in the fourteenth century, 'While the Latins steadily increased their profits and their power, the Greeks grew weaker, and every day added fresh calamity to past misfortune.'

Genoa and Venice took advantage of this situation to exploit the Empire. Genoa created the powerful trade association known as 'Mahone of Chios' which from the produce of this island and the yield of the Phocaean alum mines drew an annual revenue of from 60 to 80,000 florins. In contrast to declining Constantinople, the Genoese port of Pera was tremendously active. And whereas by the fourteenth century the Constantinople customs authority collected no more than 30,000 *hyperpera* annually, that of Galata brought in over 200,000. Even the few restrictions imposed on certain articles by the economic policy of the emperors were ineffectual, owing to clever smuggling, which still further diminished what was left of the Empire's resources.

Venice meanwhile was carrying on an immensely profitable trade throughout the East, from the Black Sea to Egypt, and from Syria to the Ionian Sea. By the beginning of the fifteenth century the day seemed near when, in the words of Doge Mocenigo, Venice was to become 'mistress of the gold of all Christendom'. Times had indeed changed since the day when Robert of Clari declared that 'Two thirds of the world's riches were in Constantinople.'

Yet Constantinople still remained the finest and busiest port in the East. Pisa, Florence, Ancona, Ragusa, Barcelona, Marseilles, Montpellier and Narbonne had flourishing colonies there, as well as Venice and Genoa; merchants came from Cadiz and Seville, and even from Bruges and London. Similarly, the Greek ports that were outlets of the great trade routes were still extremely busy. But the Byzantines did not benefit. Nicephorus Gregoras wrote in the fourteenth century, 'The Latins have taken possession not only of all the wealth of the Byzantines, and almost all the revenues from the sea, but also of all the resources that replenish the sovereign's treasury.' The Greeks could not even collect the harbour dues and the excise and customs duties from their astute rivals, the Venetians and Genoese, who had been exempted too long from such payments.

3. FINANCIAL DISTRESS

Henceforth Byzantium's financial ruin was inevitable. The two principal sources of revenue were the land tax and customs duties, and though payment was strictly enforced, the former now brought in a quite inadequate sum, while the latter were rapidly dwindling. And since the Byzantine government clung to its tradition of magnificence and display – so long the basis of its policy – and was determined to keep up appearances, it found increasing difficulty in balancing revenue and expenditure. Attempts were made to economize, regardless of the Empire's safety. Thus from the end of the thirteenth century the fleet, which Michael Palaeologus had tried to keep in good order, was allowed to decay, on the pretext that its upkeep was a needless expense, and 'a greater burden on the imperial treasury than anything else'. Other essentials such as fortresses and armaments were likewise pared away. Army estimates were reduced, regardless of the fact that by leaving the way open to invasion and piracy and by necessitating the bribery of Serbs and Turks, economic distress was aggravated and the Empire plunged further into ruin.

By these means, however, the imperial government was able to save some money for the upkeep of the court and the ostentation to which the Byzantines attached so much importance and by which they liked to think they still dazzled the world as in bygone times. There is something very pitiable about the treatise on ceremonial drawn up about the middle of the fourteenth century, containing long descriptions of the uniforms of court dignitaries, of their variously coloured hats, their different sorts of shoes, their insignia, and their hierarchic and ceremonial rank. To read this little book, one would suppose that Byzantium was still resplendent in jewels, purple and gold, and more preoccupied than ever with luxury, banqueting and ceremonial etiquette. But what were the facts?

In the middle of the fourteenth century Emperor John Cantacuzenus declared, 'There is no more money anywhere. Reserves are exhausted, the imperial jewels have been sold, and taxes bring in nothing, as the country is ruined.' The wife of this same sovereign noted that the Empire had been reduced to nothing and fallen to the lowest degree of poverty, 'so that I dare not speak of it, lest I blush before my hearers.' Another still more significant fact was that the court itself, where every effort was made to keep up an appearance of splendour, was henceforth unable to conceal its penury. At the marriage of John V Palaeologus in 1347, the wedding feast was served in vessels of earthenware and pewter, and not one item of gold or silver appeared on the table. Clothes and crowns were adorned with coloured glass instead of gems, and gilded leather took the place of gold. Nicephorus Gregoras, who tells this tale, rightly remarks, 'Anyone with any knowledge of custom will understand by this and by other breaches of etiquette how intolerable was the burden of distress.' He ends sadly, 'The bygone splendour and prosperity of Byzantium were dissipated and gone, and it is not without shame that I relate it.' For the Byzantine court to consent to such humiliation, the financial situation must have been desperate indeed. The treasury was empty. 'Nothing was to be found there', says Gregoras, 'but air and dust.'

And so the last of the Palaeologi were reduced to dire expedients. John V pawned the Crown Jewels and sold some territory for a few thousand ducats. The *Basileus* became the prey of usurers and – most humiliating incident of all – while on a journey in the West, he was arrested for debt in Venice and detained there until he paid his creditors. When we recall how transcendent a figure the Emperor of Byzantium had once been, we can appreciate the full poignancy of this account.

Everything bore witness to the same distress. In 1423 the Empire was forced to sell Thessalonica – its second city – to the Venetians for 50,000 ducats. By the beginning of the fifteenth century, the loveliest quarter of Constantinople lay in ruins, and even for the upkeep of St Sophia money was not always forthcoming. Stripped of its ancient glories and greatly diminished in population – 'there is more emptiness than fullness here,' said a fifteenth-century traveller – the dying capital seemed in mourning for the Empire; and although it still held a proud place in the world and attracted crowds of travellers and traders, foreigners alone won profit from its fine situation and from all that for so long had made it wealthy.

FOUR

The Arabs in Eclipse[1]

BERNARD LEWIS

By the eleventh century the world of Islam was in a state of manifest decay. The signs of decadence are visible even earlier, first in the political break-up, involving the loss of the authority of the central government in the remoter provinces, then in all but Iraq itself, finally in the degradation of the Caliphs to the status of mere puppets of their ministers and military commanders. In 945, the decline of the Caliphate went a step further. In that year the Buwaihids, a Persian local dynasty, advanced into Iraq and seized the capital. For the next century, the Buwaihid princes were the real rulers of the capital, assuming the title Sultan as token of secular sovereignty. Though Shī'ites, they retained the 'Abbāsid Caliphs as figureheads and as the legal source of the sovereignty of the central government over the provinces. It is perhaps significant that not long before the first moderate Shī'ite dynasty won power, the twelfth Imām pretender of the sect disappeared into eschatological concealment. The Buwaihids restored for a while the order and prosperity of the central provinces. But the signs of economic decay were increasing. The profitable trade with China dwindled and died away, partly for reasons arising from the internal conditions of that country itself. The trade with Russia and the north diminished and disappeared during the eleventh century, while the growing shortage of precious metals helped to stifle the economic life of what was ceasing to be a commercial empire.

One of the primary causes of economic decline was undoubtedly the extravagance and lack of organization at the centre. The lavish expenditure of the court and the inflated bureaucracy – at times

[1] This article was first published as chapter IX and a section of chapter X of *The Arabs in History*, Hutchinson University Library, 1960.

maintained in duplicate in the trains of contenders for power – were not met by any great technological progress or greater development of resources. Soon the shortage of ready money forced rulers to pay senior officials and generals by farming out State revenues to them. Before long, provincial governors were appointed as tax-farmers for the areas they administered, with the duty of maintaining the local forces and officials and remitting an agreed sum to the central treasury. These governors soon became the virtually independent rulers of their provinces, rendering purely legal homage to the Caliph, whose function was reduced to giving formal, and to an increasing extent *post facto*, authorization to their tenure of authority. The need to give the requisite military strength to governors and tax-farmers led to the practice of appointing military commanders to the tax-farms and this in turn to the break-up of civil and bureaucratic government and its replacement by armed pretorians governing through their guards.

By the eleventh century, the weakness of the Empire was revealed by a series of almost simultaneous attacks by internal and external barbarians on all sides. In Europe, the Christian forces advanced in both Spain and Sicily, wresting great territories from Muslim rule in a wave of reconquest which culminated in the arrival of the Crusaders in the Near East itself at the end of the century. In Africa, a new religious movement among the Berbers of southern Morocco and the Senegal-Niger area led to the creation of a new Berber Empire, formed by the conquest of the greater part of north-west Africa and those parts of Spain which had remained under Muslim rule. Farther east the two great Arab Bedouin tribes of Hilāl and Sulaim burst out of the areas of Upper Egypt where they had hitherto been living and swept across Libya and Tunisia, working havoc and devastation. By 1056–7 they were able to sack the ancient Tunisian capital of Qairawan. It is to this invasion rather than to the first Arab invasion of the seventh century that the devastation and backwardness of North Africa are to be attributed. The fourteenth-century Arab historian Ibn Khaldūn, contemplating the ruin of his native land by these nomadic invasions, elaborated what was probably the first philosophy of history in terms of the cyclic interplay of the Desert and the Sown. Of these invasions he remarks:

In Tunisia and the West, since the Hilāl and Sulaim tribes passed that way at the beginning of the fifth century (the middle of the eleventh century A.D.) and devastated these countries, for three hundred and fifty years all the plains were ruined; whereas formerly from the Negro-lands to the Mediterranean all was cultivated, as is proved by the traces remaining there of monuments, buildings, farms and villages.

From Central Asia came another wave of invaders, which in its permanent effects, was the most important of all. The Arabs had first met the Turks in central Asia and had for some time imported them to the Muslim Near East as slaves, especially of the type trained from early childhood for military and administrative purposes and later known as *Mamlūk* (owned), to distinguish them from the humbler slaves used for domestic and other purposes. We find occasional Turkish slaves under the early 'Abbāsids and even under the Umayyads, but the first to use them extensively was Mu'tasim (833–42), who collected a large force of Turkish military slaves even before his accession, and later arranged to receive a large number annually as part of the tribute from the eastern provinces. The old Khurāsāni guards of the 'Abbāsid Caliphs had become Arabized and identified with the local population. The Persian aristocracy had now found its own political outlet in the independent dynasties of Iran, and so the Caliphs found it necessary to seek a new basis of support. They found it in the Turkish Mamlūks under their Turkish commanders, expatriates with no local, tribal, family, national or religious affiliations, therefore the more devoted to the central government. From the beginning the Turks were noted for their superior military qualities, which seem to have lain mainly in their use of mounted bowmen and the nomadic speed of their cavalry. From this time on the Caliphs relied to an increasing extent on Turkish troops and commanders, to the detriment of the older cultured peoples in Islam, the Arabs and the Persians. The progressive militarization of the regime increased their strength.

By the eleventh century the Turks were entering the world of Islam, not only as individuals recruited by capture or purchase, but by the migration of whole tribes of free nomadic Turks still organized in their own traditional way. The consolidation of the Sung regime in China after an interregnum of disorder cut off the route of expansion into China and forced the Central Asian nomads to expand westwards. These Turkish invaders of Islam belong to the Oghuz tribes and are usually known as Seljuqs, after the name of the military family that led them.

The Seljuqs entered the territories of the Caliphate *c.* 970, and soon accepted Islam. Within a short time they had conquered the greater part of Persia, and in 1055 Tughrul Bey entered Baghdad, defeating the Buwaihids and incorporating Iraq in the Seljuq realm. In a few years the Seljuqs had wrested Syria and Palestine from the local rulers and from the declining Fāṭimids and, succeeding where the Arabs had formerly failed, conquered from the Byzantines a great part of Anatolia which became and remained a Muslim and Turkish land.

The Seljuqs were Sunnī Muslims, and their capture of the city of Baghdad was regarded by many as a liberation from the heretical Buwaihids. The Caliphs remained as nominal rulers, but the real sovereigns of the Empire, the greater part of which was now united under a single authority for the first time since the early Caliphate, were the Selijuq Grand Sultans, who defeated both the Byzantines and the Fātimids in the west.

The new rulers of the Empire relied largely in administration on Persians and on the Persian bureaucracy. One of the most notable figures of the age was the great Persian minister Niẓām al-Mulk, who developed and systematized the trend towards feudalism that was already inherent in the tax-farming practices of the immediately preceding period. The misuses of the previous era became the rules of a new social and administrative order based on land instead of money. Land was granted to or taken by officers. In return they furnished a number of armed men. These grants carried rights not merely to a commission on the collection of taxes, but to the revenues themselves. Though occasionally they became hereditary by usurpation, in theory and in usual practice they were granted only for a term of years, and were always revocable. The historian 'Imād ad-Dīn, writing in the Seljuq period, points out that this was the only way to give the turbulent Turkish tribesmen and soldiery an interest in the prosperity of agriculture and remarks:

H

It had been the custom to collect money from the country and pay it to the troops and no one had previously had a fief. Niẓām al-Mulk saw that the money was not coming in from the country on account of its disturbed state and that the yield was uncertain because of its disorder. Therefore he divided it among the troops in fiefs, assigning to them both the yield and the revenue. Their interest in its development increased greatly and it returned rapidly to a flourishing state.

In these few simple words he has described the long transition from a monetary to a feudal economy.

Social upheavals in such a period of change were inevitable. Landowners under the old regime were hard hit by the rise of a new class of non-resident feudal lords. Trade withered and declined. Perhaps the clearest indication of the decline of trade is to be found in the coin hoards of Scandinavia. During the ninth and tenth centuries Arabic and Persian coins are very numerous and indeed predominate in these hoards. During the eleventh century they decrease greatly in numbers; thereafter they disappear. The chief opposition movement in this period was again the Ismāʿīlīs, but in a new and changed form. In 1078 Ḥasan i Ṣabbāḥ, a Persian Ismāʿīlī leader, visited the Fāṭimid capital of Cairo. There he came into conflict with the military autocrat who was the real ruler of the Fāṭimid realms in the name of the decaying Imāms. On the death of the Fāṭimid Caliph Mustanṣir in 1094, Ḥasan i Ṣabbāḥ and his Persian followers refused to recognize the successor nominated for tameness by the military ruler, and severed connections with the emasculated organization in Cairo. The eastern Ismāʿīlīs now proclaimed their allegiance to Nizār, an elder son of Mustanṣir who had been passed over in the succession, and embarked on a new period of intense activity as an illegal revolutionary movement in the Seljuq dominions. The followers of the 'New Preaching', as the reformed Ismāʿīlism of Ḥasan i Ṣabbāḥ is known, are usually called Assassins, an Arabic word meaning takers of Hashīsh, in reference to the means by which they were alleged to have induced ecstasy in the faithful. The European meaning of the word derives from the political tactics of the sect.

In 1090 Ḥasan i Ṣabbāḥ obtained control of the inaccessible

mountain fastness of Alamūt in northern Persia. Here, and in similar bases established in Syria in the following century, the 'Old Man of the Mountain', as the Grand Masters of the sect were called, commanded bands of devoted and fanatical followers, waging a campaign of terror and 'assassination' against the kings and princes of Islam in the name of a mysterious hidden Imām. The emissaries of the Grand Masters carried out a series of daring murders of prominent Muslim statesmen and generals, including the Niẓām al-Mulk himself, in 1092. It is said that Richard Cœur de Lion was only spared by the daggers of the assassins because they did not wish to make things too easy for his rival Saladin. The terror of the assassins was not finally exorcized until the Mongol invasions of the thirteenth century, after which Ismāʿīlism stagnated as a minor heresy.

The economic reorganization of the early Seljuq period had its counterpart in religious life. In Baghdad and elsewhere theological colleges, known as *Madrasa*, were founded, which became the pattern of the many others that followed in the Islamic world. The Niẓāmīya of Baghdad, named after the great minister who founded it, and its sisters were centres of orthodox conformism, more especially of the Ashʿarī school, now becoming official, and were intended to a large extent to counter the revolutionary heterodoxy of the Ismāʿīlīs and the intellectual radicalism of the preceding period. Al-Ghazālī (1059–1111), one of the greatest of Muslim religious thinkers, taught here for a while. His works include refutations both of philosophy and of heresy.

After the death of the Niẓām al-Mulk the political fragmentation of the Near and Middle East was resumed. The Seljuq Empire broke up into a series of smaller succession states ruled by members or officers of the Seljuq House. It was during this period of weakness that in 1096 the Crusaders arrived in the Near East. Despite the idealistic aspect of this great movement, best exemplified in the ill-starred Crusade of the Children, in the perspective of the Near East the Crusades were essentially an early experiment in expansionist imperialism, motivated by material considerations with religion as a psychological catalyst. Traders from the Italian city republics following the trade they had established with Byzantium and the Fāṭimids to the sources of supply, warlike and ambitious barons, younger sons in search of principalities and sinners in search of profitable penance – these rather than the seekers of the Holy Sepulchre were the significant and characteristic figures of the invasion from the West.

For the first thirty years the disunity of the Muslim world made things easy for the invaders, who advanced rapidly down the coast of Syria into Palestine, establishing a chain of Latin feudal principalities, based on Antioch, Edessa, Tripoli and Jerusalem. This first period was one of colonization and assimilation. Conquerors and pilgrims settled in Syria, adopting local dress and customs, intermarrying with the local Christians. Fulcher of Chartres, a chronicler of the First Crusade, remarks:

> Now we who were westerners have become easterners. He who was Italian or French has in this land become a Galilean or a Palestinean. He who was a citizen of Rheims or Chartres is now a Tyrian or an Antiochene. We have already forgotten our birthplaces. Most of us do not know them or even hear of them. One already owns home and household as if by paternal and hereditary right, another has taken as wife not a compatriot, but a Syrian, Armenian, or even a baptized Saracen woman. . . . He who was an alien has become a native, he who was immigrant is now a resident. Every day our relations and friends follow us, willingly abandoning whatever they possessed in the West. For those who were poor there, has God made rich here. Those who had a few pence there, have numberless gold pieces here; he who had not a village there possesses, with God as giver, a whole town here. Why then return to the West, when the East suits us so well?

With which we may compare the remark of the twelfth-century Syrian Usāma ibn Munqidh: 'There are some Franks who have settled in our country and lived among the Muslims: they are of a better sort than those who have come recently. . . .'

But even in this first period of success the Crusaders were limited in the main to the coastal plains and slopes, always in close touch with the Mediterranean and Western world. In the interior, looking eastwards to the desert and Iraq, the reaction was preparing. In 1127 Zangī, a Seljuq officer, seized the city of Mosul for himself, and in the following years gradually built up an ever stronger Muslim state in northern Mesopotamia and Syria. His progress was at first impeded by the rivalry of other Muslim states and notably of Damascus, the ruler of which did not scruple to ally himself with the Latin Kingdom of Jerusalem against the common enemy. In 1147, the Crusaders unwisely brok the alliance, and Nūr ad-Dīn, the son and successor of Zangī, was able to take Damascus in 1154, creating a single Muslim state in Syria and confronting the Crusaders for the first time with a really formidable adversary. The issue before the two sides now was the control of Egypt, where the Fāṭimid Caliphate, in the last stages of decrepitude, was tottering towards its final collapse. The result could not long remain in doubt. A Kurdish officer called Ṣalāḥ ad-Dīn, better known in the West as Saladin, went to Egypt, where he served as Wazīr to the Fāṭimids while representing the interests of Nūr ad-Din. In 1171 Saladin declared the Fāṭimid Caliphate at an end. He restored the mention of the name of the 'Abbāsid Caliphs of Baghdad in the Mosque services and on the coinage and established himself as effective ruler of Egypt, professing an uneasy and uncertain allegiance to Nūr ad-Din. After the latter's death in 1174, leaving a minor as heir, Saladin absorbed his Syrian domains, thus creating a united Syro-Egyptian Muslim Empire. In 1187, he felt strong enough to attack the Crusaders. By his death in 1193 he had recaptured Jerusalem and expelled them from all but a narrow coastal strip which they held from the towns of Acre, Tyre, Tripoli and Antioch.

The united Syro-Egyptian state created by Saladin did not last long. Under his successors, the Ayyūbids, Syria broke up once again into a number of small states, but Egypt remained a strong united monarchy, the chief Muslim power in the Near East and the main bulwark of Islam against the West, defeating the repeated attempts of the later Crusades to recapture the Holy Land.

The chief permanent effect of the Crusades in the Near East was in trade. Colonies of Western merchants had flourished in the Levant ports under crusading rule. They survived under the Muslim reconquest and developed a considerable trade both of export and import. In 1183, Saladin, writing to the Caliph in Baghdad, justified his encouragement of this trade in these words: 'The Venetians, the Genoese, and the Pisans bring into Egypt choice products of the West, especially arms and war material. This constitutes an advantage for Islam and an injury for Christianity.' The thunder of the church in Europe against this trade and the decrees of excommunication against those who engaged in it were ineffective.

Meanwhile a new and more dangerous threat to Islam was arising in the East. Far away in eastern Asia Jenghiz Khān had, after a bitter internal war, united the nomadic tribes of Mongolia and launched them on a career of conquest which in extent must rank as one of the most remarkable in human history. By 1220 the Mongols had conquered all Transoxania. In 1221 Jenghiz crossed the Oxus river and entered Persia. His death in 1227 was followed by a pause, but in the middle of the century a new move westward was planned and executed. The Mongol Prince Hülekü crossed the Oxus river with instructions from the Great Khān of Mongolia to conquer all the lands of Islam as far as Egypt. His armies swept through Persia, overcoming all resistance and crushing even the Ismāʿīlīs, who had resisted all previous attacks. In 1258, Hülekü captured Baghdad, killed the Caliph and abolished the ʿAbbāsid Caliphate. The destruction of this great historic institution, even in decay still the legal centre of Islam and the token of its unity, was the end of an era in Islamic history. Yet in some ways the shock was perhaps not as great as is sometimes suggested. The Caliphs had long since lost almost all their real power, and secular Sulṭāns, both in the capital and in the provinces, had begun to arrogate to themselves not only the powers, but even some of the prerogatives, of the Caliphs. The Mongols did little more than lay the ghost of an institution that was already dead.

Unlike the Seljuqs, the Mongol invaders were still heathens and showed no interest in Islam, its traditions and its institutions. The destruction which they wrought in the lands they conquered has been much exaggerated. Most of it was purely strategic, not wilful. It ceased after the campaigns of conquest of which it was a part, and in Persia under Mongol rule a new period of economic and cultural development began. But in Iraq the immediate effects of the Mongol conquests were the breakdown of civil government and the collapse of the irrigation works on which the country depended, aggravated by the inroads of Bedouin tribes once the control of the sedentary power was relaxed.

Still more fatal for the prosperity of Iraq was its inclusion, as an outlying province, in an eastern empire the centre of which lay in

Persia. Henceforth the valley of the Tigris and the Euphrates, cut off from the Mediterranean provinces in the west by a frontier of sand and steel, outflanked in the east by the rise of the Persian centre to which it was subordinated, could no longer serve as channel for the East-West trade, which moved north and east to Turkey and Persia, westward to Egypt and the Red Sea, leaving Iraq and the fallen city of the Caliphs to centuries of stagnation and neglect.

Despite some raids into Syria, the direct effects of the Mongol conquest on the Arab world were confined to Iraq, which was now attached to the Mongol State centred on Persia. Syria and Egypt were saved from the Mongols by the new regime that had grown out of the Ayyūbid monarchy. Though the Ayyūbids themselves were Kurds in origin, their regime was of Turkish Seljuq type. The ruling class was a military autocracy of Turkish pretorians, often able to control the Ayyūbid Sulṭān himself.

In the middle of the thirteenth century the power of the Turkish Mamlūks in Cairo was supreme and a new regime emerged, the Mamlūk Sultanate, which ruled Egypt and Syria until 1517. In 1260, after a period of confusion following the death of the last Ayyūbid, a Qipchaq Turk called Baibars became Sultan. His career in many ways forms an interesting parallel with that of Saladin. He united Muslim Syria and Egypt into a single state, this time more permanently. He defeated the external enemies of that state, repulsing Mongol invaders from the east and crushing all but the last remnants of the Crusaders in Syria. An idea of genius was to invite a member of the ʿAbbāsid family to establish himself in Cairo with the title of Caliph. The line of ʿAbbāsid Caliphs in Cairo were mere court functionaries of the Mamlūk Sulṭāns. The Egyptian historian Maqrīzī (*d.* 1442), remarks:

> The Turkish Mamlūks installed as Caliph a man to whom they gave the name and titles of Caliph. He had no authority and no right to express his opinion. He passed his time with the commanders, the great officers, the officials and the judges, visiting them to thank them for the dinners and parties to which they had invited him.

The Cairo Caliphs represent the final stage in the decay of the Caliphate.

The Mamlūk system of Baibars and his successors was feudal and was an adaptation of the Seljuq feudalism brought into Syria and Egypt by the Ayyūbids. An officer or amir received a grant of land in lieu of pay and on condition of maintaining a certain number of Mamlūk soldiers, varying between five and a hundred according to his rank. He normally devoted two-thirds of his revenues to their upkeep. The grants were not hereditary though there were many attempts to make them so. The system was based on the permanent eviction of the Arabized descendants of the Mamlūk officers by newly imported Mamlūks, thus preventing, perhaps deliberately, the formation of a hereditary landed aristocracy. A Mamlūk officer received his grant for life or less. He did not normally reside on his estates, but in Cairo or in the chief town of the district where his fief lay. He was interested in revenue rather than possession. The system therefore developed no *châteaux* or manors or strong local authorities of the Western type. There was no subinfeudation, and even the division of the land in Egypt into fiefs was not permanent, being subject to a periodic territorial refount.

The Mamlūks themselves were bought slaves, trained and educated in Egypt. At first they were mainly Qipchaq Turks from the northern shores of the Black Sea, later they included Mongol deserters and men of other races, chiefly Circassians, with occasional Greeks, Kurds and even some Europeans. But Turkish or Circassian remained the language of the dominant class, many of whom, including some Sultans, could hardly speak Arabic. The Mamlūk State as developed by Baibars and his successors was based on a highly elaborate dual administration, civil and military, both sides controlled by Mamlūk officers with civilian staffs. Until 1383 the Mamlūk Sultans followed one another in more or less hereditary succession. Thereafter the Sultanate was held by the strongest commander. On the death of a Sultan his son succeeded as formal head during an interregnum while the real succession was decided.

In the first period the Mamlūks were threatened by Christian and Mongol enemies, and their supreme achievement is their defence of the Islamic civilization of the Near East against these enemies. During the fifteenth century a new power arose—the Ottoman Empire, rising like a phoenix from the ruins of the Seljuq Sultanate of Anatolia. Relations between the two states were at first friendly, but conflicts arose when the Ottomans, safely established in Europe, turned their attention to Asia.

The trade with Europe, and particularly the trade between Europe and the Further East via the Near East, was of vital importance to Egypt, both for the trade itself and for the customs revenues derived from it. During periods of strength Mamlūk governments protected and encouraged this trade, which brought Egypt great prosperity and a new flowering of arts and letters. But the Mongol threat, warded off by Baibars, was not yet averted. In 1400-1 the Turco-Mongol forces of Tīmūr (Tamerlane) ravaged Syria and sacked Damascus. Plague, locusts and the depredations of the unleashed Bedouin completed the work of the departed Mongols, and the Mamlūk Sultanate suffered a blow to its economic and military strength from which it never recovered.

The crises of the fifteenth century brought new fiscal policies aimed at extracting the maximum profit from the transit trade. After first encouraging Indian and even Chinese merchants to bring their wares to ports under Egyptian control, Sultan Barsbay (1422-38) had the idea that it might be even better to seize the trade than to tax it. He began by making sugar a royal monopoly, and followed it with pepper and other commodities. These policies, maintained by his successors, led to rising prices, foreign reprisals, and ultimately to general economic collapse, in which the government could survive only by currency depreciation and by drastic and violent taxation.

The historians of the period paint a vivid picture of the increasing corruption and inefficiency of the regime in its last days. One historian, speaking of the Wazirs, remarks:

> They were cruel rascals, inventors of a thousand injustices, arrogant and presumptuous. They were famous neither for their knowledge nor for their religious spirit. They were the scourges of their age, always with a causeless insult ready in their mouths. Their existence, passed exclusively in oppressing the people of their time, was a disgrace to humanity.

When Sultan Barsbay convened the four chief Qādīs of Cairo and asked them to authorize new taxes over and above those laid down by the Holy Law, one of them was reputed to have replied: 'How can we authorize the taking of money from the Muslims when a wife of the Sultan wore on the day of her son's circumcision a dress worth 30,000 dinars; and that is only one dress and only one wife.'

In 1498 came the crowning catastrophe. On May 17th of that year the Portuguese navigator Vasco da Gama landed in India, having come by sea round the Cape of Good Hope. In August 1499 he returned to Lisbon with a cargo of spices. He had opened a new route from Europe to the Further East, cheaper and safer than the old one. Other expeditions followed rapidly. The Portuguese established bases in India, and developed direct trade, dealing a mortal blow to the Egyptian route and cutting off the very lifeblood of the Mamlūk state. The Mamlūks, recognizing the immediate consequences of these events, and urged to action by their Venetian fellow-sufferers from this diversion, tried by diplomacy and then by war to avert the Portuguese menace. Their efforts were fruitless. The Portuguese fleets, built to face the Atlantic gales, were superior in structure, armament and navigational skill to those of the Muslims. Soon they were able to defeat the Egyptian squadrons, systematically destroy Arab merchant shipping in the Indian Ocean and penetrate even to the Persian Gulf and the Red Sea. In the sixteenth century, after the Ottoman conquest and the growth of European commercial enterprise, the Levant trade revived to some extent, but remained of secondary importance. The Arab Near East had been outflanked. Not until the nineteenth century did the main routes of world trade return to it.

During the long period that we have been considering three significant changes emerge. The first of these is the transformation of the Islamic Near East from a commercial monetary economy to one which, despite an extensive and important foreign and transit trade, was internally a feudal economy, based on subsistence agriculture. The second is the end of the political independence of the sedentary Arabs and Arabic-speaking people and their replacement by the Turks. In the vast but thinly peopled deserts the Arab tribes retained the independence they had recovered during the decay of the 'Abbāsids, defying repeated attempts to impose control over them and often eroding the frontiers of the cultivated land in their long struggle with the Turks. In a few mountain outposts, too, men who spoke Arabic retained their independence. But everywhere else, in the cities and in the cultivated valleys and plains of Iraq, Syria and Egypt, for a thousand years people of Arabic speech were no longer to rule themselves. So deep-rooted was the feeling that only the Turks were equipped by nature to govern that in the fourteenth century we find a Mamlūk secretary of Syrian birth addressing the Arabs in Turkish through an interpreter rather than in his mother-tongue, for fear lest he should lose face by speaking the despised language of the subject people. As late as the beginning of the nineteenth century Napoleon, when he invaded Egypt, tried unsuccessfully to appoint Arabic-speaking Egyptians to positions of authority and was forced to resort to Turks who alone could command obedience.

The third change is the shifting of the centre of gravity of the Arabic-speaking world from Iraq to Egypt. The disorganization and weakness of Iraq and its remoteness from the Mediterranean, across which both the traders and the enemies of the later period were to come, ruled that country out as a possible base. The only alternative was Egypt, the other trade-route, and the irrigated valley of a single river, which by its very nature demanded a single centralized government – the only powerful centralized state in the Arab Near East.

With the power of the Arabs went the glory. The Persian and Turkish-speaking rulers who inherited the thrones of the Arabs patronized poets who could praise them in their own languages, according to their own tastes and traditions. First the Persians then the Turks developed independent Muslim culture languages of their own, and, with the political leadership, assumed the cultural leadership of Islam. Under Seljuq and Mongol rule the Islamic arts entered new periods of efflorescence. Both Persian and Turkish literatures, while strongly coloured by the Arab-Islamic tradition, branched out on independent and significant lines. After Seljuq times the literary use of Arabic was confined to the Arabic-speaking countries, except for a limited output of theological and scientific works. The movement of the centre of gravity of the Arab world westwards gave greater importance to Syria and still more to Egypt, which now became the main centres of Arabic culture.

The development of a static society and the predominance of a static formalist theology led to a decline in independent speculation and research. The passive dependence on authority in public life found its parallel in literature, which suffered a loss of vitality and independence. The most striking feature of the time is the increased stress on form for artists, on memory for scholars. But there were still some great figures – Ghazālī (1059–1111), one of the greatest thinkers of Islam, who attempted to combine the new scholasticism with the intuitive and mystical religion of the Sūfīs; Ḥarīrī (1054–1122), still regarded by the Arabic-speaking peoples as the supreme exponent of literary form and elegance; Yāqūt (1179–1229), biographer, geographer and scholar, and in post-Mongol times a series of historians or rather historical compilers, among whom the Tunisian Ibn Khaldūn (1332–1406) stands alone as the greatest historical genius of Islam and the first to produce a philosophic and sociological conception of history.

In 1517 the weakened and decaying Mamlūk Empire crumbled before the Ottoman assault and for four hundred years Syria and Egypt formed part of the Ottoman Empire. Soon the Barbary States as far as the frontiers of Morocco accepted Ottoman suzerainty, and with the final Ottoman conquest of Iraq from Persia in 1639, almost the whole Arabic-speaking world was under Ottoman rule.

Only in a few places did the peoples of Arabic speech retain any real independence. In Arabia, the south-western province of Yemen became an Ottoman Pashalik in 1537, but recovered its independence in 1635. The Arab rulers of Mecca and the Ḥijāz, the Sharīfs, recognized Ottoman suzerainty and were dependent on Cairo rather than on Constantinople. For the rest the Bedouin of the Peninsula maintained their independence in the inhospitable deserts. In the mid-eighteenth century they produced a potent spiritual movement, in some ways resembling the rise of Islam itself. A jurist of Najd called Muḥammad ibn ʿAbd al-Wahhāb (1703–1791) founded a new sect, based on a rigid, anti-mystical puritanism. In the name of the pure, primitive Islam of the first century, he denounced all subsequent accretions of belief and ritual as superstitious 'innovation', alien to true Islam. He forbade the worship of holy men and holy places, even the exaggerated veneration of Muḥammad, and rejected all forms of mediation. He applied the same puritan austerity to religious and personal life. The conversion to the Wahhābī doctrine of the Najdī amīr Muḥammad ibn Suʿūd gave the sect a military and political focus. Soon Wahhābism spread by conquest over most of central Arabia, wresting the holy cities of Mecca and Medina from the Sharīfs who ruled them in the Ottoman name and threatening even the Ottoman provinces of Syria and Iraq. The reaction came in 1818, when an invading Turco-Egyptian army sent by Muḥammad ʿAlī, the pasha of Egypt, broke the power of the Wahhābī empire and confined Wahhābism to its native Najd. There the sect survived with somewhat diminished vigour, to reappear as a political factor in the mid-nineteenth and again in the twentieth century.

In the Lebanon a tradition of independence in the mountain areas had existed from early times, when Christian invaders from Anatolia turned the upper reaches of the mountain into a Christian island among the surrounding sea of Islam. Semi-independent local dynasties, some Christian, some Muslim, some Druse, continued to rule parts of the mountain under Ottoman suzerainty, with a degree of independence that varied with the efficacy of Ottoman government. Finally, in the Far West the mixed Arab–Berber Empire of Morocco retained its independence and developed along lines peculiarly its own.

For the rest, the subjection of the Arabs to Turkish rule, begun under the Caliph Muʿtaṣim, confirmed by the Seljuqs and Mamlūks, was maintained by the Ottomans. Such movements of independence as there were in the Arab provinces were organized more often than not by rebellious Turkish Pashas rather than by any local leaders.

In Egypt the Ottomans maintained the Mamlūk order, superimposing an Ottoman Pasha and garrison upon it. But the feudal system lost its military character and came to be based on revenue rather than on military service. Most of the fiefs became *Iltizām* – usufructuary assignments of State lands of officials and others with limited rights of succession and disposal. The assignee collected payments from non-owning peasants. Both the assignee (*Multazim*) and the peasant paid taxes. The Multazim's heirs could succeed on payment of a due. With the weakening of central control the local Beys seized power and the Pasha became a passive observer of their rivalries. Sometimes they were able to win full control.

The Ottoman conquest brought a greater degree of change to

Syria. In the early seventeenth century the country was divided into the three Ottoman Pashaliks of Damascus, Aleppo, and Tripoli, to which a fourth, Saida, was added in 1660. Each was under a Pasha who bought his post and enjoyed a large measure of local freedom of action, varying according to circumstances and personality. The Pashaliks themselves were organized on Ottoman feudal lines. Most of the land was divided among fief-holders, mainly Turks. The fiefs were semi-hereditary and carried the obligation of paying annual dues and rendering military service with retainers. The rights of the fief-holder were the collection of taxes and the exercise of some seigneurial powers over the peasantry. Many Iltizāms of crown lands were held by court dignitaries in Constantinople. The Pashas had great powers, increasing with the distance from the capital and the weakness of the government.

At first the Ottoman conquest was an advantage, bringing relative security and prosperity after the heady nightmare of late Mamlūk rule. But by the eighteenth century the decline of the Ottoman Empire brought general misrule and corruption, anarchy and stagnation. During this long period of alien rule, this mutually disadvantageous association of two cultures, each perforce entangled in the other's decline, the spirit of revolt is still discernible. The Ismā'īlī movement had dwindled into insignificance after the Mongol invasions, but other movements replaced it. Even under the Mamlūks there were sporadic revolts of the Arabic-speaking Egyptian population. Occasional movements for independence under the Ottomans were usually due to ambitious individuals, often themselves Turkish governors. The really popular opposition, in accordance with Islamic tradition, was expressed religiously, this time in Sūfism. This was at first a purely individual mystical experience, then a social movement with an extensive following among the lower orders, organized in Dervish brotherhoods, often associated with craft guilds. The Sūfīs were not formally heretical as the Ismā'īlīs had been, and were politically quietist. In religion they opposed a personal mystic faith to the dominant orthodox transcendentalism which at times they succeeded in influencing. As far as they had any direct political expression, it was hostile to the existing order. But the Sūfī revolt by infiltration failed just as the head-on Ismā'īlī assault had failed in its time. The static elements were too strong. Real change was to come from a new factor from outside, more powerful and infinitely more aggressive than the Hellenistic impulses that had quickened the intellectual ferment of medieval Islam.

The Arabs had been in contact with western Europe since the time of the first conquests. In Spain and Sicily they had ruled western European populations and had maintained military, diplomatic and commercial relations with other western European states. They had received west European students in their universities. The Crusaders had brought a piece of western Europe to the very heart of the Arab East. But these contacts, fruitful for the West which had learnt much from the Arabs, had little effect on the latter. For them the relations were and remained external and superficial and had but little influence on Arab life and culture. The geographical and historical literature of the mediaeval Arabs reflects their complete lack of interest in western Europe, which they regarded as an outer darkness of barbarism from which the sunlit world of Islam had little to fear and less to learn. 'The peoples of the north', says the tenth-century geographer Mas'ūdī,

> are those for whom the sun is distant from the Zenith . . . cold and damp prevail in those regions, and snow and ice follow one another in endless succession. The warm humour is lacking among them; their bodies are large, their natures gross, their manners harsh, their understanding dull and their tongues heavy . . . their religious beliefs lack solidity . . . those of them who are farthest to the north are the most subject to stupidity, grossness and brutishness.

An eleventh-century Qādī of Toledo, in a work on the nations who have cultivated knowledge, enumerates the Indians, Persians, Chaldees, Greeks, Romans (including Byzantines and eastern Christians), Egyptians, Arabs and Jews. Among the rest, he singles out the Chinese and the Turks as 'noble peoples' who have distinguished themselves in other fields, and contemptuously dismisses the remainder as the northern and southern barbarians, remarking of the former: 'Their bellies are big, their colour pale, their hair long and lank. They lack keenness of understanding and clarity of intelligence, and are overcome by ignorance and foolishness, blindness and stupidity.' As late as the fourteenth century no less a man than Ibn Khaldūn could still remark dubiously: 'We have heard of late that in the lands of the Franks, that is, the country of Rome and its dependencies on the northern shore of the Mediterranean, the philosophic sciences flourish . . . and their students are plentiful. But God knows best what goes on in those parts.' This attitude was at first justified, but with the progress of western Europe it became dangerously out of date.

From the beginning of the sixteenth century a new relationship between Islam and the West is discernible. The West had made great technological advances in the crafts of war and peace. It had renewed itself through the Renaissance and the Reformation. The break-up of the feudal order had freed trade and unleashed enterprise, for which the consolidation of centralized nation states provided solid and reliable political instruments, and so began the great expansion of western Europe which by the twentieth century had forced the whole world into its economic, political and cultural orbit.

In the Near East the imposing outward strength of the Ottoman Empire concealed the deep weaknesses of a military despotism with a decaying social order. The moral bond of religious unity was of diminishing effectiveness. Corruption and decay in the administration and the decline of moral values were aggravated by economic stagnation. Neither the military ruling class nor the intellectual class were interested in economic change.

FIVE

The Decline of Spain in the Seventeenth Century[1]

JAIME VICENS VIVES

THE PROBLEM OF SPAIN'S ECONOMIC DECLINE

The subject of Spanish economic decline has aroused debates of the most impassioned kind, from the time it was first broached by the *arbitristas* of the seventeenth century to the present. Legions of Spanish and foreign authors have dedicated themselves to studying it, often with open prejudice, as the American historian Hamilton has pointed out repeatedly. Thus, German writers have exaggerated the magnitude of the collapse, wishing to glorify by contrast the figure of Charles V, whose ancestry was partly German; the Italians have done the same out of a desire to put the blame for the downfall of their own country on someone else, a downfall which was coincident with and related to Spanish domination of Italy; French and Spanish authors have done so because they wanted to extol the Bourbons' economic policy; finally, the 'liberals and Protestants of every country, to stigmatize the Inquisition and the persecution of racial minorities'.

However, these exaggerations should not make us forget the coincidence of extremely abundant evidence pointing to a decline in herding, agriculture, industry and trade in the Spain of the seventeenth century. 'Aridity, deforestation, insufficient harvests, emigration, expulsions, spread of mortmain, alms-giving and ecclesiastical vocations, vagabondage, disdain for work, mania to acquire titles of nobility, *mayorazgos*, high prices, upward movement of wages, taxes, wars, weakness of royal favourites and of the

[1] This article was first published as chapters 29 and 30 of *An Economic History of Spain* (with the collaboration of Jorge Nadal Oller, translated by Frances López-Morillas), Princeton University Press, 1969.

I

sovereigns themselves . . .' are all terms used over and over to depict the country's disastrous economic situation. Nevertheless, we must point out with Pierre Vilar that 'these causes of decadence' are too numerous for us not to suspect in them the presence of stronger reasons; that is, the general economic crisis of the seventeenth century, in which converged (in the case of Spain) political impotence, incapacity for production and social disintegration. The origins of this crisis went back a long way, though it did not become clearly apparent until Philip II's death in 1589. As Hamilton writes: 'In broad terms one can say that it took Spain only a century (from the union of Castile and Aragon in 1479, to the annexation of Portugal in 1580) to attain political pre-eminence and only a century (from the death of Philip II in 1598 to that of Charles II in 1700) to fall into the rank of a second-rate power.'

DEMOGRAPHIC STAGNATION AND DEPOPULATION

We lack data which would permit us to draw up a general balance-sheet of Spanish demography at the end of the seventeenth century, like the one made by Ruiz Almansa for the last years of the sixteenth. In the case of Catalonia, for example, no census was taken during the entire century. Under such circumstances it is not surprising to observe the divergent figures given by different authors: while Ruiz Almansa holds that the population of Spain remained stationary throughout the seventeenth century, varying only slightly from the figure of 8 million inhabitants, Hamilton assigns to it a loss of about 25 per cent of its total population and concludes with von Beloch that by 1700 Spain probably had only about 6 million people.

Stagnation or depopulation, the one certain fact is the break in the ascending curve of sixteenth-century Spanish demography. On the other hand, there was a growing tendency towards a new distribution of the country's human potential: the centripetal tendency of the previous period gave way in the seventeenth century to a relationship which placed the population of the Peninsula's periphery in an ever more favourable situation. This tendency was also apparent within the smaller area of Catalonia, where settlements along the coast grew with extraordinary rapidity at the expense of population centres in the interior.

Now that we have come down to the regional level, let us give a few cases in detail. As for Castile, Domínguez Ortiz points out as probably closest to the truth a number given in a memorial of 1623 which, basing its figures on the books of the Treasury of Papal Bulls, gives Castile some 6 million inhabitants. If we compare this figure with that of approximately 1600, it would mean that in thirty years the kingdom had suffered a decline of 25 per cent. But what happened during the seventy-seven years between 1623 and 1700? Domínguez Ortiz does not attempt to answer this, but describes the exodus from rural areas and the consequent 'demographic concentration which, in certain extreme cases, reached the point in some parts of La Mancha or Andalusia where towns of many thousands of inhabitants were separated by 15 or 20 kilometres of desert,' as the characteristic feature of Castilian demography in the 1600s. He finds specific causes for this phenomenon in the terrible tax demands which fell most heavily on the village, levies of soldiers, absenteeism of rich landowners, and the oppression of hamlets and chief towns in certain districts. (For example, he says, the miserable state of the people of Las Hurdes is in large part a legacy of jurisdictional abuses originating in La Alberca.) And he points out as general factors in the population decline the decadence of the monarchy, sale of real property and of council positions, excessive number of clergy, attraction of the Indies, etc.

In the territories of the Crown of Aragon, the expulsion of the Moriscos, decreed by Philip III, occasioned the most spectacular drop in population. A memorial of 1638 states that of the 453 Valencian hamlets occupied by Moriscos up to 1609, 205 were still abandoned, while the resettlement of the remaining 248 had required the transfer of 13,000 households of Old Christians. In the Kingdom of Valencia the expulsion affected 23 per cent of its inhabitants; in Aragon, 16 per cent; and in Catalonia, where the Moriscos were concentrated along the course of the Ebro and Segre rivers, only a little over 1 per cent. As for the Principality of Catalonia, recent studies have emphasized the influence of the same factors pointed out by Domínguez Ortiz for the Castilian rural exodus. Parish registers and much other subjective evidence coincide in placing the maximum population around 1615–20; at that time, which coincides with the final stages in the great current of French immigration, the country probably had about half a million inhabitants. Later, especially from 1630 to 1660, the tendency was one of stagnation if not regression.

One more reference to the demographic trend in seventeenth-century Spain: in general, two great phases can be distinguished, one of depression during the first half of the century, and another of recuperation following the end of the great period of plague (1648–54) which, concentrated in the Western Mediterranean area, affected not only the Levant – from the Roussillon to Andalusia – but also invaded the Meseta from the south and from Aragon. We must make perfectly clear, however, that our information is inconclusive, and consequently so are any generalizations we may necessarily have drawn. In the case of Galicia, for instance, a study by Ruiz Almansa, whom we have quoted so often, has revealed that population loss was moderate during the first few years of the seventeenth century and became progressively greater after the revolt in Portugal and subsequent war. In this area, therefore, we cannot speak of recuperation during the second half of the seventeenth century.

THE PLAGUES

Those specialists who have pointed out the demographic stagnation of the seventeenth century, while they have been concerned with its causes, have generally passed over the most important of them: incidence of the plague factor on population development. Contagious diseases, which periodically intervened in the demographic process (no generation in the seventeenth century escaped their impact), decisively influenced the tendency towards decline.

The survival of a medical system which still considered Galen the supreme authority, and the persistent state of undernutrition in most of the country, caused by economic decline in general and agricultural decline in particular, explain the extraordinary virulence of seventeenth-century plagues. At that time there was a very close relationship between harvests and population figures, and the inadequate system of land transport could not cope with large-scale shipment of grain. In a closed economy, as Habsburg Spain still was, a district's food supply was reduced to what its agricultural resources could produce. Only the coastal towns could resort to importing grain in case of an insufficient harvest. Under these conditions mortality was closely linked to the ups and downs of local agricultural production. People made considerable efforts to soften the effects of these, such as storing the surplus harvest in good years, or simply resorting to biological measures. None the less, a time would come when a series of bad harvests made all these efforts insufficient, and the spectre of famine stalked the land. Then, when the disproportion between the number of men and the amount of available food became intolerable, the always latent factor of plague caused terrible ravages among the undernourished people. Jean Meuvret, in France, has demonstrated with statistics and graphs the exact coincidence in times of famine between the mortality curve and the price of wheat; when grain is lacking the curve shows a dizzying rise. There are no analogous studies for Spain, but we do have documents and proofs of the solid connection between demographic development and economic conditions.

As for the results of the plague itself, there is much evidence from persons and institutions of the period concerning the loss of one-third or one-fourth of the inhabitants of a given locality or region due to plague. That these figures are not so exaggerated as might be thought is proved from counts of deaths listed in parish records, or those which cities occasionally ordered made. Thus, the minute-book of the old Council of Barcelona permits us to follow very closely the impact of the epidemic on the Catalonian capital over a period of time. To sum up, and taking into account the fact that we do not have reliable figures for the whole country, we can at least state that the population loss in the Spanish Levant during the seventeenth century was due, more than anything else, to the constant incidence of contagious diseases, notwithstanding the counter-factor of a booming birth-rate, of the order of 40 or 50 per 1,000.

Now that we have noted the importance of the plague factor in demographic development, we need to pinpoint its appearance in time and estimate its periodicity. As on so many other occasions, we find ourselves in an area where nothing has been published, where ground has not yet been cleared, in so far as the greater part of Spanish territory is concerned. On the other hand, studies made by

Emilio Giralt and Jorge Nadal have succeeded in reconstructing the complete picture of the great plagues of the 1600s in Castile: 1589–91, 1629–31, 1650–54 and 1694. That is, in the space of one century there were four appearances of plague, with a mean periodicity of twenty-five years; this was what we meant when we said that no generation could have escaped its effects. Generally speaking, these plagues affected the entire country, producing population losses that were difficult to overcome. The most serious of all was produced by the great epidemic we have mentioned before, that of 1648–54, which came at the end of a series of catastrophic events and placed Spain in one of the most dangerous moments of her history. For the rest, the study of these plagues has corroborated the theory concerning a close relationship between undernourishment and rise in the mortality rate. When things were going badly in one region, the others, where circumstances were identical, soon saw themselves attacked as well. A good example of this is the path taken by the plague about the year 1650; it began in Andalusia in 1648, spread into Murcia and Valencia, spilled over into Catalonia and then Aragon through the passes of the Maestrazgo region, into France and finally to Majorca, Sardinia and Naples, where it still persisted in 1656.

Now that we have established the principle that plague depended on food supply, we would not be wrong in attributing the high incidence of plague to the long drought of the last few decades of the sixteenth century and the early years of the seventeenth. Aridity meant the failure of many harvests, hence undernourishment, triumph of plague and depopulation. In this respect the seventeenth century, like the fourteenth was a fateful one for Spanish demography.

THE SPANIARD AND LABOUR: THE HIDALGO MENTALITY

In the last years of the sixteenth century, the twin spectacle of a bourgeoisie ruined by its own enterprises and an inactive, though prosperous, aristocracy, had had a most unfortunate effect on the mental attitude of the Spanish working classes. Survival of the economic factors which caused this bitter paradox and the subsequent polarization of the country's social structure into two antagonistic groups – the active and the inactive – found confirmation in the seventeenth century by means of customs and laws which placed a stigma of social dishonour on the mechanical occupations, as they were called at the time.

Any number of examples, foreign as well as domestic, could be adduced to corroborate this thesis, and many authors have defined the attitude of the seventeenth-century *hidalgo* as the expression of a theory of leisure. In *Lazarillo de Tormes*, the sixteenth-century picaresque novel, just one step removed from the crisis that was to usher in the new century, we read that 'any no-good wretch would die of hunger before he would take up a trade'. This aversion to work was accompanied by a puerile pride in indolence:

> Let London manufacture those fine fabrics of hers to her heart's content; Holland her chambrays; Florence her cloth; the Indies their beaver and vicuña; Milan her brocades, Italy and Flanders their linens . . . so long as our capital can enjoy them; the only thing it proves is that all nations train journeymen for Madrid, and that Madrid is the queen of Parliaments, for all the world serves her and she serves nobody.

This absurd defence came from the pen of Alfonso Núñez de Castro in 1675 during the dark days of Charles II's minority, on the eve of the financial disaster of 1680.

Groaning under the weight of all the disadvantages (direct taxes fell exclusively upon him) and none of the advantages, it is not surprising that the poor commoner of the seventeenth century should have pinned all his hopes on changing his status and going over to the other camp by purchasing a patent of *hidalguía*, or minor nobility. The consequences of the first step – changing his status – are well known: 'People of the plebeian class disdain to work in factories, workshops, and manufactories, and steer their children into other careers in which, for one person who wins, a thousand lose'; and as a final result, 'idleness, depopulation, and an increase in the crime and indigence which are found everywhere.'

The second step was the acquisition of a patent of nobility. Literature is full of examples of the mania to attain the category of knight or *hidalgo* which obsessed the Spaniards of the seventeenth century. Let us take a look at the consequences of this mania.

Traditionally the *hidalgos*, like the lesser nobility in general, had made up for the tax exemption they enjoyed by giving military service: while the plebeian paid taxes to the Crown, the *hidalgo* defended it by force of arms. However, the creation of professional armies and the discrediting of the military profession in the seventeenth century ('the people are so convinced that all those who exercise the soldier's profession are wicked, that there is no tailor or cobbler who would not consider it a great dishonour were his son to take it up') deprived the *hidalgo* of his function; and he often used his social position 'not in order to go to war, but in order not to go'. On the other hand, the Crown's financial needs, which required the collaboration of all citizens, leaped the barrier between commoner and non-commoner and extended taxation to those privileged persons who had not paid it previously.

Thus, though the seventeenth-century Spaniard's mania for nobility continued to gain ground, the boundaries between the status of commoner and *hidalgo* grew more and more imprecise. What difference could there be between a plebeian and a *hidalgo* if, as Prieto Bances assures us, the latter was hardly a noble (since he had no power), nor necessarily free (since it was possible to be one and yet be in a state of servitude), nor a soldier by obligation (*hidalgos* formed a large part of the knightly group, but could be excused from all military service)? In reality the difference was purely formal. The *hidalgo* belonged to a higher estate in society and accepted everything on condition that his rank would not be affected. The example given by Domínguez Ortiz is significant: obliged to pay taxes by the Crown, the Castilian *hidalgo* defended his immunity as such with more fervour than he did his pocket book, which in any case was slim. The medieval idea associating taxation with dishonour and servitude was still alive in Castile, and when the *hidalgos* of the sevententh century were forced to pay taxes, they did not recognize the poll tax, which they felt to be an unworthy levy; they resigned themselves, however, to paying taxes of a general nature,

> provided that, in defence of principle, a rebate or small quantity should be returned to them, given by the State or municipal government as indemnification for the part of the *sisa* corres-

ponding to their personal consumption. Many paid taxes until they were ruined, but always insisted on observing the legal fiction that they need not be included in the list of taxpayers.

Conclusion: the Castilian *hidalgos* of the seventeenth century deprived the Spanish economy of an enormous human potential, which went into other, completely unproductive professions: 'Church, royal household, or the sea.'

DESTITUTION AND VAGRANCY: INDISCRIMINATE CHARITY

Though he did not entirely eschew work – as has been repeated so many times by those interested in presenting him as an archdrone – we will have to agree at least that the Spaniard of the Golden Century refused to put any effort into tasks which he considered plebeian (Carande). The same man who spared no effort to preserve his honour, win fame and achieve glory in Italy, Flanders, Germany, or the Indies, was quite willing to live, even under the best of circumstances, on some modest income from property, or, in the majority of cases, from some other form of parasitism, turning the country into 'an idle and vicious republic', as Cellorigo puts it. This Spanish-attitude towards life, which often displayed spectacular traits, coincides in any case with the development of the mania for nobility and the insufficient recompense given to sound work. This situation progressively decreased the needs of the poor and caused their stoicism to increase. In this respect, the literature of the period undertook to reflect faithfully the subterfuges of a society sunk in destitution and at the same time eager to hide its difficulties. On this point it is interesting to notice how closely the best literary witnesses to the crisis followed it: the two parts of *Guzmán de Alfarache*, the most important of the 'black' novels, were published in 1599 and 1604, and the first part of *Don Quijote*, the liveliest satire on the society of the time, appeared in 1605.

Destitution reached a peak during Philip IV's reign. The king himself has left proof of his concern over general food supply in his letters to Sister María de Agreda, but he was as impotent to solve this problem as the others with which he was faced. There were moments when the situation became so desperate that it resulted in dangerous popular uprisings – for example, one in Seville in 1652, known under the name of the 'Green Banner', a classic mutiny brought on by famine which kept the Feria quarter in a state of revolt for twenty-one days and had repercussions in Cordova and other Andalusian cities.

The cure proposed by the State to avoid similar movements was worse than the disease. Its supply policy was dictated by the simplistic mercantilist idea then in vogue (Viñas Mey): imposition of a price ceiling – 'cheap bread' – on staple articles, without taking into consideration that a simple price war, ignoring any compensation to the poor labourer, would merely swell the army of unemployed who had had to abandon trades that did not give them a living wage. Nor did the attitude of the clergy, who stubbornly denounced the state of destitution, respond to a more intelligent view of the problem. The free soup of the convents, distributed indiscriminately to every sort of vagabond and needy person, raised begging to the status of a *modus vivendi*, was a contributing cause to 'that sort of religious aura with which Spaniards invested the act of giving or receiving alms', and stripped beggars of 'their shamefaced appearance, for they lived in a well-organized manner and turned begging into a lucrative business' (Pfandl).

FOREIGNERS IN THE SPANISH ECONOMY

Ever since the middle of the sixteenth century, in the wake of the discoveries and colonization of America, Spain had been the gathering place for many European businessmen. At the end of the century, to the influx of precious metals was added as a further inducement the industrial decline of the country, which made provisioning of the Indies fleet dependent on foreign imports.

During the sixteenth century the most favoured merchants had been natives of countries allied with the Crown: Genoese, Flemings and Germans. We have already spoken of the advantages obtained by the former, beginning with the treaty of 1528. Their supremacy lasted exactly one century, for after 1629 they were dislodged from their Spanish positions by the Portuguese who, thanks to their African establishments, could open or close at will the supply of Negro slaves so necessary to the Indies. In fact, in 1640 there were

2,000 Portuguese traders – the majority of them Jews or *conversos* – in Seville, and to judge from the obituaries of the cathedral, their number was growing. The Portuguese *conversos* – or *marranos*, as they were called – could count on very favourable positions in the court itself and in the principal port cities on the Cantabrian Sea. Their central offices were in Hamburg, the city where they had taken refuge after the Spanish *tercios* captured Antwerp in 1585. Portugal's separation from the Spanish Crown put an end to Portuguese expansion in Spain and her colonies.

The Flemings, for their part, had relied upon the favour of Charles V. Export trade from the Low Countries to Spain was very active until the insurrection there. This event obstructed mercantile dealings. On the one hand, the Dutch became bitter enemies of Spanish shipping and commerce. Between the capture of La Brielle in 1571 and the Peace of Westphalia in 1648, Holland carved out a colonial empire at the expense of Spain and Portugal. On the other hand, the Walloons of the south, who were Catholics, and the Flemings remained loyal to Spain; but the war paralysed industry and commerce in their country, with the natural repercussions on trade with Spain. It survived, however, and even experienced a period of considerable prosperity after 1621, when Holland again went to war with Spain after the Twelve Years' Truce. The Flemish colony in Andalusia was large. We need only recall that in 1596 whole companies of Flemings could be formed to defend the city of Cádiz against English attack.

Last, the Germans, the great bankers of the Crown during Charles V's reign, appeared on the Spanish coasts as merchants and sailors beginning in the last years of the sixteenth century. This was an action carried out by the Hanseatic cities (members of the medieval German Hanseatic League). These cities took advantage of the Dutch provinces' rebellion to bring to Spain wood, grain, tools, metals, and munitions supplied by the rebels. As neutrals, the Hamburgers and other Hanseatic merchants were favoured by the governments of Madrid and Brussels and made a great success of this trade, especially at moments when England and France found themselves at war with Spain. The great risks taken by Hanseatic shipping, which, pursued by the Dutch and other adversaries of the Habsburgs, often had to sail around the north of Scotland and

Ireland, were amply compensated by the large profits to be gained. During the truce of 1609–21 Spanish-Hanseatic trade fell off considerably but later managed to recover, until recognition of the United Provinces in 1648 re-established the former situation.

The lure of profits from the Indies trade was so great that even countries who were enemies of the Spanish Crown lost no opportunity to enter the country and swell the colonies of foreign merchants in every port. The French were prominent among them. Traders from Nantes appeared in Seville, Málaga and the Canaries under the protection of those of Bilbao, whose privileges they shared because of the trade agreement existing between those two cities. Merchants from Vitré developed their contacts with Cádiz, Sanlúcar, and Puerto de Santa María after 1560. Finally, the Normans, who already thought of Seville and Cádiz as way stations on the Canaries route, stopped in those cities more frequently after the sixteenth century. We do not know the number of French citizens established in the Spanish sea-coast cities, but the presence of French consuls in Cádiz (1575 or 1581), Seville (1578), Barcelona (1578) and Valencia (1593) attests their importance.

In regard to the French, we must mention the continuation of the great stream of peasants, herdsmen and small artisans which had begun at the end of the fifteenth century. While immigration into Catalonia dropped sharply about 1620, it grew more intense in the rest of Spain. In Aragon and Valencia, French farmers assured continuation of the crops after the Morisco expulsion. In the Castilian cities, the French carried out the humblest trades, those which repelled the minds of the natives. By the end of the seventeenth century, French pressure in the large cities and towns of Spain was so considerable that there were even violent popular outbreaks against them.

The last to arrive in the deteriorating Spain of the seventeenth century were the English and Dutch. And this is understandable. Not only had they been the Spaniards' bitterest adversaries, but their Protestant status was also a barrier between them and Spain. It was necessary to seek a *modus vivendi*, however, for although the Spanish Crown owned the Indies, Amsterdam and London had the industries necessary to supply them. This fact was translated into a special regime enjoyed by Protestants in Seville, Cádiz, Málaga, and

Puerto de Santa María. By the end of the century Santander also tried to obtain this same privileged situation. But the Crown did not give its authorization.

In the second half of the seventeenth century the enormous Dutch trade with Spain, in particular with Cádiz, changed Amsterdam into Europe's chief money market: the stock of currency concentrated in the city became so considerable that it permitted, against the rules of the mercantile system, export of previous metals and coins not only to India for its own trade, but even to a number of Western countries. Already active during the Thirty Years' War, this trade reached its apogee after the peace of 1648, when Hispano-French rivalry induced the Spaniards themselves to favour the business dealings of their late enemies, the Dutch. In the last decades of the seventeenth century Dutch and English merchants appeared in Catalonian ports as active buyers of the brandy made from Panedés and Maresme wines.

Owing to Spain's weakness in the seventeenth century, the activity of these foreigners was prejudicial to the country's interests. When we take up in detail the matter of trade we shall see how they monopolized almost all the great maritime traffic, especially that carried on with the Indies. Contemporary Spaniards, were well aware of this process, and there were a great many complaints by *arbitristas* and even literary testimony to the situation. Both coincided in repeating *ad infinitum* the 'desubstantization' of Spain through its effects. We shall conclude by quoting the opinion of Sancho de Moncada, who alleged that foreigners enjoyed the largest incomes in the nation: 'more than a million in *juros* (bonds on public revenue) an infinite number of *censos* (bonds on private debts), all the funds of the Crusade, a great number of of prebendaries, *encomiendas*, benefices, and annuities.'

DECLINE OF AGRICULTURE: EXPULSION OF THE MORISCOS

Early in the seventeenth century the Spanish soil, always so neglected because of the traditional predominance of herding, received a rude blow. The expulsion of the Moriscos (former Mudéjares forced to convert in 1502 in the Crown of Castile and in 1525 in the Crown of Aragon), decreed in 1609–11, deprived agriculture of the most skilled manpower it possessed. (Article 5 of the expulsion decree exempted 6 per cent of the Moriscos 'so that dwellings, sugar mills, rice harvests, and irrigation systems may be preserved, and so that they may give instruction to the new settlers'.) How was such an unfair decision arrived at? We shall quote Pierre Vilar's reply to the question:

> They (the Moriscos) were a residue of the conquered Moors, converted by force but not assimilated; sometimes shopkeepers, more often farmers, formed into closed communities at the service of the great lords of the Reconquest: a colonial problem on home soil which Spain had borne for two centuries without solving. About 1600, after so many revolts, repressions, expulsions and mass displacements, the danger of a general uprising was probably only a myth. But suspicion towards the crypto-Christian, 'bad blood', the spy, the marauder, the businessman who laid his hand on too many ducats, turned the Morisco into an all-too-obvious scapegoat in a moment of crisis. He was considered too prolific and too frugal: those were the real charges.

Let us examine the results of the expulsion. In the demographic sphere a new loss occurred which was difficult to recoup. The most reliable figures (Lapeyre's) give the following balance sheet of expelled persons:

CROWN OF CASTILE

	Absolute figures	Per cent of total population
Central and intermediate zone (Old and New Castile, León, La Mancha and Extremadura)	45,000	0·9
Southern zone (Murcia and Andalusia)	37,000	2·0

CROWN OF ARAGON

	Absolute figures	Per cent of total population
Aragon	64,000	16·0
Catalonia	5,000	1·0
Valencia	135,000	23·0

In other words, the number of expelled persons came to nearly

300,000 persons altogether, equivalent to about 3 per cent of all Spaniards. But the expulsion did not affect the different regions equally, so that those composing the Crown of Aragon, especially Valencia, were much more seriously damaged. In these regions the problem of resettlement became extremely urgent; but this does not mean that it was always solved. In Valencia, for example, almost half the Morisco villages abandoned in 1609 were still uninhabited in 1638. In Aragon, conversely, French immigration succeeded in 'filling in', as the expression of the period was, the void left by the expelled Moriscos.

In the economic sphere the consequences were even more important. Essentially, disappearance of the agricultural *élite* (as early as May 1610, the *Audiencia* of Valencia lamented the 'scarcity of labourers caused by the expulsion of those very Moriscos who were so extremely hard-working') meant the disappearance of the *revenues* with which these vassals' lords paid their interest charges, or annuities obtained from mortgage loans (*censos* and *censales*), contracted with the speculators of the cities (*censalistas*). If we recall the extraordinary enthusiasm of moneyed people to invest their capital in *censos al quitar*, or annuities, we will easily understand the collapse produced in this parasitic society by the departure of the Moorish peasants who, in the last instance, supported it. Reglá, the first historian to bring this important question into focus, transcribes an essential document proving that contemporaries of the expulsion were well aware of its consequences in the economic sphere. The Archbishop of Valencia wrote to a minister of Philip III in 1608:

> All those who are necessary to the Republic, for its government and spiritual and temporal adornment, depend on the services of the Moriscos and live from the mortgages with which they or their ancestors have burdened the Morisco towns; and thus, when they see that they are unable to live, they will have to make an appeal to their rights and call upon His Majesty, lamenting their indigence and destruction.

To prevent this 'indigence and destruction' the landholding aristocracy, not content with seizing the property of the expelled Moriscos, finally obtained a reduction of the interest on *censales* to 5 per cent. Thus the cycle was complete: the measure which began by affecting agricultural economy made its immediate effects felt on the feudal economy, and finally affected the bourgeois economy which was its creditor. We may therefore conclude that, despite Hamilton's optimistic theory, the whole Spanish economic system suffered from the expulsion.

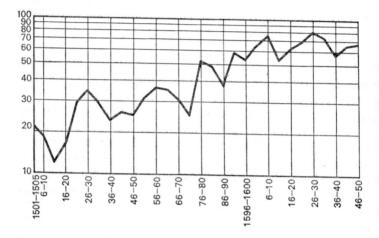

EVOLUTION OF WHEAT PRICES IN PALMA DE MALLORCA
FROM 1501 TO 1782,
EXPRESSED IN QUARTERLY WAGES AND FIVE-YEAR AVERAGES
(*after* J. FONTANA, using documents of the Royal Majorcan Economic
Society of Friends of the Country).

Along with the expulsion of the peasants who made a speciality of irrigation farming came the definitive victory of the old feudal concept that the basis of agrarian economy was cereals, olives and vines. The only other crops that continued to be cultivated were sugar cane and cotton, in the southern part of Granada; silk in this same region, Valencia and Murcia; linen and hemp in a number of regions in the North, and rice along the Mediterranean shore. No notable progress was made in a century which, to make matters worse, witnessed a constant drop in the price of agricultural products.

DECLINE OF HERDING AND OF THE MESTA

One of the incontrovertible facts of Spanish economy in the seventeenth century is the loss in livestock. Although continuous statistical series do not exist, we know through Klein that during the second half of the century the number of head of sheep controlled by the Mesta was less than 2 million, a fact which confirms the diminution in numbers which had begun a century before. There were many causes for this phenomenon. Some authors attribute it to a period of drought undergone by the Mediterranean climate in the last decades of the sixteenth century and the early years of the seventeenth. Others add to this factor the disturbances which took place in the development of herding because of the wars in Catalonia and Portugal (1640–1), interrupting use of the customary pastures and sheepwalks. And finally, we must not forget the attacks levelled against the Mesta, precursors of those which were to ruin it in the eighteenth century.

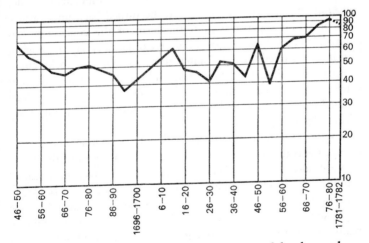

In this interesting graph, despite the insular nature of the place under observation, the great fluctuations of the international trade cycle can be observed, especially the two inclines of the sixteenth-century price revolution, the seventeenth-century decline, and eighteenth-century recovery.

K

In the seventeenth century open warfare was declared on the Honourable Assembly of the Mesta. This powerful organization, so feared but at the same time so respected, became the target of every sort of criticism. Opposition to the privileged members of the Mesta arose from delegates to the Cortes, from the chanceries, the defenders of agriculture and enclosures, and from the great creditors of the Crown. The attacks converged particularly on the powers of the *Alcalde Entregador*, or President, who saw his powers limited on all sides and his jurisdiction questioned.

The Mesta gave way before these attacks inch by inch. Its chief support was its alliance with the monarchy, which, though in 1619, in exchange for the *millones* tax, it had granted the Pragmatic of Belén declaring entrance into the stockbreeders' brotherhood a voluntary act and limiting the functions of the organization's judges, had compensated the Mesta in 1633 by re-establishing all its privileges and granting full protection to its grazing grounds. The royal cedula of 1633 prohibited ploughing up new ground and ordered all arable land granted since 1590 – private as well as municipal, public, common and uncultivated lands – to be turned back into pasture with or without permission, if the term of the concession had expired. 'The carrying out of this decree of famine,' says Colmeiro, 'for it condemned men to suffer want so that the flocks could prosper', necessitated a demarcation and survey of such lands, thus originating an infinite number of lawsuits and litigations which aroused many passions and plunged agriculture and non-migratory herding into a calamitous condition.

In spite of this monopolistic legislation it was no longer possible to change the course of events, for the herding crisis pushed the Mesta into a dead-end street. Klein observes that after 1685 the threat of imminent bankruptcy can be seen in the Mesta's account books. In this last phase the great livestock trust could count less and less on royal support: 'The impecunious later Habsburgs were quite as ready to dicker with the opponents of the Mesta for subsidies as they were to bargain for "loans" from a scarcely solvent organization. . . .' Thus, throughout the seventeenth century the defeat of this formerly all-powerful herding organization was slowly being prepared.

COLLAPSE OF CASTILIAN INDUSTRY

'Even if we did not find convincing proof,' wrote Colmeiro in 1863, 'in the Parliamentary papers and the royal decrees, of the weakness and collapse of Spanish industry from the middle of the sixteenth century to the beginning of the eighteenth . . . we would be more than convinced of the sad truth by the inquiry of the Council of Castile in 1619, the very urgent *junta* of 1620 (though it bore no fruit because of Philip III's untimely death), and the efforts, pleas, and importunings of the impoverished and ruined cities, mainly Toledo, Cordova, Seville, Granada, and Valencia, which in 1655 were trying to bargain with the Court for a cure, or at least some relief from their troubles.'

Though detailed studies are lacking, there are numerous memorials of the period (as for example Martínez de la Mata's, giving the list of seventeen guilds disbanded in 1655) which provide unequivocal evidence of this industrial decline. In particular, the table below, taken from Larraz, shows population decline in the old industrial and mercantile cities of Castile.

City	Heads of Families			
	1530	*1594*	*1646*	*1694*
Burgos	1,500	2,665	600	1,881
Valladolid	6,750	8,112	3,000	3,637
Palencia	1,364	3,063	800	972
Salamanca	2,459	4,953	2,965	2,416
Avila	1,523	2,826	1,123	965
Segovia	2,850	5,548	—	1,625
Toledo	5,898	10,933	5,000	5,000
Cuenca	—	3,095	800	1,641

The population loss for Toledo and Segovia is particularly significant as an index of Castilian industrial evolution. The recovery of Burgos and Cuenca at the end of the seventeenth century has a possible connection with renewed export of raw wool.

One of the few encouraging events in this moribund seventeenth century was the establishment of ironworks for casting cannon and munitions in Liérgana and La Cavada (Santander). Assisted by the policies of the Count-duke of Olivares, the Belgian Jean Curtius and the Luxembourger Georges Labande set up an excellent metallurgical works in those towns in the year 1622.

This seems the appropriate place to sum up, with Larraz, the different factors contributing to the decline of Castilian manufactures: (1) industrial superiority of the Low Countries, England, and France over Castile, (2) the deviation of Spanish prices from European ones as a consequence of the influx of American silver, (3) the lesser capitalistic spirit of Castile in the sixteenth and seventeenth centuries, (4) the unhappy results of the Habsburgs' European intervention.

A realization of this process of decline was so widespread that by the end of the century, during the reign of Charles II, there was a general desire for recuperation, and many projects to attain it were devised. In Castile, among the excellent proposals of the Count of Oropesa one at least survived: the *Junta de Comercio y Moneda*, or Board of Trade and Currency, created in 1679, which gave fruitful results in the following century. In 1674 thirty-two Aragonese deputies joined under the presidency of Don John of Austria to try to restore the kingdom's economic potential, but the committee was stalemated by a serious controversy over freedom versus limitation of trade. In Catalonia the efforts of a generation of men united around the doctrines of Narcis Feliu de la Penya obtained positive results with the aid of foreign technicians. Finally, in a general sense, the Royal Pragmatic of 1682 was – as Colmeiro says – the first step toward the rehabilitation of arts and trades, when it declared that possessing or having possessed factories for weaving silk, cloth, woollens, or other textiles was not unworthy of the nobility.

THE GUILDS AND INDUSTRIAL DECLINE

The guilds are usually blamed for the stagnation into which Spanish industrial production fell in the seventeenth century. Echoing the diatribes of the enlightened thinkers of the eighteenth, even apologists for the guilds attribute the stagnation of industry to them, because of the restrictions on entry into trades and the system of privileges enjoyed by the guilds.

The history of guilds under the Habsburgs has not yet been

written. The amount of material, both published and unpublished, is immense. But the published material is not very useful, for its authors based their studies on an idealistic view of the past and were unaware of even the rudiments of the economic life from which the guilds had sprung and out of which they developed. Just as they considered the institution to be very ancient – and we have already pointed out its relative modernity, even in Catalonia – they believed that its progress had been uniform, disregarding the tenacious opposition that had existed ever since the sixteenth century between the guilds of the old privileged cities and those which had arisen in the towns around them precisely to escape their monopolistic prerogatives. The relationship between the trade cycle and guild activity has also been forgotten, and, what is still more important, the State's tendency to submit guilds to uniform rules and strict control, not out of industrial policy but out of an obvious desire for tax revenue.

Now that we have cleared up these points, we can concentrate on guild history under the Habsburgs and gauge its supposed responsibility for the country's industrial decline. After Ferdinand and Isabella's measures, which gave form to guild life in Catalonia and Valencia and encouraged creation of guilds in the Crown of Castile, the sixteenth century was characterized by the appearance of a considerable number of guild corporations. The motive was Spain's industrial expansion in the wake of the expanding economy of the period. A simple examination of the known foundations shows us that most modern guilds were founded in the second half of the sixteenth century, especially after 1530, starting point of the upward trend. In Burgos, for example, the market gardeners received their charter in 1509; the tanners in 1512; cobblers, 1528; and masons, 1529; after 1540, embroiderers (1544), dealers in skins (1545), shoemakers (1552), thong-makers (1570), charcoal-burners (1574), hatters (1589), and gamekeepers (1591). In Toledo, to the guild of the wax workers, recognized in 1446, were added the dyers (1530), butchers (1560), pastrycooks (1580), locksmiths (1582), sieve-makers (1588), and straw workers (1598). The same phenomenon is found in Saragossa (1540, blacksmiths; 1550, wool-combers; 1556, harness-makers, mattress-makers, locksmiths, and hatters; 1565, linen-weavers; 1567, wool-weavers; 1584, glass-blowers; 1590, carters), and even in Barcelona and Valencia, where numerous similar lists could be made.

Simultaneously, the guilds appeared in towns of secondary importance. Economic prosperity caused journeymen to move from the cities, where a mastership was difficult to obtain, and set themselves up as masters in nearby towns and even villages. Little attention has been paid to this phenomenon in Spain. However, its strength is undeniable. There is evidence of it in Catalonia (for example, foundation of the wool-weavers' guild in Sabadell in 1558, competing with the powerful wool-dressers' association of Barcelona). More examples could no doubt be found in other regions.

During the prosperous phase of the trade cycle there was no guild problem. It arose when Spanish foreign trade began to decline, and with the decline came a reduction in labour activity. Then the guilds became organizations of resistance to the contraction of economic life. Such is their history – a very unflattering one – in the seventeenth century. Caught between the devil of business stagnation and the deep sea of the State's tax demands, the guild corporations lived miserably and poorly, generally speaking, with the all-too-predictable sequel of obstructionism, oppression, fraud, oligarchic monopolies, and so on. Gradually people began to think of them as a dead weight, especially in places where they had been established relatively recently. In 1678 voices were raised in the Cortes of Calatayud asking for their suppression. However, in places where money was abundant the guilds continued to prosper; this was the case of those in Madrid. It was, in fact, during the seventeenth century that the Five Greater Guilds of Madrid were established, whose importance in Spanish economic life will be taken up in the next chapter.

The Crown's interest in keeping the guilds under strict control became accentuated in this same century, as its fiscal needs continued to grow. It was essential to the plans of the reformers of the Spanish treasury at the time to have an assured tax base. Hence, when the Board of Trade and Currency was created in 1679 the guilds came under its jurisdiction in administrative and economic matters. With the exception of the Catalonian and Valencian guilds, which maintained their traditional independence, the life cycle of the guilds was over: they returned fully to the control of the State which had created them, and in the end the State itself decreed their elimination.

STAGNATION OF COMMERCIAL LIFE

The view of mercantile law 'as a statute . . . of persons who destroyed the harmony of mediaeval life and sowed restlessness in the human soul' is, according to Beneyto, what characterizes the abundant specialized literature of the Spanish Golden Age. Naturally there were some exceptions, especially in Catalonia and Valencia where, beginning with Eiximenis in the fourteenth century, a theological tradition more favourable to the world of business was kept alive. But the attack of the Dominicans, zealous continuers of Scholastic tradition against this Mediterranean type of deviationism, permits us to state in broad terms that in this area ethical prejudices reinforced those of the *hidalgo* mentality against economic activity in general. These several prejudices were linked to agricultural and industrial decline, and constituted the factors responsible for the downfall of Spanish commerce in the 1600s.

As for the interior of the Peninsula, Colmeiro points out 'the thousand impediments derived from opinion and from laws' which hindered the development of trade: lack of roads and transport, the disdain with which the nobles treated merchants, the supply policy, monopolies, pre-emptive rights, intervention of *regatones* (the black-marketeers of the period), internal customs duties (turnpike and municipal taxes, apart from those enjoyed by private persons by right of inheritance, and certain regional privileges designed to prevent the introduction of products and foodstuffs from neighbouring regions), price-fixing, alterations in the currency, etc.

External trade did not cease, but it passed almost entirely into the hands of foreigners. We have already studied the settlement of foreign businessmen in Spain, and the results of the illicit traffic with America encouraged by them. But, as Larraz points out, foreigners also gained control of regular trade with the Indies, hampered as it was by strict laws and administrative regulations. The flow of legal trade, constantly dwindling as contraband grew in importance, fell almost totally under their influence. And here we notice the industrial and mercantile superiority of other countries, the bad effects of Spain's tax system and its unsatisfactory customs organization. A memorial of French origin, quoted by Haring, See and Larraz, sums up the consequences of this situation. According to it, in 1691 participation of the various countries in American trade, which officially continued to be Spain's exclusive monopoly, was distributed in the following manner: French, 25 per cent; Genoese, 21 per cent; Dutch, 19 per cent; Flemings, 11 per ent; English, 11 per cent; Hamburgers, 7.6 per cent; and Spaniards, 3.8 per cent. We need not accept these figures as absolutely accurate, but if we recall that as early as 1619 Sancho de Moncada complained that 'nine out of ten parts of the Indies trade are carried on by foreigners', we may conclude without fear of contradiction that Spain had lost by a very wide margin the game she was playing with other European nations for the possession of American riches.

Decline was equally noticeable on the other routes of Spanish trade. There are no detailed studies on the extent of this decline, but we can find symptoms of the phenomenon. Thus, we are told by Smith and Basas that in Burgos the number of marine insurance policies drawn up between 1594 and 1619 (that is, a period of twenty-five years) did not exceed 200, while the annual average in the middle of the sixteenth century had been more than 1,000; or, through mercantile records, we can see that maritime trade in Barcelona between 1630 and 1660 was largely in the hands of the French and Genoese, and that its radius was growing smaller and smaller, ending in Lisbon and Sicily.

DECLINE OF SHIPPING AND FAULTY COMMERCIAL POLICY

The situation we have just described is even less comprehensible when we recall that up to 1640 the united empire of Spain and Portugal was the centre of world trade, and possessed, in Seville and Lisbon, the chief points of contact between the colonial world and continental Europe. Even after the political unity of the Peninsula was dissolved, the Spanish-American bloc continued to have a great deal of influence on the economies of all European nations.

We can realize this if we examine the centres of trade activity which were linked with the Peninsula. Indispensable colonial products converged on Seville and Lisbon: in the first place silver, and then sugar, cocoa, pepper, hides and various dye plants. To these must be added the products of Spanish soil: silk, iron and wool. And in the opposite direction, wheat and other foodstuffs, war and naval equipment and a large number of manufactured products came into the Peninsula destined for use by Spaniards and by the colonies. From the Far East and the New World, an intense commercial life circulated along the chief maritime trade routes, which included the most important French, English, and Dutch ports, the Baltic trading posts, Central Europe by way of Hamburg, and even reached as far as Archangel in northern Russia. On the other hand, Spanish sea-ports controlled the best routes in the Western Mediterranean, especially that of Leghorn in Italy.

Certainly, and this was one of the fundamental causes of the Spanish economy's profound decline in the seventeenth century, maritime trade had fallen into the hands of foreigners. Chaunu has pointed out the tremendous difficulties undergone by the Spanish administration in order to organize the Indies trade within its own monopolistic area. After 1610 the number of ships in the Indies trade kept getting smaller and smaller, reaching its lowest tonnage in 1640. In fact, ever since 1590 the Portuguese fleet had helped to ensure Atlantic service. The freight crisis brought on by the recession of 1640 could not be overcome, even though foreign ships were used for the first time. Perhaps this phenomenon had something to do with the change in navigation brought about by the disappearance of the galleon in favour of the lighter and more seaworthy *nave*, and the difficulties experienced by Spanish sailors in adapting themselves to the new type of ship, which the Dutch and English introduced everywhere. If this occurred in the Atlantic area, it is useless to ask what happened in places which were not closed to foreigners. The French controlled trade in the Levant; the British, trade between the North Sea and the Western Mediterranean; the Hanseatic League, in the Baltic Sea; and the Dutch everywhere, for Holland was the great sea power of the seventeenth century. To gain some idea of the decline of the Spanish merchant fleet during this period, suffice it to say that the Catalans, whose sea power in the later medieval centuries had been undisputed, now went to Marseilles to pick up Eastern goods and to Leghorn to buy Baltic wheat brought there by the English. The same thing happened in the

Cantabrian ports, whose principal needs were served by foreign vessels.

Of course, Spain would have been able to defend herself against the danger which threatened her shipping if she had used heroic measures, such as a navigation act like the one promulgated by Cromwell in defence of English ports. But this would have forced the country first into a war with Holland, and then with England. In regard to Holland, Spain blundered at the Treaty of Münster in 1648, not only accepting Holland's *de jure* independence, which was already obvious, but also acceding to a disadvantageous commercial treaty by the terms of which Spain was left wide open to Dutch trade. At the same time, a tariff schedule susceptible to all kinds of illicit dealings was set up, based on weight of merchandise. Thanks to this policy of concession, the government of Philip IV obtained Holland's neutrality in the war it had undertaken with France and shortly afterward with England. The military defeat also carried with it a new economic recession. In 1659, by the terms of the Peace of the Pyrenees, France obtained the right to bring goods into Catalonia free of customs duty; and soon after, in 1667, by means of a commercial agreement with England (called Eminente's Agreement from the name of its negotiator), Spain opened her borders to British goods, with extremely unfavourable tariffs also based on weight.

The fatal result of these two tendencies – decline of the Spanish merchant fleet and opening of the internal market to foreign goods – could have been avoided only by a vigorous export policy. Unfortunately this did not take place. On the contrary, just at that time the traditional products sold abroad encountered brisk competition both in quantity and quality. About the middle of the seventeenth century Spanish wool was replaced by Irish wool in many Northern markets, at the same time as Swedish iron began to move out of the Baltic area into England and France. Silk also beat a retreat in the fact of the ever-increasing progress of the Piedmontese in this product.

In consequence, the tariff-free system set up by the Habsburgs turned out to be of very little advantage to the country's interests.

TRADE MONOPOLIES: SEVILLE AND CÁDIZ

Another very serious drawback affecting seventeenth-century Spanish economy was the preservation intact of the monopoly system in American trade. We have already analysed the causes which brought about the implanting of this monopoly, and the choice of Seville as the centre of colonial economic activity. If we follow the Andalusian capital's development under the Habsburgs, we shall see the best example of the virtues and defects of mercantilist economic policy in general.

In principle, monopoly of the Indies trade meant that, at a time when sea transport was extremely expensive, a premium was placed on the export of Sevillian products; this fact, and the abundance of available capital due to the presence of the monopoly itself, aided the industrial development of the city. Thus, sixteenth-century Seville, which had become the largest city in Spain (150,000 inhabitants), had the second largest shipbuilding industry in the country after Biscay, and was its chief manufacturer of silk: it had ships to supply the Indies trade and high-grade cloth for export. At the same time, since in spite of this development it was unable to supply the American market, the Andalusian capital also played the role of intermediary between the industrial powers of Northern Europe and the new lands which had been brought under exploitation. A great number of foreign vessels were constantly docking in the port of Seville, bringing in manufactured products and taking away gold and silver from Mexico and Peru: some figures from 1604, a period of maximum prosperity, tell us that imports were almost double exports. 'This figure alone explains why silver became so scarce only a few weeks after the galleons' arrival; it took the route of merchandise in reverse, for the lack of equilibrium in the balance of trade could be resolved only by exporting precious metals.'

This imbalance between incoming and outgoing trade grew ever larger as the rise in Spanish prices compared to foreign ones placed the industry of Seville in a position of obvious inferiority. Guilds of shipwrights, caulkers and rope-makers (an Andalusian speciality) almost disappeared, and the number of silk looms decreased very noticeably (for the reasons described and also because of the sumptuary laws which limited industries producing luxury goods).

Under these circumstances the Crown adopted the practice of sequestering the treasure of private individuals brought by the fleet (Charles V had already done this), of declaring itself bankrupt (beginning with Philip II), or simply by devaluing the currency (beginning with Philip III). These unilateral measures were especially damaging to Seville, the port where the galleons dropped anchor and where the chief bankers lived. Therefore the State's own mercantilist regulations, which had forged Seville's prosperity in the sixteenth century, also brought about its bankruptcy in the seventeenth.

Aside from the causes we have enumerated, there were others of a strictly local nature. In this area 'the event which marked the irretrievable decline was the plague of 1649' (some 60,000 dead, almost half of the entire population), exhausting the city's demographic reserves. Cádiz took advantage of this misfortune to win the last attack in her fierce mercantile competition with the city on the Guadalquivir. Let us follow with Domínguez Ortiz the development of this struggle between the two great Southern commercial cities: Cádiz was one of the nine ports authorized in 1529 to send ships directly to the Indies; it is true that this arrangement had very unfavourable results and was finally abolished by another royal cedula in 1573, so that those ports, situated mostly in the North, never participated importantly in overseas trade. But Cádiz was more fortunate thanks to her geographical position: since it was absurd that merchandise loaded on the shores of the Bay of Cádiz (including most of the wine consumed in America) should have to be taken to Seville simply to fulfil administrative formalities there, measures of tolerance in this respect were soon taken; there were numerous ships which, with or without a licence, sailed directly from Cádiz for the Atlantic crossing. In 1558 vessels coming from Hispaniola and Puerto Rico laden with hides and sugar were authorized to unload in Cádiz. Three years later this concession was amplified to include damaged ships which could not cross the Sanlúcar sandbar, provided that gold, silver and pearls were taken to the House of Trade.

On the other hand, legal decrees could not alter the fact that the larger ships in the fleet came up the river with great difficulty, especially if they were heavily laden; and the practice grew up that large ones came no farther than Sanlúcar, or left Seville half-loaded and finished loading in Sanlúcar or Cádiz. From force of habit, this led to the practice of assigning to Cádiz a third of the fleet's total tonnage for its own merchandise. The diversion of sea traffic resulted in diversion of merchandise, and finally the transfer of the officials themselves. After 1547 there was a *Juzgado*, or magistracy, in Cádiz, a sort of branch of the House of Trade. By the middle of the seventeenth century Seville's monopoly was purely nominal, while Cádiz's volume of business increased for the following reasons: foreigners preferred it, for they wished to escape the vigilance of the Sevillian administrative bodies and found the Bay of Cádiz more convenient for contraband than the inland port of Seville; the difference in tariffs owing to the individual practices of those who framed the customs, for they were interested in attracting the foreign merchants who came to Cádiz, and treated the obligatory and assured clientele of Seville more perfunctorily; and the demographic disaster of 1649, which stripped Seville of all her strength.

The rivalry between the two cities continued to be keen during the rest of the seventeenth and early eighteenth centuries, until in 1717 the activities of a well-known citizen of Cádiz, Andrés de Pez, governor of the Council of the Indies, assured the victory of his own city by obtaining from Patiño the decree transferring the House of Trade to Cádiz. In the end, Seville and Cádiz changed positions: now Seville retained only a judge delegated from the House, the 'third of tonnage', and the right to appoint two consuls.

DECLINE OF BURGOS AND RISE OF MADRID

Another important phenomenon in Castilian economic life in the seventeenth century was the rapid decline of Burgos as Castile's co-ordinating centre. We have spoken before of the pernicious effects of the 1575 financial crisis on life in Burgos. The disorganization of the Medina del Campo–Antwerp connection gravely affected all the cities which had formed part of the circuit, Burgos as well as Bilbao and Santander. Another factor was soon added to this: the decline in wool exports, to which we have also alluded. According to statistics of 1622, export through the port of Santander was not even a shadow of what it had been fifty years before: eleven ships and 605 sacks of wool annually compared to sixty-six and 17,000 respectively. Burgos suffered very severely from the consequences of contraction in the wool trade. This was why it sought so insistently the centralization of the Castilian wool market in the city (for example, during Charles II's reign), accusing the Cantabrian ports of fraud in trade with foreigners. This attitude stemmed from the great period of discord between Burgos and Bilbao, and therefore did not have great importance in a period of general decline.

Actually, Burgos had been reduced to the size of a large village in the course of the first forty years of the seventeenth century. From the 20,000 inhabitants it had possessed in 1575, the number had dropped successively to 13,000 in 1594, 7,600 in 1611, and 3,000 in 1646. Nazario González states the chief cause of this regressive phenomenon: the rise of Madrid as the economic capital of the Spanish State. Many natives of Burgos abandoned their trades and businesses to move to Madrid, where it was easy to do business and to prosper.

In fact, in the latter years of the sixteenth century Madrid had become an extraordinary human concentration by the standards of the time (14,000 inhabitants in 1570, 108,000 in 1617). When the crisis caused by the transfer of the Court to Valladolid (1603–6) was over, Madrid continued to develop extraordinarily up till 1660 (340,000 inhabitants?), in response to the law of creation of huge urban centres in countries of low population density and impoverished agriculture. This accumulation in the city of revenues from the great latifundist aristocracy, especially the Andalusian aristocracy, the management of public finance, and the interests of the American empire, stimulated monetary circulation and commercial life. Hence important mercantile bodies arose which gained great strength from the proximity and needs of the administration. Such corporations demanded adoption of a free-trade policy, based especially on the import of luxury goods.

The basic pressure in this regard was not exercised by the Consulate of Madrid, installed in 1632 as one more organ of the State's bureaucratic machinery (it was, in fact, a dependency of the Royal Council, whose members were appointed by the king); the lever which really set the wheels in motion was the *Cinco Gremios Mayores*, or Five Greater Guilds. Their history is really the economic history of Madrid under the Habsburgs and in the eighteenth century. Humbly born during the fifteenth century, by the middle of the seventeenth these guilds were powerful groups which stood out above the multitude of smaller ones. They were – it should be carefully noted – commercial rather than industrial corporations; the woollen merchants, the silk merchants of the Guadalajara Gate, the jewellers of the Calle Mayor, the spice merchants of the Calle de Las Postas and the cloth merchants. Woollen merchants, silk, merchants, jewellers, spice merchants and drapers all benefited greatly from the installation of the capital in Madrid and slowly separating themselves from the smaller guilds, joined forces in defence of their interests. With the exception of the woollen merchants, we find them acting together in a number of lawsuits after 1667; in 1679, year of the creation of the Board of Trade, they formed a compact group; on 23 March 1686, the ordinances were laid down which defined their particular field of action. They were well on the way, then, to becoming united in a single and powerful body, an aim not achieved legally until 1731 with the formation of the *Diputación de Rentas*, or Council on Revenues, of the Five Greater Guilds. But after the end of the seventeenth century the fiscal factor linked them more and more closely into a coherent whole from which each guild member gained new and fruitful advantages.

Thus Madrid, closely linked with Cádiz, was the new star which arose in Spanish commercial life during the seventeenth century. Firmly linked to latifundist economy and the free-trade tendencies of the Five Guilds, it foreshadowed through its bureaucracy the country's industrial rebirth by means of a controlled system. This was to be its great undertaking during the eighteenth century.

TAXES AND ECONOMIC LIFE

Following Sureda's example, we shall divide the Royal Treasury's revenues in the Crown of Castile into *ordinary revenues not deriving from taxation* and *tax revenues*. Among the first, the most outstanding were those coming from royal ownership of salt beds, mines, the tunny-fisheries of Cádiz and revenues from masterships of military orders (incorporated into the Crown by Ferdinand and Isabella).

In the second group, revenue from taxes, we can point out:

Taxes levied by Apportionment and governed by the personal circumstances of the taxpayers. They were as follows: *servicio*, both ordinary and extraordinary; *moneda forera* (the tax paid by all vassals in recognition of the royal overlordship); *chapín de la reina* (150,000 maravedís on the occasion of the king's marriage), The so-called *vecinos pecheros*, or commoners, were obliged to pay these, the nobles and clergy being exempt. In compensation, the latter estate had to pay the *ecclesiastical subsidy*.

Excise Taxes, levied on the transport and production of goods. They included three subgroups:

(1) *Levies on transit of merchandise or customs duties:* sea tithes, revenue of inland ports, sale of provostships, revenues from wool, the export–import tax of Seville and of the Indies, a tax on sales of coarse cloth, one on Málaga raisins, and 1 per cent of the customs receipts in Málaga and Cádiz.

(2) *General sales taxes:* the *alcabala* and the *hundreds*. The *hundreds* were four charges of 1 per cent on sales, created successively in 1626, 1639, 1656, and 1663. In 1686 they were reduced to four $\frac{1}{2}$ per cent payments. The *alcabala*, one part in ten 'on everything sold', was the amplification of the 5 per cent tax on the value of any transaction which had been conceded to the kings of Castile in the Middle Ages. The universal character of these taxes was not diminished by a few personal exemptions and a very few exceptions made on the transfer of certain articles.

(3) *Taxes on special articles of consumption.* Of these, some were set up in the form of a legal monopoly on the sale of certain articles (for example, those on salt, quicksilver, tobacco, playing cards and chocolate were the ones which brought in the largest revenues), while others were *in the form of a levy*.

This usually took the form of the *sisa*, or excise (a sum reserved for the treasury out of merchandise fully paid for), in the places where the merchandise was sold, or by *fee* (payment of a certain percentage per unit of measure of the article taxed) in the places where it was produced or harvested.

The total of these taxes on consumption was very important, because together they brought in the majority of the revenues necessary to pay the *servicio de millones*, so-called because it was counted in millions of ducats instead of in maravedís as was customary in all *servicios* requested by the king. The *servicio de millones* was granted by the Cortes after it had heard the royal proposal, in which the state of the treasury and its needs were explained. Once this proposal had been studied the Cortes agreed on the sum to be granted, indicating the taxes by means of which it was to be collected and imposing the condition that the *servicio* be used to meet the expenses for which it had been requested: hence, the official documents of the *servicio de millones* represented the beginnings of a budget system. The first *servicio* was granted to Philip II in 1590, for the sum of 8 million ducats to be paid within six years. In 1600 there was a new *servicio* of 18 million, also payable in six years. This was the largest of the *servicios* and was successively renewed throughout the seventeenth century with a number of variations (2,500,000 annually from 1608 to 1610, 2 million annually from 1612 to 1632, and 4 million annually after that date). But it was not the only one granted, for after 1632 the Cortes voted other *servicios de millones* which ran concurrently.

Subrogatory or Diversification Taxes on patrimonies or certain classes of revenue. In general these came from revenues belonging to the ecclesiastical class, exempt from all taxes except those on sales. In this group were: the *Bulls of the Holy Crusade*, granted by Julius II in 1500; the *subsidy on galleys* (420,000 ducats coming from ecclesiastical revenues), granted by Pius IV in 1561; and the *excusado* or tithe of the chief establishment of each parish, granted by Pius V in 1567. The *tercios reales*, or royal thirds of medieval origin, still remained in force and consisted of two-ninths of the ecclesiastical tithes.

This is a general sketch of tax organization in the sixteenth and seventeenth centuries. Its main bases were the *servicios*, both ordinary and extraordinary, the *alcabalas*, and the *millones*. As the monarchy was plagued by constantly rising financial requirements, fiscal policy kept squeezing more and more taxes from the coffers of the taxpayers. The table below, taken from Larraz, refers to Philip II's tax policy regarding *alcabalas* and *millones*, the two great indirect taxes of the period:

L

| | INDEX NUMBERS | | |
Year	Collected from alcabala and millones (1)	General price index (2)	Difference (1–2)
1504	100	100	0
1535	117	129	− 12
1562	160	239	− 79
1575	489	273	+ 216
1578	357	258	+ 99
1590	537	300	+ 237
1596	537	307	+ 230

The interpretation of these figures is quite clear: after 1575, the curve of the tax index is considerably higher than that of the general price index; after that year the treasury not only made up for the loss in purchasing power of money, but also greatly increased tax pressure. This increase becomes more significant if we keep in mind that Castilian industry and agriculture were less active in the last quarter of the sixteenth century. Hence, the treasury contributed towards aggravating the condition of national production.

Is it not clear that the burden of taxation on economic life in the seventeenth century became even more grievous when the *servicio de millones* reached its maximum?

STATE MERCANTILISM

Medieval economy, with its meagre circulation of money, considered it axiomatic that an abundance of money intensified business, while restriction of currency depressed it. The maintenance of this principle at all costs by the Spanish State of the sixteenth and seventeenth centuries, completely inundated by American silver, was the initial cause of the country's ruin.

The identification of money with wealth established by Spanish mercantilists and statesmen of the period, dazzled by the abundance of American metal, could scarcely be equalled by any other nation. The measures taken with the prime objective of increasing and maintaining the stock of money can be classified into three groups:

Measures to stimulate discovery and exploitation of American gold and silver mines. Both natives and colonizers were guaranteed ownership in all claims involving personal property; tools and equipment could not be seized for private debts; royal officials took special care to supply mining districts, etc., so that 100 per cent of the metal extracted would reach Castile; trade among the different colonies was restricted, and a rigid system of transport and monopolies established.

Stockpiling of metal in Spain by means of a ban on its export to other countries. With this object in mind.

Castile repeatedly altered the bimetallic ratio, the weight, fineness and tariff of gold and silver coins, deflated vellon; and prohibited imports of debased foreign money in an effort to curb the outflow of treasure. At least 75 per cent of the innumerable petitions in the Cortes and the pragmatics affecting money in the sixteenth and seventeenth centuries stated specifically that limitation of specie exports was a goal. [Hamilton]

During the reigns of Philip III and Philip IV, the draining off of gold and silver, accelerated by uncontrolled inflation of vellon (bad money driving out good), and by the disparity between Spanish and foreign prices, brought the strictness of prohibitive measures to their maximum point: after 1624, the death penalty was applied as a punishment for exporting specie.

Notwithstanding these measures, currency always had a legal loophole through the numerous licences for exporting money to settle the debts contracted by the Crown with foreign money-lenders.

Restrictions on export of raw materials through imposition of high customs duties. This measure was intended to favour national industry, whose development would have prevented the expenditure of part of the currency used in acquiring products from other countries. But it must be noted that these limitations were in the long run a financial manœuvre rather than a protectionist measure properly speaking. Protective duties – says Hamilton – had little place either in the theory or practice of Castilian mercantilism, and the same could be said of the Crown of Aragon. On the other hand we should recall, with Larraz, that the circulation of Castilian currency and bullion to other countries, in spite of the prohibitions on exporting money, kept foreign exchange from fluctuating with sufficient elasticity to make up for the differences between internal and external price levels; so that imports into Castile were very much at a premium, and exports consequently at a disadvantage.

This observation brings us to a mention of the *results of Spanish mercantilism*. Hamilton emphasizes as the most important ones the sacrifice of general colonial interests in favour of the Sevillian monopoly system – created in large part to raise to a maximum and protect metal imports – and the sacrifice of some American territories (among them the La Plata region) because of Castile's gravitation toward the mining zones of America (Zacatecas-Potosí); the harmful rise in Spanish prices compared with foreign ones as a consequence of the artificial accumulation (that is, not produced by a favourable trade balance) of gold and silver; the illusion of prosperity created by an abundance of these metals, which gave fuel to the Habsburgs' aggressive and ruinous foreign policy; disdain for work; and other phenomena which contributed to Spanish economic decline in the seventeenth century.

MONETARY INFLATION IN CASTILE: THE COPPER REVOLUTION

One of the culminating factors in the disintegration of seventeenth-century Spanish economy, added to the many we have just described, was the monetary confusion produced by that international phenomenon which Spooner has recently baptized with the name of 'the copper revolution'. The end of the silver era began after 1621 with the first symptoms of exhaustion in American mines; twenty years later, the paralysation of silver's influence on world monetary activity was a consummated fact. From that moment up till 1680, when the appearance of Brazilian gold re-established the situation of the two great precious metals, there was a considerable drop in the circulation of specie and a throttling of exchange which surprised and disquieted all the financial centres. During these sixty years, that is, in the heart of the seventeenth century, the metal which saved the situation, in spite of its modest origin, was copper: no longer copper mixed with silver, like the medieval 'dark' coins, but pure copper. Europe overcame the crisis by forcing into circulation the copious mintings of this metal, even though an inflationary process was instituted in the nations which used this instrument incautiously. One of these was, as a matter of fact, the Crown of Castile. There was a second price revolution within its borders during the seventeenth century, brought on this time by copper, now the credit weapon of an impoverished economy. The incapacity of the later Habsburg governments to control the inflationary spiral, their lack of courage to resist the temptations of a monetary policy too easy not to be dangerous, explain the disastrous downfall into which the Castilian economy plunged during the last decades of the seventeenth century.

The stages in this process are known, thanks again to Hamilton's work. Putting his information together with Spooner's view, we shall now present the great phases of copper inflation in Castile. Let us first recall that the ordinance of Medina del Campo dictated by Ferdinand and Isabella in 1497 was the basis of a new monetary system which, along essential lines, remained in force until 1598. During the course of the intervening century only three reform measures were taken. Two of these affected gold currency. In 1537 Charles V heeded the Cortes' reiterated pleas that Spanish gold must be prevented from leaving the country. He reduced the tale of the excelente of Granada (or ducat) from 24 to 22 carats, and its nominal value from 375 to 350 maravedís. With this measure, which made the fineness of Castilian gold money equal to French, the profit obtained from exporting Spanish gold coins was wiped out. In 1566 Philip II proceeded to a new increase in gold prices, corresponding to the drop in the price of silver produced by the constant influx of American shipments of this metal. To adjust its nominal value to the market price, the tariff of the escudo (the name given to the devalued ducat of 1537) rose from 350 to 400 maravedís.

The third measure taken in the sixteenth century affected vellon. In 1552 there was an attempt to adjust the price of copper money to that of silver, which was falling as the stock of silver grew. Since the rise in copper prices compared with those of silver threatened to bring about the flight of the copper coinage minted in former times (when this metal was cheaper), the real value of vellon was lowered (leaving its weight and nominal value unchanged): the silver content in these coins dropped 21·43 per cent.

Beginning of the Inflationary Period (1599–1630)

Faced with a contant rise in expenditures, Philip II attempted all sorts of solutions, not even excluding a declaration of bankruptcy; but he always resisted debasing the currency. It must be said that he possessed an excellent asset with which to manœuvre: American silver. When this began to dwindle, his successor, Philip III, had no recourse but to turn to copper. Thus the copper revolution of the seventeenth century began both for Castile and for Europe.

In fact, given the Crown's needs, there was no hesitation about resorting to successive mintings of copper. The era of vellon was unleashed in 1599. In a few years (1599–1606) 22 million ducats were minted. A decrease in the quality of vellon coincided with this process; thus, as early as 1599 the silver in this type of metal had been suppressed, and copper, which after that time was the exclusive substance used in vellon coinage, underwent a reduction in weight of 50 per cent (140 former maravedís now rose to 280).

Public opinion was aroused and prevented any serious inflation from 1606 to 1617. On 22 November 1608, the Cortes extracted from Philip III the promise that he would not mint any more vellon for the next twenty years; in compensation, the delegates voted a *servicio* of 17,500,000 ducats requested by the king.

The Crown's difficulties after the expulsion of the Moriscos were so great that in 1617 there was a new coinage of vellon, this time by permission of the Cortes, which released the monarch from his promise of 1608 and allowed him to mint enough vellon to obtain a net profit of 600,000 ducats, on condition that the minting did not exceed 800,000. That is, it was admitted *a priori* that the treasury would receive a profit of 75 per cent from this minting. However, the total minted was far above the authorized figure. By 1619 some 5 million ducats had been produced. In the face of this situation there were new protests from the Cortes, which in June 1619, wrested a new promise from the king (as in 1608) not to mint vellon coinage for twenty years. However, the Crown's needs were so pressing (imminent war with Holland) that by January 1621, more vellon was being struck in the mint at Toledo. From 1621 to 1626 some 14 million ducats were placed in circulation.

Deflationary Interval (1627–34)

This succession of inflationary measures resulted in placing the premium or overvaluation of silver in the 45 per cent range, and vellon prices went up accordingly. The crisis came to a head in 1627, when a scarcity of wheat and of livestock, combined with inflation, resulted in extraordinarily high prices. This situation required a change in the monetary policy which had been followed until then. That same year, as a measure to contract circulation, a banking company directed by Italians was formed, with broad commercial privileges and the function of taking part of the vellon out of circulation by buying it up with silver at 80 per cent of its nominal value, plus interest of 5 per cent. But this project failed because the long-suffering Castilians had no confidence in it, and refused to part with their vellon.

Once this project had failed, the first effective deflationary measure since the days of Ferdinand and Isabella was passed in 1628: the nominal value of copper vellon currency was reduced by 50 per cent. Holders of devalued vellon were not reimbursed.

Great Inflationary Phase (1634–56); Crisis of 1641

After all possible solutions had been exhausted, the return to inflation began in 1634, this time based not only on putting a larger quantity of money into circulation, but also on simple increase in the nominal value of coinage by means of the *resello* (or restamping a greater value on existing coins). The new inflationary race started in 1634 by means of a decree doubling the value of *calderilla* (vellon with an admixture of silver, and therefore minted before 1599), until then excluded from currency changes. Since profits from this restamping were divided between the Crown and the owners of the coins, the latter lost in this operation 25 per cent of the value of the coins delivered for restamping. Soon after, in 1636, despite the royal promise 'never to increase the tale of copper vellon' made in 1628, a new restamping was decreed, tripling its tariff. Later, following an unsuccessful attempt to withdraw vellon from circulation completely, the revolutions in Catalonia and Portugal simply hastened the inflationary process. Then the inflationist phenomenon of 1641

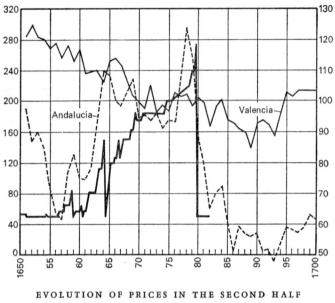

EVOLUTION OF PRICES IN THE SECOND HALF
OF THE SEVENTEENTH CENTURY

Heavy black line: curve of the silver premium over copper
(index numbers at left). The other lines represent price evolution
in Andalusia and Valencia (index numbers at right). Index,
100 = 1671–1680.

occurred. In February, restamping of the 4-maravedí coin to double
its nominal value was agreed upon: these coins had been restamped
once already in 1603. In October came the restamping, at triple their
nominal value, of all 2-maravedí coins and those of 4 maravedís
minted after 1603.

The prodigious increase in vellon prices and the fabulous rise in
the silver premium (190 per cent by early August, 1642) which
followed the inflation of 1641, obliged the government to carry out
a brutal deflation. This was accomplished at the end of 1642: it
reduced the 12- and 8-maravedí coins to 2, those of 6 and 4 maravedís to 1, and those of 1 maravedí to one-half.

Philip IV's promise to maintain the deflationary measure of 1642
was broken because of the expenditures necessary to reinforce his

armies in Milan and Flanders. Forced to take action by extreme necesssity, in 1651 Philip IV decreed the restamping, at four times its nominal value, of the 2-maravedí coin. This was accompanied by the minting of 100,000 ducats of pure copper in coins of 2 maravedís, weighing one-fourth as much as the old coins of this denomination which were now being restamped.

However, this bungling measure did not last long, and in 1652 there was a return to the line of 1642. The 8-maravedí pieces were again valued at 2, and the 2-maravedí coins minted in 1651 were tariffed at 1, as were 4-maravedí coins. On the other hand, and contrary to what had happened in 1628 and 1642, in 1652 holders of vellon were compensated for the reduction of its nominal value by means of bonds pledged by revenues from tobacco.

The Monetary Catastrophe (1656–80); Crisis of 1680

About the year 1650 a third phase in the depreciation of copper began throughout the world. This fact was what caused a change in monetary policy during the last years of Philip IV's reign, and the early years of Charles II's. Castile's financial ship was adrift, lashed by the gales of inflation, foreign wars, governmental inefficiency, administrative corruption, and the collapse of agriculture, industry and trade. This explains the crisis of 1680, when the economy of Castile foundered completely.

New currency disturbances had begun in 1654. That was the year in which *calderilla* regained its old value (it had been retired in 1653): it was restamped and its owners were given half its value, the other half being retained by the king. In 1658 restamping of the 1- and 2-maravedí pieces was decreed, giving them double value. In May 1659, this measure was suspended and an effort was made to retire such coins from circulation. But this attempt at a radical contraction in the circulation of vellon failed, because people preferred the depreciated coins to the bonds offered in exchange by the monarchy. Finally, in October 1660, there was a decree calling for turning in all *calderilla* and copper vellon which had not circulated at par for forty years, in order to melt it down and remint it in 'rich' vellon. It was hoped that this would put an end to the monetary disorder. In spite of this measure, inflation continued its course, spurred by the government itself, which continued to issue new mintings of vellon currency. Hamilton says that there was a flood of bad money, with the result that the premium on silver went up to 150 per cent (in 1650 it had still been 50 per cent). It was the road to catastrophe. To avoid it, in 1664 the value of the coins minted only three years before was reduced by half. The premium on silver went down to 50 per cent.

With Charles II's ascension to the throne the inflationary process knew no bounds, until the currency crisis of 1680 occurred. By 1665 the silver premium had gone up sharply to 120 per cent, and about the middle of the year 1669 it rose to 180 per cent. For the next six years the situation remained relatively stable; but from 1675 to 1680 abuses in mintings of low fineness, introduction of counterfeit money and the need for making foreign payments produced a new rise, to 275 per cent. The outcry was so great that in March 1680, the government decreed devaluation of vellon coinage to half its nominal value; that is, one-fourth of its tale in 1664. This measure produced the collapse of wholesale prices, which dropped 45 per cent in a few months. If we remember that in the great crash of 1929 American prices fell only 38 per cent, we will have an idea of the magnitude of the disaster to which the monetary chaos had led.

It was a harsh but inevitable measure, followed by the order of 22 May 1680 strictly limiting mintings of vellon. Steps were taken at the same time to retire copper from circulation by using it to manufacture various articles and tools. In 1686 the situation could be considered stable. The revaluation of silver, aided by the appearance of Brazilian gold, contributed to the success of the operation. Vellon mintings ceased in 1693. The copper revolution was over.

THE ARBITRISTAS AND THE ECONOMY

Awareness of economic crisis, which spread over Spain at the moment of its greatest political splendour, was general around 1600. And with it came a proliferation of the literature of the *arbitristas*, who attempted to diagnose the country's ills and to propose suitable remedies for them. This abundant production, which shuffled 'the prescriptions of the technician, the lament of the guild, and the thought of the patriot, worked out in the office of the jurist or the cell of the monk', has been satisfactorily summarized by Larraz. He divides these authors into two major groups according to whether or not they show themselves favourable to economic planning.

In the first group, those who along general lines were in accord with the economic policies of the time, Larraz points out the writers who called for adjustment of Spanish foreign policy to the demands of their economic planning. They were the heirs of the spirit of the sixteenth-century *comuneros*, defenders of the national interest as opposed to Castile's interference in European affairs. In their opinion, the restoration of the country required a change from offensive to defensive wars, from the policy of European expansion to one of preserving the American empire. With this change in attitude, they argued, would come realization of the supreme idea inherited from the Middle Ages: to concentrate and retain in the mother country the enormous shipments of American precious metals. Most of the public shared this view, as was periodically demonstrated in the Cortes. Among the writings which favoured this opinion we should recall those of Baltasar de Álamos y Barrientos (1598), Pedro López de Reino (1624), accountant of the Council of the Indies, and, to a degree, Fernández de Navarrete, chaplain and secretary to the royal family.

The conformist writers, who clung to the principles of the mercantilist theory, took issue with them. They formed the more numerous group and stoutly defended the growth and preservation within Spain of the stock of precious metals. *Memorial Against the Flight of Money From These Realms* (*Memorial para que no salgan dineros de estos Reinos*, 1558) was the title of a work by the first Spanish mercantilist, the accountant Luis Ortiz. In order to carry out his objective, he worked out a complete plan of development of all resources based on the following principle: a ban on export of raw materials and on import of manufactured products through establishment of the appropriate customs system. Ortiz is an isolated and forgotten author of the sixteenth century. It was in the following century that Spanish mercantilist literature reached its apogee. Doctor Sancho de Moncada, professor of Holy Writ in the University of Toledo, was its chief exponent. In his writings (1619), he developed a detailed economic plan based on the same principles as Ortiz's. Later, Martínez de la Mata (1659) proposed to raise public funds or banks to the category of the fundamental element in mercantilist policy, for the purpose of financing industrial and agricultural development.

It is not difficult to discover the contradiction of the Spanish mercantilists' noble proposals. The very historical reality of Spain was sufficient to demonstrate that when domestic prices climbed much higher than foreign ones, the monopoly of America metals was incompatible with the healthy progress of production of wealth.

Larraz singles out three central groups among the *arbitristas* opposing the economic policy practised by the monarchy. In the first, we find the authors who attacked the accumulation of precious metals. They are the ones who, following the lead of the quantity school of Salamanca (which formulated for the first time the relationship between increase in the amount of currency in circulation and the rise in prices, as Larraz and Grice-Hutchinson indicate, demonstrating that they do not share the ignorance displayed by most foreign authors), reacted against the ideal of accumulation of money and campaigned for the reconsideration of productive labour as the basic element in wealth. On the other hand, these authors – Cellorigo (1600), Pedro de Valencia (1605), Fernández de Navarrete (1616), and Caxa de Leruela (1627) – who so skilfully described the effects of the discovery of America, were incapable of finding the formula that would solve the technical problems presented by exploitation of the Indies.

Another group is composed of authors who attacked the large profits earned by exporting to the Indies. When they confronted the problem which the previous group had been unable to solve, the members of the second – outstanding among whom was Father Tomás de Mercado – grasped the need for establishing a relationship between export to the colonies and import of metals from them. In fact, they realized that American gold and silver should be no more than a medium of payment, and the circulation of money an instrument for developing the economy of the home country.

Finally, there were some authors who attacked the whole theory of economic regulation. The thought of Alberto Struzzi, a foreign employee of the Spanish Crown writing in 1624, reflects this position. His doctrine has its origin in a doubly pessimistic assumption: Castile's incapacity to supply the American market herself or to prevent the disruption of economic planning based on a monopoly system. Taking as his point of departure the status quo of legal infraction so typical of Castile's economic policy, Struzzi defended freedom of trade with America.

GOVERNMENTAL APATHY AND BUREAUCRATIC IMMOBILITY

The transcendental fact of the beginning of American colonization took place at a moment when neither Castile nor the other European countries were prepared to cope with its vast economic repercussions. Consequently, the errors committed in the early years are excusable, even including the rigid monopoly on American metal which placed Spanish products in a position of inferiority. But by the end of the sixteenth century the Spanish ruling class was in the position of being able to make improvements: the immense possibilities of the Empire of the Indies had been recognized, and the quantity school of Salamanca had demonstrated its opposition to the simple identification of money with wealth.

At this crucial point, when Philip II might have acquired a sense of the need for changing his aims, the burden of his foreign policy prevented him from doing so. More and more involved in undertakings of war instead of putting his attention on intelligent exploitation of the Indies, the 'Prudent King' walled himself up in the traditional system which at least would provide him with abundant and immediate supplies of silver. The country's interests were sacrificed to this need for money at a given moment – at an unbroken succession of given moments: in this regard let us remember that the tariff reform of 1566–7 was of a fiscal rather than a protective nature. At the end of his reign Philip II made public the catastrophic result of his policies by declaring to the Cortes in 1592 that, after having gone through his own patrimony and his subjects' (remember the bankruptcies of 1557, 1575 and 1590), he owed more than 13 million ducats.

This inherently destructive economic regimen acquired its most dramatic traits during the course of the seventeenth century. The incapacity of the kings, the ruin of sources of production and the constant increase in fiscal needs justified the most arbitrary unilateral measures. To the lamentable debasements of money we have mentioned, we must add, for example, the damage done to public credit: Colmeiro, with all the passion of a nineteenth-century liberal, points out the disorder, immorality, injustice and scandal of an administration which betrayed its trust by arbitrarily altering the interest rate on *juros* (bonds on public debt).

And so it happened that the State argued in a vicious circle which made any solution impossible. This was clearly seen when in June 1618, Philip III had his famous consultation with the Council of Castile. Six years of reforming effort (1618–24) served only to see traditional regulation confirmed and even reinforced (Larraz). In the long run, the seventeenth-century Spanish State sacrificed the economy to the treasury, and the interests of its subjects to its own interests. Obsessed by the idea that each individual must give it more money (unbearable tax pressure) and keep less for himself (profusion of sumptuary laws fixing a limit on private expenditures), in the end the State neglected to develop the country's interests and trampled on the ethic which should have ruled its relations with its subjects.

If administrative inefficiency and immorality had taken control of the large cogs in the governmental machinery, we can imagine what happened to the smaller ones. The extremely bad example from above easily spread through a too numerous body of bureaucrats, imbued with all the prejudices of the *hidalgo* and obliged to too many expedients to subsist even from hand to mouth. On the other hand, the growing centralization of the State's machinery provided occasion for the worst of abuses. Some authors have given us ample description of the most outstanding of these. Thus, Uztáriz describes the extremely damaging practice of farming out the customs, which gave rise, among other anomalies, to the appearance on the scene of the famous Francisco Eminente who, together with his relatives, proceeded to exploit the revenues under his control from 1667 to 1717 'without feeling the slightest qualm over the public damage which resulted'. Within this same area, Colmeiro points out the abuses and excesses of tax-farmers of all kinds who, since they had to give satisfaction to a treasury which grew ever more exigent, had no recourse but to compensate themselves as best they could, and 'changed the lightest tax into an insupportable burden'. In the last instance, the figure of 150,000 fiscal employees cited by Alcázar de Arriaza, giving as his authority the accountant Antolín de la Serna, or the figure of 9,000 persons employed solely in the administration and collection of the Bull of the Holy Crusade cited by Luis Valle de la Cerda, chief accountant of this section, are sufficiently eloquent for us to conclude that if the depreciation of productive work through the effects of the economic collapse produced the conversion of large sectors of Spanish society from activity to inactivity, the structure of the State assured the permanence of this process.

Only at the end of the century, when the feeling of disaster was inescapable, did the good faith of a few worthy members of the ruling class indicate a need for reform. The excellent plans of the Count of Oropesa were a failure, but one organization remained which in the following century was to give fruitful results: the Board of Trade and Currency, founded in 1679. Most important among its concepts were simplification of the working-class structure (the Cortes of Calatayud, in 1678, had requested abolition of the guilds) and the idea of bringing Spain more into line with other European countries.

SIX

The Decline of Spain[1]

J. H. ELLIOTT

By the winter of 1640, the empire, which had dominated the world scene for the best part of a century seemed at last, after many a false alarm, to be on the verge of collapse. In October of that year, after the revolt of Catalonia but before the revolt of Portugal, the English ambassador in Madrid wrote home of 'the state of Christendom, which begins already to be unequally balanced'.[2] Six months later he was writing: 'Concerning the state of this kingdom, I could never have imagined to have seen it as it now is, for their people begin to fail, and those that remain, by a continuance of bad successes, and by their heavy burdens, are quite out of heart.'[3] Olivares' great bid between 1621 and 1640 to turn back the pages of history to the heroic days of Philip II had visibly failed; and, like everything about Olivares, his failure was on the grand scale. The man whom eulogists had portrayed in the days of his greatness as Atlas, supporting on his shoulders the colossal structure of the monarchy, was now, Samson-like, bringing it crashing down with him in his fall.

[1] This article was first published in *Past and Present*, No. 20, 1961.

An earlier version of this article was read as a paper to the Stubbs Society at Oxford, and I have deliberately left it as a contribution to discussion, based on a general survey of the present state of knowledge, rather than attempting to transform it into a detailed analysis. I have treated the period 1598–1648 in closer detail in a chapter on the Spanish peninsula in the forthcoming vol. iv of the *New Cambridge Modern History*. Any reader of this article will appreciate how much I, in company with other historians of Spain, owe to the ideas of M. Pierre Vilar in his 'Le Temps du Quichotte', *Europe* (Paris), xxxiv (1956), pp. 3–16.

[2] P[ublic] R[ecord] O[ffice, London] SP 94.42 f. 51, Hopton to Windebank, 22 Sept./2 Oct. 1640.

[3] PRO SP 94.42 f. 144, Hopton to Vane, 3/13 April 1641.

The dissolution of Spanish power in the 1640s appears so irrevocable and absolute that it is hard to regard it as other than inevitable. The traditional textbook approach to European history of the sixteenth and seventeenth centuries has further helped to establish the idea of the inevitability of Spain's defeat in its war with France. Spanish power is first presented at its height under Philip II. Then comes, with the reign of Philip III, the *decline of Spain*, with the roots of decline traced back to Philip II, or Charles V, or even to Ferdinand and Isabella, depending upon the nationality, or the pertinacity, of the writer. After the lamentable scenes that have just been portrayed, the early years of Philip IV come as something of an embarrassment, since the ailing patient not only refuses to die, but even shows vigorous and unexpected signs of life. But fortunately the inexplicable recovery is soon revealed as no more than a hallucination. When a resurgent France under Richelieu at last girds itself for action, Spain's bluff is called. Both diagnosis and prognostication are triumphantly vindicated, and the patient dutifully expires.

It is not easy to reconcile this attractively simple presentation of early seventeenth-century history with our increasing knowledge of the discontent and unrest in Richelieu's France.[1] If Spain may still be regarded as a giant with feet of clay, France itself is coming to seem none too steady on the ground. This naturally tends to cast doubt on the validity of any concept of a French triumph in the first half of the century as being a foregone conclusion. Yet the lingering survival of the traditional view is easily understood. France had a population of some 16 million, as against Spain's 7 or 8, and it is commonly argued that, in the end, weight of numbers is bound to tell. It is also argued that the fact of Spain's decline is notorious and irrefutable, and that a power in decline will not win the final battle.

The argument from the size of populations is notoriously dangerous when used of a period when governments lacked the resources and the techniques to mobilize their subjects for war. Victory in war

---

[1] See B. P. Porchnev, *Die Volksaufstände in Frankreich vor der Fronde*, (Leipzig, 1954) and R. Mousnier, 'Recherches sur les Soulèvements Populaires en France avant la Fronde', *Revue d'Histoire Moderne et Contemporaine*, v (1958), 81–113.

ultimately depended on the capacity of a state to maintain a continuing supply of men (not necessarily nationals) and of credit, and
this capacity was by no means the exclusive prerogative of the large
state. But the decisive argument in favour of an inevitable French
victory is obviously the second: that Spain was in a state of irrevocable decline.

The phrase *decline of Spain* automatically conjures up a series of
well-known images. Most of these are to be found in Professor Earl
J. Hamilton's famous article,[1] which remains the classic statement
of the theme: 'the progressive decline in the character of the rulers';
mortmain and vagabondage, the contempt for manual labour,
monetary chaos and excessive taxation, the power of the Church
and the folly of the government. These so-called 'factors' in the
decline of Spain have a long and respectable ancestry, and both their
existence and their importance are irrefutable. Most of them can
indeed be traced back to the writings of seventeenth-century
Spaniards themselves – to the treaties of the economic writers or
arbitristas, of whom Hamilton says that 'history records few instances
of either such able diagnosis of fatal social ills by any group of moral
philosophers or of such utter disregard by statesmen of sound
advice'. The word *decline* itself was used of Spain at least as early as
1600 when González de Cellorigo, perhaps the most acute of all the
arbitristas, discussed 'how our Spain . . . is subject to the process of
decline [*declinación*] to which all other republics are prone'.[2] Vigorously as González de Cellorigo himself rejected the determinist
thesis, the condition of Spain seemed to his contemporaries graphic
evidence of the validity of the cyclical idea of history, of which the
concept of decline formed an integral part.

The skilful dissection of the Spanish body politic by contemporary
Spaniards, each anxious to offer the patient his own private nostrum,
proved of inestimable value to writers of later generations: to
Protestants of the later seventeenth century, and to rationalist
historians of the eighteenth and nineteenth, who saw in the decline

---

[1] 'The Decline of Spain', *Econ. Hist. Rev.*, 1st ser., viii (1938), pp. 168–179.
[2] Martin Gonzalez de Cellorigo, *Memorial de la Politica necesaria y útil Restaura-
cion a la República de España* (Valladolid, 1600), p. 1. I am indebted to Man-
chester University Library for the loan of a microfilm of this important work,
of which I have been able to find no copy in this country.

of Spain the classic instance of the fatal consequences of ignorance, sloth and clericalism. Apart from its important additions on Spanish wages and prices, and its rejection of the traditional thesis about the grave results of the expulsion of the Moriscos, Hamilton's article would seem to belong, in content as in approach, to the eighteenth- and nineteenth-century historiographical tradition.

It would be pleasant to be able to record that, in the twenty years since Hamilton's article was published, our knowledge and understanding of seventeenth-century Spain have been significantly enlarged. But, in most of its aspects, our picture of the reigns of Philip III and IV remains very much as it was drawn by Martin Hume in the old *Cambridge Modern History* over fifty years ago. The one significant exception to this story of historiographical stagnation is to be found in Hamilton's own field of monetary history. Whatever the defects either of Hamilton's methods or of his generalizations, both of them subject to growing criticism, historians now possess a vast amount of information on Spanish monetary history which was not available to Hume; and the work of a generation of historians, culminating in the monumental study of Seville and the Atlantic by M. and Mme Chaunu,[1] has revealed much that is new and important about the character of Spain's economic relations with its American possessions.

It could, however, be argued that these advances in the fiscal and commercial history of Habsburg Spain have been achieved only at the expense of other equally important aspects of its economic life. Hamilton's pioneering example has encouraged an excessive concentration on the *external* influences on the Spanish economy, such as American silver, to the neglect of *internal* economic conditions.[2] Little more is known now than was known fifty years ago about Spanish forms of land tenure and cultivation, or about population changes, or about the varying fortunes of the different regions or social groups in the peninsula. It could also be argued that Hamilton's lead, together with the whole trend of contemporary historical writing, has produced a disproportionate concentration on *economic*

---

[1] H. and P. Chaunu, *Séville et l'Atlantique* (1504–1650), 8 vols. (Paris, 1955–9).
[2] This point is well made in the useful bibliographical survey of recent work on this period of Spanish history: J. Vicens Vives, J. Reglá and J. Nadal, 'L'Espagne aux XVIᵉ et XVIIᵉ Siècles', *Revue Historique*, ccxx (1958), pp. 1–42.

conditions. Explanations of the decline in terms of Spanish religious or intellectual history have become unfashionable. This is understandable in view of the naïveté of many such explanations in the past, but it is hard to see how an adequate synthesis can be achieved until detailed research is undertaken into such topics as the working of the Spanish Church, of the Religious Orders and the educational system. At present, we possess an overwhelmingly economic interpretation of Spain's decline, which itself is highly arbitrary in that it focuses attention only on certain selected aspects of the Spanish economy.

If this leads to distortions, as it inevitably must, these become all the greater when, as so often happens, the decline of Spain is treated in isolation. The very awareness of crisis among late sixteenth- and early seventeenth-century Spaniards prompted a flood of pessimistic commentaries which helped to make the subject exceptionally well documented. The extent of the documentation and the critical acuteness of the commentators, naturally tended to encourage the assumption that Spain's plight was in some ways unique; and this itself has led to a search for the origins of that plight in specifically Spanish circumstances and in the dubious realm of allegedly unchanging national characteristics. But considerably more is known now than was known twenty or thirty years ago about the nature of social and economic conditions in seventeenth-century western Europe as a whole. Much of the seventeenth century has come to be regarded as a period of European economic crisis – of commercial contraction and demographic stagnation after the spectacular advances of the sixteenth century – and certain features which once seemed peculiarly Spanish are now tending to assume a more universal character. The impoverished *hidalgos* of Spain do not now seem so very different from the discontented *hobereaux* of France or the gentry of England. Nor does the contempt for manual labour, on which historians of Spain are prone to dwell, seem any longer an attitude unique to the peninsula. A study like that by Coleman on English labour in the seventeenth century[1] suggests how 'idleness', whether voluntary or involuntary, was a general problem of European societies of the time, and can be regarded as the consequence

[1] D. C. Coleman, 'Labour in the English Economy of the Seventeenth Century', *Econ. Hist. Rev.*, 2nd ser., viii (1956), pp. 280–295.

as much as the cause, of a backward economy: as the outcome of the inability of a predominantly agrarian society to offer its population regular employment or adequate remuneration for its labour.

Seventeenth-century Spain needs, therefore, to be set firmly back into the context of contemporary conditions, and particularly conditions in the Mediterranean world, before recourse is had to alleged national characteristics as an explanation of economic backwardness. It may be that idleness *was* in fact more widespread, and contempt for manual labour more deep-rooted, in Spain than elsewhere, but the first task must be to *compare:* to compare Spanish conditions with those of other contemporary societies, and then, if it is possible to isolate any features which appear unique to Spain, to search for their origins not only in the realm of national character, but also in the conditions of the soil and the nature of land-holding, and in the country's social and geographical structure.

Some of the difficulties in breaking free from traditional assumptions about the decline of Spain must be ascribed to the powerful connotations of the word 'decline': a word which obscures more than it explains. Behind the phrase *decline of Spain* there lurk different, although interrelated, phenomena. The decline of Spain can, in the first place, be regarded as part of that general setback to economic advance which mid-seventeenth-century Europe is said to have experienced, although the Spanish regression may well prove to have been more intense or to have lasted longer. Secondly, it describes something more easily measured: the end of the period of Spanish hegemony in Europe and the relegation of Spain to the rank of the second-rate powers. This implies a deterioration in Spain's military and naval strength, at least in relation to that of other States, and a decrease in its ability to mobilize the manpower and credit required to maintain its traditional primacy in Europe.

Any attempt to analyse the reasons for the decline of Spanish *power* in the middle decades of the seventeenth century must obviously begin with an examination of the foundations of that power in an earlier age. Olivares, between 1621 and 1643, was pursuing a foreign policy which recalls that of Philip II in the 1580s and 1590s. The general aims of that policy were the same: the destruction of heresy and the establishment of some form of Spanish hegemony over Europe. The nominal cost of the policy was also the same, though the real cost was greater. Philip III's ministers maintained that Philip II was spending nearly 13 million ducats a year between 1593 and 1597; Philip IV's ministers in 1636 estimated an expenditure of just over 13 million for the coming year,[1] and estimates were always liable to prove too conservative, in view of the rising premium on silver in terms of Castilian *vellón* (copper coinage), and of the sudden emergency expenses that invariably arose in time of war.

While the policy, as well as its nominal cost, remained the same under Philip IV as under Philip II, the basis of Spanish power under the two kings was also unchanged. It was, as it had always been, the resources of the Crown of Castile. Philip IV's best troops, like Philip II's, were Castilians. Philip IV's principal revenues, like Philip II's, came from the purse of the Castilian taxpayer, and Philip IV relied, like his grandfather, on the additional income derived from the American possessions of Castile.

The primacy of the Crown of Castile within the Spanish monarchy, stemming as it did from its unique value to its kings, was obvious and acknowledged. 'The King is Castilian and nothing else, and that is how he appears to the other kingdoms,' wrote one of the most influential ministers at the Court of Philip III.[2] Olivares found himself as dependent on Castile as Philip II had been. But the assistance that Castile could render Olivares proved to be less effective than the assistance it rendered Philip II, and was extracted at an even greater expense. From this, it would seem that we are faced with a diminution of Castile's capacity to bear the cost of empire, and consequently with the problem, in the first instance, not so much of the decline of Spain as of the *decline of Castile*, which is something rather different.

Three principal foundations of Castile's sixteenth-century primacy were its population, its productivity and its overseas wealth. If the process by which these foundations were slowly eroded could be

[1] A[rchivo] G[eneral de] S[imancas] Hacienda l[egajo] 522–750 no. 231, Consulta, 23 Aug. 1636.
[2] AGS Cámara de Castilla leg. 2796 Pieza 9 Inquisición f. 329, Don Pedro Franqueza to Dr Fadrique Cornet, 22 Jan. 1605.

traced in detail, we should have a clearer picture of the chronology of Castile's decline. But at present our knowledge is fragmentary and inadequate, and all that is possible is to suggest something of what has been done, and the areas still to be investigated.

Spain's great imperial successes of the sixteenth century had been achieved primarily by the courage and vitality of the surplus population of an overcrowded Castile. Figures for the population of sixteenth-century Spain are scanty and unreliable, but it would probably now be generally agreed that Castile's population increased during much of the century, as it increased elsewhere in Europe, with the fastest rate of increase in the 1530s. The population of the peninsula, excluding Portugal, in the middle of the sixteenth century is thought to have been about 7½ million, of which 6½ million were to be found in Castile.[1] But perhaps even more significant than the overwhelming numerical predominance of the Castilian population is its superior density. As late as 1594 there were 22 inhabitants to the square kilometre in Castile, as against only 13·6 in the Crown of Aragon. The great empty spaces of modern Castile seem so timeless and so inevitable, that it requires an effort of the imagination to realize that Castile in the sixteenth century was relatively more populous than the rich Levantine provinces; and here, indeed, is to be found one of the fundamental changes in the structure of Spanish history. In the early 1590s the central regions of Castile accounted for 30·9 per cent of the population of Spain, whereas they now account for only 16·2 per cent. The political preponderance of Castile within Spain therefore rested in the sixteenth century, as it now no longer rests, on a population that was not only larger but also more densely settled.

This relatively dense Castilian population, living in an arid land with a predominantly pastoral economy – a land which found increasing difficulty in feeding its rising numbers – provided the colonists for the New World and the recruits for the *tercios*. It is not known how many Castilians emigrated to America (a figure of

[1] For this and the following information about population figures, see J. Vicens Vives, *Historia Económica de España* (Barcelona, 1959), pp. 301 ff.; Ramón Carande, *Carlos V y sus Banqueros*, i (Madrid, 1943), p. 43; and J. Ruiz Almansa, 'La Población Española en el Siglo XVI', *Revista Internacional de Sociologia*, iii (1943), pp. 115–36.

150,000 has been suggested for the period up to 1550), nor how many died on foreign battlefields; nor is it even known how many were required for the armies of Philip II. Although foreign troops already represented an important proportion of the Spanish army under Philip II, the contrast between military conditions under Philip II and Philip IV is none the less striking. Native Castilians, who formed the *corps d'élite* of the army, were increasingly difficult to recruit. By the 1630s, Olivares was desperate for manpower. Provincial governors were reporting the impossibility of raising new levies, and the majority of the recruits were miserable conscripts. 'I have observed these levies', wrote the English ambassador in 1635, 'and I find the horses so weak as the most of them will never be able to go to the rendezvous, and those very hardly gotten. The infantry so unwilling to serve as they are carried like galley-slaves in chains, which serves not the turn, and so far short in number of what is purposed, as they come not to one of three.'[1]

The explanation of this increased difficulty in recruiting Castilian soldiers may be found to lie primarily in changed military conditions. Philip IV had more men under arms than Philip II, and the demand on Castile was correspondingly greater; better chances of earning good wages or of obtaining charity at home may have diminished the attractions of military service abroad; the change from the warrior Charles V to a sedentary, bureaucratic monarch in Philip II, no doubt had its influence on the Castilian nobles, whose retreat from arms would in turn add to the difficulty of recruiting their vassals for war. All these problems deserve investigation,[2] but, in the search for the origins of Olivares' troubles over manpower, it would be natural to look also to the exhaustion of Castile's demographic resources.

Here, contemporary accounts may be misleading. There are numerous complaints of depopulation in late sixteenth-century Castile, but some of these can be explained by movements of population within the peninsula rather than by any total fall in

[1] B(ritish) M(useum) Egerton MS. 1820 f. 474, Hopton to Windebank, 31 May 1635.
[2] Some of them are in fact now being examined by Mr I. A. A. Thomspon of Christ's College, Cambridge, who is researching into the Spanish military system in the late sixteenth and early seventeenth centuries.

numbers. There was a marked drift of population from the country-side to the towns, most of which grew considerably between 1530 and 1594; and there was also, during the course of the century, a continuous migration from *North* Castile – the most dynamic part of the country under Ferdinand and Isabella – into central Castile and Andalusia. This southwards migration, which may be regarded as a continuation by the populace of the *reconquista*,[1] was not completed before 1600. For all those Castilians who could not themselves cross the Atlantic, Andalusia became the El Dorado. The population of Seville, the gateway to the Atlantic, rose from 45,000 in 1530 to 90,000 in 1594, and, between those dates, the populations of all but two of the larger towns of the southern half of Spain increased, while several of the northern towns, like Medina del Campo, recorded a marked decline.

A survey of conditions in North Castile alone might therefore provide a false picture of the state of the population in the Crown of Castile as a whole, and it does not seem on present evidence that an overall decline in population can be established before the end of the 1590s. All that *can* be said is that Castile's population became concentrated in the towns, particularly those of the centre and south, and that it lost some of its most vital elements through emigration and military service. Then, in 1599 and 1600, famine and plague swept up through Andalusia and Castile, causing fearful ravages in the countryside and in the densely packed cities. Unfortunately, there are no figures for the losses of these years. One village, near Valladolid, reported that no more than 80 inhabitants survived out of 300,[2] but it is impossible to say how this figure compares with others elsewhere.

Although the traditional view of its importance has recently been questioned,[3] it is hard to avoid the conclusion that the plague of 1599–1600 marks the turning-point in the demographic history of Castile. Hamilton's figures, while too unsatisfactory as a series for the immediate years of the plague to allow of any comprehensive statistical deductions, do at least point to a very sharp increase of wages over prices in the following decade, and suggest something

[1] Chaunu, *Séville et l'Atlantique*, vii (1) pp. 257–8 and 265.

[2] AGS Hacienda leg. 293–409 no. 222, Consulta, 27 Aug. 1601.

[3] Chaunu, op. cit., viii (2), Pt. 2, pp. 1267–8.

of the gravity of the manpower crisis through which Castile was passing.

This crisis was exacerbated by the expulsion of the Moriscos ten years after the plague. The figures of the expelled Moriscos used to range to anything up to one million. Hamilton reduced them to 100,000. The recent meticulous study of the size and distribution of the Morisco population by M. Lapeyre,[1] shows that between 1609 and 1614 some 275,000 Moriscos were expelled from Spain. Of these 275,000 perhaps 90,000 came from Castile and Andalusia, and the rest from the Crown of Aragon – above all, Valencia, which lost a quarter of its population. If Hamilton underestimated the number of the Moriscos, he also underestimated the economic consequences of their expulsion. The consequences to the Valencian economy were very grave,[2] but it is important to remember that the Valencian and Castilian economics were distinct, and that Castile would be only marginally affected by the disruption of the economic life of Valencia. But Castile also lost 90,000 Moriscos of its own. These Moriscos, unlike those of Valencia and Aragon, were predominantly town-dwelling, and they undertook many of the more menial tasks in Castilian life. Their disappearance would naturally produce an immediate dislocation in the Castilian economy, which is reflected in the relationship between prices and wages for the crucial years of the expulsion, but it is not known how far this dislocation was remedied by Old Christians taking over the jobs previously occupied by Moriscos.

The present picture of the Castilian population, therefore, suggests a rapid increase slackening off towards the end of the sixteenth century, and then a catastrophic loss at the very end of the century, followed by the further loss of 90,000 inhabitants through the expulsion of the Moriscos. After that, almost nothing is known. Figures available for towns in 1646 show heavy losses, and there was another disastrous plague between 1647 and 1650. Where Hamilton suggests a 25 per cent decline during the course of the seventeenth century, there are others who believe that the population remained stationary rather than actually diminishing. All that can be said at

[1] Henri Lapeyre, *Géographie de l'Espagne Morisque* (Paris, 1959).
[2] See J. Reglá, 'La Expulsión de los Moriscos y sus Consecuencias', *Hispania*, xiii (1953), pp. 215–67 and 402–79.

present with any certainty is that Olivares was making heavy demands on the manpower of a country whose population had lost its buoyancy and resilence, and had ceased to grow.

In so far, then, as Castile's primacy rested on its reserves of manpower, there was a marked downward turn in its potentialities after the 1590s. Castile's national wealth, on which the Habsburgs relied for the bulk of their revenues, also shows signs of depletion. One of the principal difficulties involved in measuring the extent of this depletion is our ignorance of economic conditions in Castile in the first half of the sixteenth century. It is hard to chart the descent when one is still trying to locate the summit. But the researches of Carande and of Lapeyre[1] have gone far to confirm that the first half of the sixteenth century is a period of quickened economic activity in Castile and Andalusia, presumably in response to a growing demand. This was a time of population increase and of sharply rising prices. Indeed, Dr Nadal has recently shown, on the basis of Hamilton's own figures, that there was a faster proportional rise of prices in the first half of the century than in the second, although American silver shipments were much greater in the second half than in the first.[2] The average annual rise in prices from 1501–62 was 2·8 per cent, as against 1·3 per cent from 1562–1600, and the highest maximum rise in any decade occurred between 1521 and 1530, long before the discovery of Potosi. This sharp upswing in prices during Charles V's reign may be attributable to a rising scale of aristocratic expenditure, to the dramatic growth of Charles V's debts, which he financed by the distribution of *juros*, or credit bonds, and to a vastly increased demand: an increased demand for food from Castile's growing population, an increased demand in North Europe for Castilian wool, and an increased demand for wine and oil and textiles, and for almost all the necessities of life, from the new American market. This was the period which saw the development of large-scale wine and oil production in Andalusia,

---

[1] Carande, op. cit.; Henri Lapeyre, *Une Famille de Marchands: les Ruiz* (Paris, 1955); and see Ladislas Reitzer, 'Some Observations on Castilian Commerce and Finance in the Sixteenth Century', *Journal of Modern History*, xxxii (1960), pp. 213–23 for a detailed bibliography.

[2] Jorge Nadal Oller, 'La Revolución de los Precios Españoles en el Siglo XVI', *Hispania*, xix (1959), pp. 503–29.

and of cloth production in the towns of Castile, to meet the needs of the New World; and it was also the great age of the Castilian fairs – international institutions which linked the Castilian economy to that of Italy and Northern Europe in a complicated network of reciprocal obligation.

If it is accepted that the reign of Charles V represents a period of economic expansion for Castile, the first clear signs of a check to this expansion appear in 1548, when the country was experiencing one of the five-year periods of highest price increase for the entire sixteenth century. In that year the Cortes of Valladolid, moved by the general complaint of high prices, petitioned the Crown to forbid the export of Castilian manufactures, even to the New World, and to permit the import of foreign goods, which would be less expensive for the Castilian consumer than Castile's own products.[1] The assumption that the export trade was pushing up Castilian prices above the general European level appeared sufficiently convincing for the Crown to agree to the Cortes' request in 1552, except in so far as Castilian exports to the Indies were concerned. The consequences of the new anti-mercantilism were exactly as might have been expected, and six years later, the prohibition on exports was lifted at the request of the Cortes themselves. The whole episode, brief as it was, augured badly for the future of Spanish industry.

During the reign of Philip II foreign merchants succeeded in forcing wider and wider open the door that they had suddenly found so obligingly ajar in the 1550s, and Castile's industries proved unable to resist the pressure. Professor Hamilton gave the classic explanation of this industrial failure in his famous argument that in Spain, unlike France or England, wages kept pace with prices, and that therefore Spain lacked the stimulus to industrial growth which comes from a lag between wages and prices in an age of price revolution.[2] This argument, if correct, would naturally furnish a vital clue to the *decline of Spain*; but the evidence behind it has recently been critically examined, and the whole argument has been increasingly ques-

[1] José Larraz López, *La Epoca del Mercantilismo en Castilla (1500–1700)* (Madrid, 1943), pp. 31 ff.
[2] Hamilton, 'The Decline of Spain', and 'American Treasure and the Rise of Capitalism (1500–1700)', *Economica*, ix (1929), pp. 338–57.

tioned.[1] Professor Phelps Brown has shown how Hamilton's own figures would indicate that a Valencian mason's wages by no means kept pace with the rising cost of living, and indeed lagged further behind prices than those of his English equivalent[2] (although, if comparisons of this kind are to be really satisfactory, they require a knowledge of comparative diets and household budgets such as we do not yet possess). Hamilton does not provide sufficiently connected series to allow similar calculations for other parts of the peninsula, but his hypothesis that Spanish wages kept abreast of prices would seem so far to be quite unfounded. Indeed, further investigation may well show a marked deterioration in the living standards of the mass of the Castilian population during the first half of the century. Such a deterioration, combined with the high level of Castilian prices in relation to those of other European states, would go a long way towards explaining the peculiar structure of Castile's economy by the end of the century: an economy closer in many ways to that of an East European state like Poland, exporting basic raw materials and importing luxury products, than to the economies of West European states. In so far as industries survived in Castile they tended to be luxury industries, catering for the needs of the wealthy few and subject to growing foreign competition.

Castile's industrial development, then, would seem to have been hampered not only by the Crown's fiscal policies and by unfavourable investment conditions, but also by the lack of a sufficiently large home market. This lack of a market for cheap manufactures points to an economy in which food prices are too high to leave the labourer and wage-earner with anything more than the bare minimum required for their housing, fuel and clothing. One of the most important reasons for the high price of food is to be found in

[1] David Felix, 'Profit Inflation and Industrial Growth', *The Quarterly Journal of Economics*, lxx (1956), pp. 441–63. See also for criticisms of Hamilton: Pierre Vilar, 'Problems of the Formation of Capitalism', *Past and Present*, no. 10 (1956), pp. 15–38; Ingrid Hammarström, 'The "Price Revolution" of the Sixteenth Century', *Scandinavian Econ. Hist. Rev.*, v (1957), pp. 118–54; and Jorge Nadal Oller, 'La Revolución de los Precios'.

[2] E. H. Phelps Brown and Sheila V. Hopkins, 'Builders' Wage-rates, Prices and Population: Some Further Evidence', *Economica*, xxvi (1959), pp. 18–38.

the agrarian policies pursued by the kings of Castile even before the advent of the Habsburgs. Their traditional practice of favouring sheep-farming at the expense of tillage – a practice vigorously continued by Ferdinand and Isabella – meant that Castile entered the sixteenth century with a dangerously unbalanced economy. While the demand for corn increased as the population grew, the sheep-owners of the *Mesta* continued to receive the benefits of royal favour. The corn-growers, on the other hand, were positively hampered, not only by the presence of the ubiquitous and highly privileged sheep, but also by the *tasa del trigo* – a fixed maximum for grain prices, which, after being sporadically applied in the first years of the century, became a permanent feature of the Crown's economic policy from 1539.[1]

The consequences of this short-sighted policy towards the agricultural interest, at a time of rapid population increase, require no comment. Professor Braudel has shown how, in the last decades of the century, Castile, in common with other South European states, became heavily dependent on grain supplies from northern and eastern Europe.[2] Castilian agriculture was simply incapable of meeting the national demand for food. What is not clear is whether agriculture was expanding, but not expanding fast enough to keep pace with the population, or whether agricultural production for the home market was actually falling off in the later sixteenth century. There are indications that more land was being cultivated in south Spain after the middle years of the century, but this may have been more to meet the needs of the American market than to satisfy home demand. The debates of the Castilian Cortes under Philip II give an impression of mounting agrarian crisis, characterized by large-scale rural depopulation, but unfortunately, apart from the tentative pioneering survey by Viñas y Mey,[3] agrarian questions in this period remain unstudied. There are signs that the smaller

---

[1] See Eduardo Ibarra y Rodriguez, *El Problema Cerealista en España durante el Reinado de los Reyes Católicos* (Madrid, 1944), and Carande, op. cit., i, pp. 78–9.

[2] F. Braudel, *La Méditerranée et le Monde Méditerranéen à l'époque de Philippe II* (Paris, 1949), pp. 447–70.

[3] C. Viñas y Mey, *El Problema de la Tierra en la España de los Siglos XVI–XVII* (Madrid, 1941).

landowners in Castile were being squeezed out in the later sixteenth century: it was harder for them than for the large landowners to survive the misfortunes of bad years, and they were liable to run into debt and find themselves compelled to sell out to their more powerful neighbours. This still further encouraged the concentration of land in the hands of a small number of powerful landowners, at a time when mortmain and the entail system were working powerfully in the same direction. It is customary to find historians frowning upon this process, as if the consolidation of estates in a few hands was in itself necessarily inimical to agrarian progress. But a large landlord is not automatically debarred from being an improving landlord. It would be very useful to know how far, if at all, improving landlords *were* to be found among the great lay and ecclesiastical landowners, and also to what extent they were diverted from corn-growing by the profits of sheep-farming, or by the production of wine and coil for the American market.

The discussion in the Castilian Cortes of 1598 on agrarian conditions suggests that by this time the crisis was acute,[1] and certainly the movement of the great Castilian nobles to take up residence at Court after the accession of Philip III did nothing to lessen it. Philip III's government found itself vainly legislating against absentee landlords, in the hope that an overcrowded Court could be cleared overnight, and the lackeys and servants who thronged the streets of Madrid would be compelled to return to the land. But much more than legislation against absentee landlordism was required to save Castilian agriculture. If the real causes of rural depopulation are to be found, they must be sought, in the first instance, at the level of village life. It is here that the dearth of good local histories in Spain becomes particularly serious. Apart from what can be learnt from the discussions of the Cortes, and from one useful but necessarily general article by Professor Dominguez Ortiz,[2] little can so far be said about the exact nature of the crisis that was overwhelming Castilian rural communities in the late sixteenth and early seventeenth centuries.

It is, however, clear that the Castilian village was pitifully

[1] *Actas de las Cortes de Castilla*, xv. (Madrid, 1889), pp. 748 ff.
[2] 'La Ruina de la Aldea Castellana', *Revista Internacional de Sociologia*, no. 24 (1948), pp. 99–124.

unprotected. There was, for instance, the little village of Sanzoles, which in 1607 addressed to the Crown a petition that has survived at Simancas.[1] It raised a loan for municipal purposes, to place itself under royal jurisdiction instead of that of Zamora cathedral, and then, as the result of a series of bad harvests, found itself unable to pay the annual interest. The creditors moved in on the village and so harassed its inhabitants that eventually, out of ninety householders, no more than forty remained. Communal indebtedness was frequent among Castilian villages, and it obviously became particularly grave when even a handful of villagers moved away, and the reduced population found itself saddled with obligations that it was now even less able to meet. But the money-lender and the powerful neighbour were only two among the many natural enemies of Castilian villages. They were exposed also to the merciless attentions of the tax-collector, the recruiting-sergeant and the quartermaster. Unfortunately we do not yet possess the information to tell us what proportion of a seventeenth-century villager's income went in taxes. A speaker in the Cortes of 1623 suggested that, in a poor man's daily expenditure of 30 maravedís, 4 went in the *alcabala* and *millones* alone,[2] and besides these and other taxes paid to the Crown – taxes which the peculiar fiscal structure of Castile made particularly heavy for the peasant – there were also dues to be paid to landlords and tithes to the Church. Then, in addition to the purely fiscal exactions, there were all the vexations and the financial burdens connected with the quartering and recruiting of troops. Villages along the principal military routes, particularly the road from Madrid to Seville and Cadiz, were dangerously exposed, and billeting could be very expensive – 100 ducats a night for a company of 200 men, according to a report made in the 1630s.'[3]

The persistence of these many afflictions over a long period of time left the villager of Castile and Andalusia very little inducement to remain on the land. He would therefore either move with his family and become swallowed up in the blessed anonymity of the great towns, or he would join the army of vagabonds that trudged the roads of Castile. We have, then, the spectacle of a nation which, at

[1] AGS Hacienda leg. 345–473, Consulta, 25 March 1607.
[2] *Actas de las Cortes*, xxix, p. 142.
[3] BM Add. MS. 9936, Papeles tocantes a las Cortes, f. 2.

the end of the sixteenth century, is dependent on foreigners not only for its manufactures but also for its food supply, while its own population goes idle, or is absorbed into economically unproductive occupations. Accusing fingers are commonly pointed at Church and bureaucracy as important agents of decline, in that they diverted the population from more useful employment. But is it not equally likely that the growth of Church and bureaucracy was itself a consequence of contemporary conditions: of the lack of incentive to agricultural labour at the village level, and of the inability of the Castilian economy to provide its population with adequate employment? The nature of the economic system was such that one became a student or a monk, a beggar or a bureaucrat. There was nothing else to be.

What could be done to revitalize a flagging economy, and increase national productivity? There was no shortage of ideas. The *arbitristas* – the economic writers – of the early seventeenth century, men like González de Cellorigo, Sancho de Moncada, Fernández Navarrete, all put forward sensible programmes of reform. Royal expenditure must be regulated, the sale of offices halted, the growth of the Church be checked. The tax system must be overhauled, special concessions be made to agricultural labourers, rivers be made navigable and dry lands irrigated. In this way alone could Castile's productivity be increased, its commerce be restored, and its humiliating dependence on foreigners, on the Dutch and the Genoese, be brought to an end.

The ideas were there; and so also, from the truce with the Dutch in 1609, was the opportunity. This opportunity was thrown away. The ineptitude of the Lerma régime, its readiness to dissipate the precious years of peace in a perpetual round of senseless gaiety, is one of the tragedies of Spanish history, and goes far to explain the fiasco that finally overwhelmed the country under the government of Olivares. But behind this inert government, which possessed neither the courage nor the will to look its problems squarely in the face, lay a whole social system and a psychological attitude which themselves blocked the way to radical reform.

The injection of new life into the Castilian economy in the early seventeenth century would have required a vigorous display of personal enterprise, a willingness and ability to invest in agrarian and

N

industrial projects, and to make use of the most recent technical advances. None of these – neither enterprise, nor investment, nor technical knowledge – proved to be forthcoming. 'Those who can will not; and those who will, cannot,' wrote González de Cellorigo.[1] Why was this?

The conventional answer, useful so far as it goes, is that the social climate in Castile was unfavourable to entrepreneurial activity. The Castilians, it is said, lacked that elusive quality known as the 'capitalist spirit'. This was a militant society, imbued with the crusading ideal, accustomed by the *reconquista* and the conquest of America to the quest for glory and booty, and dominated by a Church and an aristocracy which perpetuated those very ideals least propitious for the development of capitalism. Where, in Castile, was that 'rising middle class', which, we are told, leavened the societies of northern Europe until the whole lump was leavened? 'Our republic', wrote González de Cellorigo, 'has come to be an extreme contrast of rich and poor, and there is no means of adjusting them one to another. Our condition is one in which there are rich who loll at ease or poor who beg, and we lack people of the middle sort, whom neither wealth nor poverty prevents from pursuing the rightful kind of business enjoined by Natural Law.'[2]

These words were published in 1600, and accurately describe Castilian society at that time, but they cannot be said to describe it in 1500. For, however uncapitalistic the dominant strain in sixteenth-century Castilian life, there *were* vigorous 'people of the middle sort'. in the Castile of Ferdinand and Isabella and of Charles V. The towns of north Castile at that time could boast a lively bourgeoisie – men like Simón Ruiz, willing to engage their persons and their fortunes in commercial enterprise. But the decay of commercial and financial activity in north Castile, which is patent by 1575, suggests the disappearance of such people during the course of the century. What happened to them? Doubtless they acquired privileges of nobility. The passion for *hidalguía* was strong in Castile, and a title secured not only enhanced social standing, but also exemption from taxation. Yet it is hard to believe that this is an adequate explanation for the disappearance from the Castilian scene of men like Simón Ruiz. All over Europe it was the practice of merchants to buy their

[1] *Memorial de la Politica*, p. 24 v.   [2] Ibid., p. 54.

way into the nobility, and yet it was not everywhere so economically stultifying as it proved to be in Castile.

It would seem desirable to press further than this, and to turn away for a time from repeating the conventional arguments about contempt for commerce and the strength of the aristocratic ideal, to the technical and neglected subject of investment opportunities.[1] What was happening to wealth in sixteenth-century Castile? Much of it was obviously going, as it was going elsewhere, into building and jewellery, and all the expensive accoutrements connected with the enjoyment of a superior social status. But it was also being invested, and unproductively invested, in *census*, or personal loans, and in *juros*, or government bonds. Sixteenth-century Castile saw the development of a highly elaborate credit system – a system which no doubt received much of its impetus from the exigencies of the Crown's finances. Anyone with money to spare – a noble, a merchant, a wealthy peasant – or institutions, like convents, could lend it to private persons, or municipal corporations, or else to the Crown, at a guaranteed 5, 7 or 10 per cent. A proper study of *censos* and *juros* in Spain could tell us much about the reasons for its economic stagnation, especially if related to similar studies for other parts of Europe. *Censos* and *juros* might almost have been deliberately devised to lure money away from risky enterprises into safer channels, of no benefit to Castile's economic development. Indeed, in 1617 the Council of Finance complained that there was no chance of a Castilian economic revival as long as *censos* and *juros* offered better rates of interest than those to be gained from investment in agriculture, industry or trade.[2]

To this unwillingness to engage one's person and one's money in risky entrepreneurial undertakings, there must also be added Castile's increasing technological backwardness, as an explanation of its failure to stage an economic recovery. This backwardness is suggested by the failure of Spanish shipbuilders between the 1590s and the 1620s to keep pace with the new techniques of the North

---

[1] An indication that this question may at last be arousing attention is provided by the pioneering article of Bartolomé Bennassar, 'En Vieille-Castille: Les Ventes de Rentes Perpétuelles', *Annales. Economies, Sociétés, Civilisations*, xve année no. 6 (1960), pp. 1115–26.

[2] AGS Hacienda leg. 395–547 no. 58, Consulta, 3 Sept. 1617.

European dockyards.[1] It was commented upon by foreign travellers, like the Frenchman Joly, who remarked in 1603 on the backwardness of the Spaniards in the sciences and the mechanical arts,[2] and Olivares himself in the 1630s was complaining of the ignorance of modern engineering techniques: 'I am certain that no Spanish man who comes from abroad to see Spain can fail to blame us roundly for our barbarism, when he sees us having to provision all the cities of Castile by pack-animal – and rightly so, for all Europe is trying out internal navigation with great profit.'[3]

While these technical deficiences can presumably be attributed in part to the general lack of business enterprise in Castile, they should also be related to the whole climate of Castilian intellectual life. Here we are seriously hampered by the lack of a good study of the Castilian educational system. Why was it that science and technology failed to take root in Spain, at a time when they were beginning to arouse considerable interest elsewhere in Europe? It may be that further investigations will show a greater degree of scientific interest in Spain than has hitherto been assumed, but at present there is no evidence of this.[4] Indeed, such evidence as does exist points in an opposite direction – to the gradual separation of Habsburg Spain from the mainstream of European intellectual development. Early sixteenth-century Spain was Erasmian Spain, enjoying close cultural contacts with the most active intellectual centres of Europe. From the 1550s there was a chilling change in the cultural climate. The *alumbrados* were persecuted, Spanish students were forbidden to attend foreign universities, and Spain was gradually sealed off by a frightened monarch from contact with the contagious atmosphere of a heretical Europe. The conscious transformation of Spain into the redoubt of the true faith may have given

[1] See A. P. Usher, 'Spanish Ships and Shipping in the Sixteenth and Seventeenth Centuries', *Facts and Factors in Economic History for E. F. Gay* (Harvard University Press, 1932), pp. 189–213.

[2] 'Voyage de Barthélemy Joly en Espagne (1603–1604)', ed. L. Barrau-Dihigo, *Revue Hispanique*, xx (1909), p. 611.

[3] BM Add. MS. 25,689 f. 237, Consulta del Conde Duque a SM.

[4] A collection of essays on Spanish science, of very varying quality, was published in Madrid in 1935 under the title of *Estudios sobre la Ciencia Española del Siglo XVII*, but they have not been followed up.

an added intensity to Spanish religious experience under Philip II, but it also served to cut Spain off from that powerful intellectual current which was leading elsewhere to scientific inquiry and technical experiment.[1]

The period between 1590 and 1620, then, sees a rapid erosion of two of the principal foundations of Castile's sixteenth-century primacy, and consequently of Spain's imperial power: a decline both in Castile's demographic vitality and in its productivity and wealth. Recent investigations have also confirmed that it sees the erosion of the third foundation of Castile's primacy, in the form of a drastic reduction in the value, both to the Crown and to Castile, of Castile's possessions overseas. The great convoy of volumes launched by M. and Mme Chaunu has brought home to us the enormous significance of trade between the port of Seville and Spanish America. It is, they suggest, in the 1590s that the *Carrera de las Indias* shows its first signs of serious strain. In 1597 it became clear for the first time that the American market for European goods was overstocked, but already from about 1590 the upward trend of Seville's trade with the Indies was losing speed. Although the trade fluctuated round a high level between the 1590s and 1620, its whole character was changing to the detriment of the Castilian economy. As Mexico developed its industries and Peru its agriculture, the colonies' dependence on the traditional products of the mother country grew less. There was a decreased demand in America for the Spanish cloth, and for the wine, oil and flour which bulked so large in the transatlantic shipments of the sixteenth century. The consequences of this were very serious. The galleons at Seville were increasingly laden with foreign goods, although unfortunately we do not know the relative proportions of Spanish and non-Spanish cargoes. With less demand in American for Castilian and Andalusian products, less of the American silver carried to Seville is destined for Spanish recipients, and it is significant that Spanish silver prices, which had moved upwards for a century, begin their downward movement after 1601. Moreover, the changes and the stresses in the

[1] For the intellectual isolation of Spain as a factor in the decline, see especially Santiago Ramón y Cajal, *Los Tónicos de la Voluntad*, 5th edn. (Buenos Aires, 1946), pp. 203 ff.; and Claudio Sanchez-Albornoz, *España, Un Enigma Histórico* (Buenos Aires, 1956), ii. p. 553.

transatlantic system began to undermine the whole structure of credit and commerce in Seville.

The principal beneficiaries of this crisis were the foreigners – the hated Genoese ('white Moors' as an irate Catalan called them),[1] the Portuguese Jews and the heretical Dutch. Foreign bankers ran the Crown's finances; foreign merchants had secured a stranglehold over the Castilian economy, and their tentacles were wrapping themselves round Seville's lucrative American trade. Castile's sense of national humiliation was increased by the truce with the Dutch in 1609, and bitterness grew as the Dutch exploited the years of peace to prise their way into the overseas empires of Spain and Portugal. The humiliating awareness of the sharp contrast between the dying splendour of Castile and the rising power of the foreigner is one of the most important clues to the psychological climate of Philip III's Castile. It helps to accentuate that sense of impending disaster, the growing despair about the condition of Castile which prompts the bitter outbursts of the *arbitristas*; and it turns them into fierce patriots, of whom some, like Sancho de Moncada, betray a hysterical xenophobia.

The resulting mental climate goes far to explain some of the more baffling characteristics of the age of Olivares. Insufficient attention has been paid to the many signs of a revival of aggressive Castilian nationalism between 1609 and 1621 – a nationalism that would seem to have been inspired by Castile's growing sense of inferiority. Consciously or subconsciously Castilians were arguing that peace with heretics, itself deeply humiliating, was politically and economically fruitless, since it had done nothing to check the advance of the English and the Dutch. Yet, if the foreigner triumphed in the contemptible arts of commerce, Castile could at least evoke the spirit of its former greatness – its military prowess. The answer to its problems was therefore a return to war.

This appears to have been the attitude of the great Castilian Viceroys of Philip III's reign, the Osunas and the Alcalás, and it was in this climate of aggressive Castilian nationalism, with its strong messianic overtones, that Olivares came to power in 1621. In the person of Olivares one finds curiously blended the two dominant

[1] Acadèmia de Bones Lletres, Barcelona. Dietari de Pujades i. f. 135, 1 Dec. 1602.

strains of thought of the reign of Philip III: the reforming idealism of the *arbitristas* and the aggressive nationalism of the great Castilian proconsuls. With his boundless confidence in his own powers, Olivares determined to combine the programmes of both. He would restore Castile to economic vigour, and simultaneously he would lead it back to the great days of Philip II when it was master of the world.

But the ambitious imperial programme of the Conde Duque depended, as the imperial programme of Philip II had depended, on the population, the productivity and the overseas wealth of Castile, and each of these had undergone a serious crisis between 1590 and 1620. It would conventionally be argued also that Philip II's imperialism was dependent, and indeed primarily dependent, on the flow of American silver coming directly to the Crown; and in so far as that flow had diminished by the second and third decades of the seventeenth century, the attempt to revive Spain's imperial greatness was in any event doomed. Here, however, the popular conception of the role played by the king's American silver supplies can be misleading. The silver remittances to the Crown at the end of Philip II's reign averaged about two million ducats a year. This was little more than the annual sum raised by ecclesiastical taxation in the king's dominions, and under a third of the sum which Castile alone paid the Crown each year in its three principal taxes.[1]

The American remittances were important, in the long run, less for their proportionate contribution to the Crown's total income than for the fact that they were one of the few sources of revenue not pledged for many years in advance. Their existence assured a regular supply of silver which was necessary if the bankers were to continue to provide the king with credit. During the decade 1610–20 the remittances began to fall off. Instead of the two millions of the early 1600s, the President of the Council of Finance reported in December 1616 that 'in the last two years hardly a million ducats have come each year',[2] and by 1620 the figure was as low as 800,000. It recovered in the 1620s, but between 1621 and 1640 $1\frac{1}{2}$ million ducats

[1] This can be deduced from papers and *consultas* of the Council of Finance in AGS Hacienda for the years 1598–1607, and particularly leg. 271–380.
[2] AGS Hacienda leg. 391–542 no. 1, Don Fernando Carillo to King, 23 Dec. 1616.

represented an exceptional year, and not more than a million ducats could be expected with any degree of confidence; in fact, about half the sum that Philip II could expect.

This was serious, but it was not crippling in relation to the overall revenues of the Crown. Under Philip IV, as under Philip II, it was not America but Castile that bore the main burden of Habsburg imperialism, and Castile was still paying its six, seven or eight million ducats a year in taxation. But during the 1620s it became increasingly expensive for Castile to raise these sums. Since 1617 large new quantities of *vellón* coinage had been manufactured, and by 1626 the premium on silver in terms of *vellón* had risen from 4 per cent in 1620 to some 50 per cent.[1] This meant in practice that a tax collected in *vellón* would now buy abroad only half the goods and services for which it was nominally supposed to pay.

Olivares tried to compensate for the disastrous drop in the purchasing power of Castilian money by raising the level of taxation in Castile and inventing a host of ingenious fiscal devices to extract money from the privileged and the exempt. In many ways he was extremely successful. The Castilian aristocracy was so intensively mulcted that a title, so far from being a badge of exemption, became a positive liability, and the Venetian ambassador who arrived in 1638 reported Olivares as saying that, if the war continued, no one need think of possessing his own money any more since everything would belong to the king.[2] While this fiscal policy, when applied to the Castilian nobles, caused no more than impotent rumblings of discontent, it proved to be self-defeating when adopted towards what remained of the Castilian merchant community. The long series of arbitrary confiscations of American silver remittances to individual merchants in Seville, who were 'compensated' by the grant of relatively worthless *juros*, proved fatal to the town's commercial life,[3] Olivares' tenure of power saw the final alienation of

[1] Earl J. Hamilton, *American Treasure and the Price Revolution in Spain, 1501–1650* (Harvard University Press, 1934), Table 7, p. 96.

[2] *Relazioni degli Stati Europei*, ed. Barozzi and Berchet. Serie 1. Spagna, ii. (Venice, 1860), p. 86.

[3] See Antonio Dominguez Ortiz, 'Los Caudales de Indias y la Politica Exterior de Felipe IV', *Anuario de Estudios Americanos*, xiii (1956), pp. 311–83. The same author's *Politica y Hacienda de Felipe IV* (Madrid, 1960), is an impor-

Spain's native business community from its king, and the final defeat of native commercial enterprise in the name of royal necessity. The crumbling of the elaborate credit structure of Seville and the collapse of Seville's trading system with the New World between 1639 and 1641,[1] was the price that Olivares had to pay for his cavalier treatment of Spanish merchants.

In spite of Olivares' ruthless exploitation of Castile's remaining resources, there was never enough to meet all his needs. Castile's growing inability to meet his demands for manpower and money naturally forced him to look beyond Castile for help. To save his beloved Castile, it became imperative for him to exploit the resources of the peripheral provinces of the Iberian peninsula, which had been undertaxed in relation to Castile, and which were under no obligation to provide troops for foreign service. It was this determination to draw on the resources of the Crown of Aragon and Portugal which inspired Olivares' famous scheme for the Union of Arms: a device which would compel all the provinces of the Spanish monarchy to contribute a specified number of paid men to the royal armies.[2]

Olivares' scheme of 1626 for the Union of Arms was in effect an implicit admission of a change in the balance of economic power within the Spanish peninsula. Behind it lay the contemporary Castilian assumption that Castile's economic plight was graver than that of the other regions of Spain. How far this assumption was correct, it is not yet possible to say. The various regions of the peninsula lived their own lives and went their own ways. A decline of Castile does not necessarily imply the simultaneous decline of the Crown of Aragon and Portugal, both of them living in different economic systems, and shielded by separate monetary systems from the violent oscillations of the Castilian coinage.

Yet, if we look at these peripheral kingdoms, we may well think that the prospects were a good deal less hopeful than Olivares

tant contribution to the study of the Crown's financial policy in the reign of Philip IV, based as it is on previously unused documents from Simancas.
[1] Chaunu op. cit., viii (2), Pt. 2, pp. 1793–1851.
[2] For the Union of Arms, see my chapter in the forthcoming *New Cambridge Modern History*, vol. iv, and my *The Revolt of the Catalans. A Study in the Decline of Spain (1598–1640)* (Cambridge, 1963).

believed them to be. Aragon: a dry, impoverished land. Valencia: its economy dislocated by the expulsion of the Moriscos. Catalonia: its population growth halted about 1625,[1] its traditional trade with the Mediterranean world contracting after the plague of 1630. Portugal: its Far Eastern empire lost to the Dutch under Philip III, its Brazilian empire in process of being lost to the Dutch under Philip IV.

Even if Olivares overestimated the capacity of the other territories of the peninsula to bring him the help he needed, he none the less knew as well as anyone else that he was engaged in a desperate race against time. If France could be beaten swiftly, the future would still be his. Then at last he could undertake the great reforms which only awaited the return of peace, and which would enable Castile to devote itself as effectively to the task of economic reform as it had already devoted itself to the successful prosecution of the war. In 1636, at Corbie, he very nearly achieved his aim. A little more money, a few more men, and French resistance might have crumbled. But the gamble – and Olivares knew it *was* a gamble – failed, and, with its failure, Olivares was lost. The Franco-Spanish war inevitably turned after Corbie into the kind of war which Spain was least able to stand: a war of attrition, tedious and prolonged. Such a war was bound to place heavy strains on the constitutional structure of the Spanish monarchy, just as it placed heavy strains on the constitutional structure of the French monarchy, since Olivares and Richelieu were compelled to demand assistance from, and billet troops in, provinces which had never been assimilated and which still possessed their own semi-autonomous institutions and their own representative bodies. The Spanish monarchy was particularly vulnerable in this respect, since both Catalonia in the east, and Portugal in the west, were uneasily and unsatisfactorily yoked to the central government in Madrid. When the pressure became too great, as it did in 1640, they rose up in arms against that government, and Castile – for so long the predominant partner in the monarchy that it took its superiority for granted – suddenly discovered that it no longer possessed the strength to impose its will by force.

The great crisis in the structure of the monarchy in 1640, which

[1] Catalan population problems are admirably treated in J. Nadal and E. E. Giralt, *La Population Catalane de 1553 à 1717* (Paris, 1960).

led directly to the dissolution of Spanish power, must therefore be regarded as the final development of that specifically Castilian crisis of 1590–1620 which this article has attempted to describe; as the logical dénouement of the economic crisis which destroyed the foundations of Castile's power, and of the psychological crisis which impelled it into its final bid for world supremacy.

It seems improbable that any account of the *decline of Spain* can substantially alter the commonly accepted version of seventeenth-century Spanish history, for there are always the same cards, however we shuffle them: mortmain and vagabondage, governmental ineptitude, and an all-pervading contempt for the harsh facts of economic life. Instead of continuing to be indiscriminately scattered they can, however, be given some pattern and coherence. Yet even when the reshuffling is finally done and all the cards are fairly distributed, it remains doubtful whether dissent will be possible from the verdict on Spain of Robert Watson's *History of the Reign of Philip III*, published in 1783: 'her power corresponded not with her inclination';[1] nor from the even sterner verdict of a contemporary, González de Cellorigo: 'it seems as if one had wished to reduce these kingdoms to a republic of bewitched beings, living outside the natural order of things'[2] – a republic whose most famous citizen was Don Quijote de la Mancha.

[1] p. 309.   [2] *Memorial de la Politica*, p. 25 v.

SEVEN

The Economic Decline of Italy[1]

CARLO M. CIPOLLA

At the beginning of the seventeenth century, Italy, or rather Central and Northern Italy, was still one of the more highly developed regions of Western Europe, with an exceptionally high standard of living for that time. Towards the end of the same century, that is around 1680, Italy had become a backward and depressed area; her manufacturing industry had collapsed, there were too many people for the available resources; agriculture had become by far the predominant section of the economy. To study this tragic example of economic decline there are no very elaborate statistics. However, there is enough information to make it possible at least to understand in a general way how far things had changed.

Venice, at the beginning of the seventeenth century, produced annually an average of more than 20,000 cloths, with an upper limit of around 29,000 cloths in 1602. At the end of the century annual production had declined to little over 2,000 cloths.[2]

At the beginning of the century Como had about sixty firms, producing an average of about 8,000 to 10,000 cloths a year. In 1650 there were only four firms, with a total output of about 400 cloths a year. At the beginning of the eighteenth century, the production of woollen cloths had almost entirely ceased.

In Como at the beginning of the seventeenth century the silk

---

[1] This article is translated from 'Il declino economico dell' Italia' printed in *Storia dell' economia italiana*, published by Boringhieri, Turin (1959). It is a revised and expanded version of an article which originally appeared as 'The decline of Italy: the case of a fully matured economy', in *The Economic History Review*, second series, Vol. V (1952). The translation is by Janet Pullan.

[2] D. Sella, 'Les mouvements longs de l'industrie lainière à Venise aux XVIe et XVIIe siècles', *Annales*, 12 (1957), p. 32.

industry had thirty active looms. By 1650 there were only two – one of which worked for only six months of the year. At the beginning of the eighteenth century there were no longer any looms working.

The story is not very different in other industrial areas: the number of firms in the Como group of minor guilds seems to have suffered, between 1600 and 1650, a reduction of about 50 per cent, and the capital invested seems to have diminished correspondingly. After 1650 decline continued. At the beginning of the eighteenth century there was widespread and chronic unemployment in Como.[1] At Torno at the end of the seventeenth century 'vines now grew in places where once were factories'.[2]

In Milan at the beginning of the seventeenth century there were between sixty and seventy firms making woollen cloths, with an overall output averaging 15,000 cloths a year. By 1640 the number of firms had dropped to fifteen, and the overall annual average output to about 3,000 woollen cloths, By 1682 the number of firms was reduced to five. By 1709 there was but a single firm with an average annual production of around 100 cloths.[3]

At the end of the sixteenth century Milan had more than 500 firms with workers in silk and gold cloth. In the eighteenth century there were only thirty-two.[4]

[1] A.S.C., *Relazione fatta dal questore D. G. Larriatequi* (30 August 1650) (in print); A.C.M., *Materie*, b. 268, *Consulta a S.C.C.R. Maestà circa l'estimo del mercimonio*, 7 June 1732, Chapter 52. On this theme cf. also B. Caizzi, *Il Comasco sotto il dominio spagnolo* (Como, 1955), pp. 83–110. From Larriatequi's *Relazione* it appears that in the woollen industry 'if a piece of cloth was worth 400 lire, more than half would be spent on working it, and in making a piece of serge the cost of labour amounts to 75 per cent'. Cf. V. Pitti, p. 131, n. 2.
[2] Caizzi, op. cit., p. 109.
[3] G. M. Tridi, *Informatione del danno proceduto a S.M. et alle città dello Stato di Milano* (Milan, 1641), several printed copies in A.C.M., *Materie*, b. 268; P. Verri, *Considerazioni sul commercio dello Stato di Milano*, ed. C. A. Vianello (Milan 1939), p. 57; *Consulta a S.C.C.R. Maestà*, 7 June 1732, Chapter 52.
[4] University Library, Pavia, Mscr. Aldini 30; likewise R. Rossi, in his *Memoria del 1641*, A.C.M., *Materie*, b. 268, asks us 'to consider that the making of silk cloths has declined in this city . . .', and he talks of 'the scarcity of activity, especially in the woollen and silk industries, and workers are emigrating to other states and countries'. Cf. also Verri, *Considerazioni sul commercio dello stato di Milano*, ed. C. A. Vianello (Milan, 1939), p. 51; also M. Daverio, 'Saggio storico sulle sete e serifici nello stato di Milano (1807)', *Economisti minori del Settecento Lombardo*, ed. C. A. Vianello (Milan, 1942), p. 446.

We have no detailed statistics for other economic activities, but there is no doubt that, in Milan, the metallurgical and building industries also showed a long and drastic decline.[1]

In Cremona in 1615, 187 people were registered in the woollen guild, and local tax officials taxed the making and selling of woollen cloths at the annual rate of 742 lire. In 1648 the number of people registered was down to twenty-three, and the assessment was down to ninety-seven lire.[2] Post-plague recovery after 1630 raised the assessment to 164 lire in 1663, but decline then began again. In the first half of the eighteenth century, woollen cloths manufactured in Cremona amounted only to a few barracans made by a couple of merchants.[3]

In Cremona, again, the fustian-makers' guild had ninety-one men on the register in 1615, and the tax quota for fustians in that year was 240 lire. In 1648 there were only forty-one on the register, and the tax quota was down to twenty-nine lire.[4]

In 1648 the merchants' corporation in Cremona noted the 'shortage of merchants and businesses, which are getting fewer every day to the grave detriment of this state'.[5] If one ventures to take the fiscal assessments of the total trade of the city as an indication, however rough, of the economic activity of the city itself, one can say that while Pigliasco's survey in 1580 attributed to Cremona trade valued at about 8 million lire, in 1647 the valuation was only about 2 million. After 1647 the decline continued without interruptions.[6]

In Monza in 1620 there were still twenty firms producing woollen cloths. By 1640 they had all disappeared.[7]

[1] Tridi, op. cit.; Rossi, op. cit.; *Consulta de Tribunale di Provvisione*, 23 December 1641, and *Consulta a S.C.C.R.*, Maestà, 7 June 1732: all in A.C.M., *Materie*, b. 268.

[2] U. Meroni, 'Cremona fedelissima', Vol. II, *Annali della Biblioteca Governativa e Libreria Civica de Cremona*, Vol. 10 (Cremona, 1957), p. 19.

[3] Meroni, op. cit., p. 21, n. 1.

[4] Ibid., p. 20.

[5] Ibid., p. 105.

[6] Meroni, op. cit., p. 16 and Fig. 1 on pp. 8–9. The level of prices in 1647 cannot have been much lower than in 1580. For the decline of Cremona in the seventeenth century, cf. also Caizzi, 'I tempi della decadenza economica di Cremona', *Studi in onore di A. Sapori*, Vol. II (Milan, 1957), pp 1009–19.

[7] Tridi, op. cit.

In Pavia in 1635 there were still twenty-five master silk workers. By 1700 there were only ten.[1]

In Genoa the silk industry was in full decline by the last decades of the sixteenth century. A seventeenth-century tradition holds that, whereas there had been 18,000 silk looms in the territory of the Republic, by 1608 there were only 3,000, and scarcely more than 2,500 in 1675.[2] The total of 18,000 weavers for the middle of the sixteenth century must be considered an exaggeration.[3] However, there can be no doubt that the silk industry did decline during the course of the century.[4]

Throughout the seventeenth century the paper and wool[5] trades in Genoa were contracting at the same time as the silk industry. The general activity of the port also declined. At the beginning of the seventeenth century the annual value of goods imported and exported by the port must have totalled around 9 million lire. At the end of the century it had fallen to 3 million lire. It is true that the historian must take into account the long decline of prices which took place during the century if he is to evaluate the true significance of this reduction; but there is no doubt that a decisive reduction in the volume of trade took place.

In Florence, between 1560 and 1580, the annual production of woollens was round about 30,000 cloths. Between 1590 and 1600

[1] G. Aleati and C. M. Cipolla, 'Il trend economico nello Stato di Milano durante i secoli XVI e XVII: il caso di Pavia', *Bollettino società pavese di storia patria*, Vol. 50 (1950), pp. 28, 29, 31.

[2] For all this, cf. H. Sieveking, 'Die genueser Seidenindustrie im XV und XVI Jahrhundert', *Schmollers Jahrbuch*, 21 (1897), p. 124, n. 1, and p. 127, n. 1. According to more detailed information in Signorina G. Sivori's *Il declino della manifattura serica genovese nel secolo XVII* (unpublished), it seems that in Genoa in 1675 there were 252 master weavers with 480 looms, of which 260 were not working; in the Riviera di Levante, 1,614 master weavers with 2,059 looms. No information is available for the Riviera di Ponente.

[3] The problem is dealt with in Sivori, op. cit.

[4] See note above.

[5] There is a mention of the decline of the Genoese woollen industry in a *Relazione* dated 23 December 1608 (A.S.G., Sala 50–1, Scansia 67, *Arte della Seta*, for the years 1432–1771, N. 161). The theme is repeated in documents of 1653 and 1698 cited by G. Giacchero, *Storia economica del Settecento Genovese* Genoa, 1951), p. 241, n. 8, and p. 269.

the average had been reduced to between 13,000 and 14,000 cloths. Towards the middle of the seventeenth century it was down to 6,000 cloths. Again, in Florence, the annual average production of *tele macchiate* was around 13,000 pieces at the beginning of the seventeenth century. By mid-century it was 6,000 pieces.[1] There are no precise figures for the second half of the century. But we do know that the decline continued. Towards the end of the seventeenth century, Florence was riddled with unemployment.[2]

In Naples the silk industry went from bad to worse throughout the seventeenth century. In 1687, talking of its complete decay, an observer said that 'the silk industry did not die of a violent fever, but wasted away of a slow consumption.'[3]

Likewise in Sicily the silk industry had entered a critical phase in the first decades of the seventeenth century, and it continued to decline throughout the century.[4] By the beginning of the eighteenth, silk or wool was not being manufactured anywhere in the whole of Sicily. 'Raw silk is exported in bulk, and (what is worse) it is

---

[1] See R. Romano, 'A Florence au XVII siècle: industries textiles et conjoncture', *Annales: économies, sociétés, civilisations*, 7 (1952), pp. 508–11. In addition, see the *Rappresentanze* of V. Pitti in 1619 and 1628 (in M. Lastri (ed.), *L'osservatore fiorentino sugli edifizi della sua patria*, 3rd edition with the addition of various notes by G. del Rosso, Vol. 8, Florence, 1821, t. 6, pp. 163–7), from which interesting information can be drawn. Indeed the *Rappresentanze* of Pitti show that in the period 1590–1604 there were about 120 Florentine woollen firms, employing 878 men and 1,457 women, with 1,420 looms. The output was around 13,000–14,000 cloths (slightly more than half being 'coarse serges and rich cloths, and the rest *perpignani*') with a total value of about 900,000 crowns. As for the relative costs, it is calculated that about 500,000 crowns represented labour costs ('taking account of the fact that in wool working the manufacturing costs amounted to 55 per cent or more') and most of the rest was 'the value of the wool' and the entrepreneurial activity. In 1610 the number of firms had declined to 112. In 1619 there were only eighty, 'and the capital involved was not more than 520,000 crowns'. In 1628 there were only fifty-two firms, 'with a capital of around 360,000 crowns, with 782 looms and 378 male weavers, of whom only 268 were actually working, 110 being engaged in other work, and there were 1,315 women'.
[2] R. Galluzzi, *Istoria di Toscana*, Vol. 4 (Florence, 1781), pp. 197 ff.
[3] L. de Rosa, *I cambi esteri del Regmo di Napoli dal 1591 al 1707* (Naples, 1955), p. 62.
[4] P. Pieri, *La storia di Messina nello sviluppo della sua vita communale* (Messina, 1939), pp. 233 and 243.

returned worked, for here there is no master who knows how to do a good job. Wool is exported because there are no clothworkers here.'[1]

It must be admitted that the figures cited here tend to exaggerate the economic decline of Italy. This is mainly because we are dealing with one of the sectors worst hit – the textile industry – and discussing only the major centres. We know for certain that while in most of the big cities there was a drastic decline, in minor centres, or rural ones, there was some expansion of industry. For example, between 1600 and 1700 the production of woollen cloths drastically contracted in Venice, but tended to expand in Treviso, Padua, and above all in Bergamo.[2] Between 1620 and 1700, many activities contracted in Como, but grew in Tremezzo, Menaggio, Bellagio and the Valtelline.[3] From the beginning of the seventeenth century, the silk industry, which was in a critical state in Milan, Genoa, Bologna, and Pavia, was developing in Verona, Pisa, Piacenza and Vigevano, and in various smaller centres of the Ligurian Riviera.[4] The manufacture of fustians was in crisis in Cremona, but was expanding in Monticelli, Busseto and Parma, and in the Mantuan countryside.[5] As for Milan, a contemporary observed that 'commerce has moved to other places in the Duchy'.[6]

[1] L. La Rocca, 'Relazione al Re Vittorio Amedeo II di Savoia sulle condizioni economiche, sociali e politiche della Sicilia alla fine del dominio spagnolo', *Archivio Storico Sicilia Orientale* (1914), p. 417.

[2] A.S.V., S. Mr. b. 124, fasc. Treviso; b. 125, fasc. 4 (3 June 1678) and fasc. 2 (22 March 1725).

[3] *Consulta a S.C.C.R. Maestà*, 7 June 1732, Chapter 52.

[4] For Verona, see Pavesi, *Memorie*, p. 106. For Pisa and Piacenza cf. a report dated 1676 which discusses the crises in the Genoese silk industry: '. . . considering the great quantity which in times past we used to sell, it has been calculated that now we only make about a quarter of what we used to, because the said silk industry has been introduced into Pisa and Piacenza', A.S.G., *Traffico ed arti* Miscellanea for the year 1676, N. 160, Scansia 67, Sala 50–1. Ibid., also for smaller centres of the Ligurian Riviera. For Vigevano, cf. P. Landrini, *La Lomellina* (Rome, 1952), p. 197.

[5] *Consulta a S.C.C.R. Maestà*, 7 June 1732, Chapter 52.

[6] D de Capitanei de Sondria, *Processo*, p. 13. The report dates from 1659. Cf. also S. Pugliese, 'Condizioni economiche e finanziarie della Lombardia nella prima metà del sec. XVIII', *Miscellanea di storia italiana*, serie 3, Vol. 21, Turin, 1924, p. 85 ff.

Later I shall try to explain the causes and the significance of these changes in the siting of manufacturing industries. Here, I only wish to point out that, although we have no precise statistical information, the general impression is that, however great the development of manufacturing industries in minor places and in rural districts, it could not have been sufficient to compensate either in volume or in value for the drastic decline in manufacturing in the major centres.[1] Further, in the major centres there was also a decline in services such as banking and shipping, for which there was no compensation in the minor centres or in the villages.

How can this tragic collapse of the Italian economy during the seventeenth century be explained?

First we must be clear that, even at the end of the sixteenth century, as in previous centuries, the economic prosperity of Italy was fundamentally dependent on massive exports of manufactured articles (above all, textiles), and on a huge volume of invisible exports such as banking and shipping services. The entire economic structure of the country depended on being able to sell abroad a large proportion of the goods it manufactured and of the services it could provide.

With the second half of the sixteenth century other nations were developing on a large scale, and with new methods were expanding their industrial, banking and maritime activities. Their products and services came to compete and triumph over Italian ones, and from the beginning of the seventeenth century Italy saw one after another of her foreign markets being closed. English and Dutch cloth and French silk, for example, not only ousted Italian textiles from French, Dutch and English markets, but between 1600 and 1680 imposed themselves inexorably on other European, North African and Near Eastern markets which had until then been supplied with Italian goods.

Venetian and Genoese documents can give us some idea of the collapse of Italian exports that took place during the seventeenth century. As for Genoa, we know that one of the duties on the export of silken cloth, the so-called 'additione del 1565', when it was

[1] It must be realized that the capacity and equipment for exporting of the smaller centres were slight, and thus the possibility of external sale was much reduced.

introduced yielded round about 5,000 silver crowns, while towards
the end of the century it yielded only around 800 silver crowns a
year on average,[1] although there was no change in the rate of
taxation. We also know that much of this collapse occurred because
Genoese silks could no longer find an outlet in the markets of France,
England and Germany.

As for Venice, we know that at the beginning of the seventeenth
century Venetian industries provided the Near East with nearly all
the woollen cloths it needed, and that much Near Eastern commerce was in Venetian hands. It appears that during the first years of
the seventeenth century Venice was able to export to Mediterranean ports something like 25,000 cloths – that is, almost her entire
output of woollens. A hundred years later, according to the Venetian
ambassador at Constantinople, Venice was exporting not more than
100 cloths a year to that area, about fifty to Constantinople, and the
same number to Smyrna. The total volume of Venetian trade in
these two centres had declined to an average of some 600 thousand
ducats a year, while French trade was around the 4 million mark and
English not much less than the French.[2]

The fundamental reason why Italian goods and services were
supplanted by those offered by foreigners was always the same:
English, French and Dutch services and goods were offered at lower
prices.[3] But why then this disparity in prices?

[1] A.S.G., Sala 37, *Porto Franco*, Archivio Segreto, N. 1011, year 1701: 'particularly in the last century the export of manufactured silk brought in a great
revenue. It is known that the extra duty imposed in 1565 (which did not
account for more than one quarter of everything that was collected) originally
yielded 5,000 crowns of silver a year, while in these most recent years it has
barely produced 800. . . .'

[2] Sella, op. cit., pp. 38–9, n. 4. A.S.V., S. Mr., b. 125, fasc. 2, letters of 10 April
1713 and 14 November 1725, and the accounts of the *Compagnia della nuova
institutione* (21 May 1723).

[3] Rossi, in his *Relazione* (1641), noted that foreign woollen cloth 'costs less to
the buyer' than Milanese cloths, and that silk cloths 'were sold at a lower price
than ours'. Cf. similar statements in *Replica dei possessori del perticato* (1640), in
de Capitanei di Sondria, op. cit. In 1611 the Venetian ambassador, Simone
Contarini, warned that British textiles were chosen in the Turkish markets in
preference to Venetian because they cost much less (A. Segre, *Storia del commercio*, Vol. 1 (Turin, 1923), p. 482). In 1671, an important Venetian business-
man specifically stated that if Venetian woollen cloths were no longer sold

Generally, Italian goods were of a higher quality. Italian industry, partly because of its proud tradition, but mainly because it was controlled by traditionalistic guild regulations, persisted in producing by ancient methods excellent goods which were now outdated.[1] In the field of textiles, for instance, the English, Dutch and French invaded the international market with lighter, less hard-

in the Levant 'this was because foreign goods were more beautiful and cost less' (*Scrittura inedita de Simone Giogalli intorno la decadenza del commercio di Venezia*, ed. E. Cicogna, (Venice, 1856), p. 16). In the same year another Venetian source stated that Dutch and English cloths were 'very moderate in price' compared with Venetian (A.S.V., *Senato Rettori, filza* 82, 21 January 1671). Again in Venice in 1678, it was said that woollen cloths were no longer sold because they were too costly compared with English and Dutch ones (A.S.V., S. Mr., sez. comm., b. 214, fasc. Venice, doc. 27 September 1678). Other evidence is quoted in Sella, op. cit., pp. 39–40.

In Genoa, towards the middle of the seventeenth century, it was stated that 'in Spain French cloths were being sold at so much lower prices that it was necessary either to learn how to make them at less expense or to cease to make them at all'. Other documents of the same period state that French competition in the silk trade made it difficult to sell Italian products, because the French 'could offer them at moderate prices'. (I was shown these documents by Signorina G. Sivori.) In 1698 the Government of Genoa, having to buy cloth, decided to buy French goods because they were less costly than local products (cf. Giacchero, *Storia economica del Settecento genovese*, (op. cit.), p. 269). For the higher cost of Italian shipping and insurance services compared with English and Dutch see, with many references, Sella, op. cit., p. 44, n. 3.

[1] For much of the seventeenth century in Venice the statutes of the woollen guild forbade the production of anything but 'Venetian cloths of the old standard'. Not until 1673, under the pressure of events, was it decided to allow 'the free introduction in to the city of cloths of the Dutch types as Venetian work' (A.S.V. sez. comm. b. 124, fasc. Venice, doc. dated 27 September 1698). Cloths of the Dutch and English type were called *londrine*. In Genoa, by 1640, the English consul, in a letter addressed to the Genoese government, pointed out that damage to the export of Genoese silks to England arose out of the insistence with which Genoese silk manufacturers continued to make products of the old type. 'In England they have introduced cheap plushes made in France *di portate* 31$\frac{1}{2}$, and because in the British Isles, as elsewhere, they are more concerned with the usefulness than the quality of the goods, all other silks are put at a disadvantage, which causes loss to this city, where the law permits the manufacture only of silks *di portate* 63' (A.S.G., *Arti ed industrie secc. XV–XVI*, N. 187, Scansia 68, Sala 50–1). For Genoa again, see another document quoted by Sieveking, *Seidenindustrie*, p. 124, n. 1.

wearing and more colourful products.[1] There is no doubt that the quality of these goods was much poorer than the Italian; but they cost less and pleased more.

However, Italian goods cost more not only because they were of a better quality. The costs of production, other things being equal, were higher in Italy than in England, Holland, or France. There were three reasons for this:

(a) Excessive control by the guilds obliged Italian manufacturers to continue to use outdated methods of production and organization.[2] There is no doubt that the guilds had become

[1] Rossi in his *Relazione* (1641), points out for example that foreign silk cloths were 'lighter and less well made, deceiving the eyes of purchasers with their colours and selling cheaper than ours . . . while ours could not be sold at the same price because they contained more material, were better made and had been dyed better – although they could not compete with these foreign stuffs in brightness . . . and today it is usual to think that whatever is cheapest is best.'

In 1611, the Venetian ambassador, S. Contarini, noting that Venetian woollen cloth was dearer than English, remarked that it was nevertheless better in quality (Segre, loc. cit.). Another Venetian ambassador at Constantinople in 1723 stated that the only way to increase Venetian exports to the Levant would be to produce a lighter, cheaper type of cloth, with brighter colours. According to the same ambassador the misfortunes of the Venetian industry arose from the fact that, while foreign competitors had kept up to date, Venice had never changed its type of products (A.S.V., S. Mr., b. 125). Cf. also similar observations by the *Compagnia della nuova institutione* (A.S.V., S. Mr., b. 125, letter of 21 May 1723). Other evidence is quoted by Sella, op. cit., pp. 39–40.

According to Venetian documents, it was originally the English and Dutch whose competition ruined the Venetian textile merchants in the markets of the Levant. Towards the end of the seventeenth century the French succeeded in producing at Carcassonne types of textiles which were even lighter, cheaper and brighter in colour than the English and Dutch types. This new French product competed strongly and successfully with English and Dutch textiles.

For the Genoese industry, cf. the letter of the English consul in 1640, quoted in the footnote above. Cf. also the report of 1676 (A.S.G., Sala 50-1, Scansia 67, *Traffico ed Arti*, Miscellanea 160), in which the export difficulties of the Genoese industries were attributed to the fact that the Genoese products were of the old type: better quality, more durable, but by that time outdated.

[2] E.g., in 1570 Paolo de Simone, a silk spinner, asked permission to have a dyer in his own shop so that he could check 'with his own eyes' the dyeing of the cloth. The guild of dyers opposed his request for fear that it might

constitute a precedent and that consequently all other artisans might take dyers to work in their own shops under their own supervision, 'keeping them like slaves and making them work for whatever wages the manufacturers liked'. The guild's resistance was supported by the State (Sella, op. cit., p. 42, n. 3).

Again, in Venice, for almost the whole of the seventeenth century, the statutes of the guild prevented cloth being made of the English and Dutch type, which had had so much success on the international markets. Moreover, the guild statutes not only demanded the production of a traditional type of goods, but also prevented the adoption of new methods of making these old products. On 3 June 1678 the representatives of the Collegio del Lanificio of Venice proposed that the various masters should be allowed to produce cloths in the way that they considered most convenient, and without any other restrictions. They proposed, too, that they should be allowed to produce cloths of the shape, colour and quality which seemed most appropriate; and that in the process they should be free to use whatever type and whatever quantity of raw materials they wanted (A.S.V., S. Mr., b. 125, fasc. iv: in the same *fascicolo*, cf. interesting reports of 9 June 1676 and 4 September 1677, which indicate in detail how production costs could be reduced by employing new techniques).

In Genoa in 1640 the English consul suggested that to boost exports of local silks it was necessary to lift the existing legislative restrictions concerning the type and method of production (cf. p. 204, n. 1). A report of 1676 saw the repeal of many of the restrictive guild practices as the only solution to the difficulties of the industry (A.S.G., Sala 50–1, Scansia 67, *Traffico ed Arti*, Miscellanea 160). A printed report of 11 July 1651, commenting on the many regulations which compelled the manufacturers to follow traditional methods of production, observed that 'it is imperative that the seller should adapt himself to the needs and taste of his customers, both in the quantity and in the price. Nor should he attempt to export three-pile velvets if he is asked for stiffened velvets or *penine* of the French type, or close-woven cloths of high quality if the customers want soft cloth of the Luccan type, or taffetas at 42 *soldi* a length if they want them at 28 *soldi* only. . . .' (A.S.G., Sala 50–1, Scansia 67, *Arte della Seta*, N. 161).

Only after long pressure of events, and usually when it was too late and the markets were lost, was it decided to allow greater freedom to the manufacturers, as for example in Genoa in 1651, when the guild of woollen workers established that 'it shall be lawful for the said Magistracy to permit the manufacture of new cloths for any purpose in order to enable the clothiers to improve the trade. . . .' (Giacchero, op. cit., p. 241, n. 8).

The entire body of guild legislation was mainly designed to prevent any kind of change. At the very time when other nations were introducing numerous changes in their industrial organization, the paralysing action of the local guilds put Italian industry at a disadvantage, reflected in higher production costs.

associations primarily designed to prevent competition between associates, and they constituted a formidable obstacle
to any possible innovations.[1]

(b) The pressure of taxation in Italian states seems to have been
too high, and badly conceived.[2]

[1] To understand the guilds' general resistance, amply documented above,
two sets of circumstances must be considered. (a) Traditionalism and pride in
one's own tradition. Accustomed for centuries to predominance and international fame for their products, many manufactuers and government officers
of the time deluded themselves that 'by maintaining the old quality' one could
overcome foreign competition which catered for the 'new fashions'. When
they realized their error it was too late. (b) Guilds aimed essentially at the
control and prevention of competition between associates. There were even
guilds which determined the total amount of work which a member could
undertake, in order to maintain a set distribution of work between all the
members. There were frequent cases of guilds determining the maximum
number of assistants or journeymen that a master could employ (with the
double purpose of preventing too much business accumulating in one firm
and of limiting competition between masters for journeymen). It is evident
that, in such an atmosphere, the adoption of any new method or technique of
production or organization was considered as the means by which one
producer could beat his competitors of the same guild – whether through a
change in the product or through a reduction in costs. To prevent this the
guild automatically turned itself into an organization protecting marginal
producers, and impeded all progress.

[2] Nearly every document of the period mentions the excessive burden of
taxation as one of the major causes of the high costs of production. It is
impossible to record here all the documents which discuss or refer to the
problem. However, it seems appropriate to mention at least the reports of
Tridi and Rossi for Milan, and those of Larriatequi for Como, and the various
files of the S. Mr. for Venice.

Naturally one must go carefully in evaluating the significance and truthful-
ness of these protests. But several other things show that there was much
truth in them. In Venice the same state organizations recognized that taxation
was excessive, especially by comparison with other countries (Sella, op. cit.,
p. 43). In Genoa a *Relatione pro arte serica* (A.S.G., Sala 50, *filze* 161 and 187)
pointed out that, because of the heavy duties imposed on leaving the harbour,
'counting all the expenses incurred between here and Lyons, a chestful of our
velvets pays over 1,000 lire more in duty than one of theirs'. Moreover, many
producers abandoned the industry because of excessive taxation. At Como,
Larriatequi refers to several instances of this; for example, Giovanni Pietro
Caramazzo, 'who, in the year 1637, left the trade of wool merchant because
he saw that this work was so much in decline that if a merchant sold 10–12
crowns' worth of goods, instead of buying more again he had to pay the sales

(c) Labour costs seem to have been too high in Italy in relation to the wage levels in competing countries.[1]

tax in the city; and, not being able to bear this taxation, he was pushed out of business' (*Relazione* of Larriatequi, (30 August 1650).

It appears that in territories subject to Spain the negative effects of an excessive fiscal burden were accentuated by the way in which the taxes themselves were apportioned among the various groups of contributors. The system in force was that of quotas. It was decided what the total yield should be, and this was apportioned among large groups of people (especially land-owners, wool merchants, silk merchants, etc.) according to an approximate evaluation of their 'capital' and of the 'trade' of each one of these groups. Within these groups the men themselves (through the guild organizations) were responsible for dividing the tax between them. The assessments, however, were made 'once and for all' (with the Pigliasco operations of 1580), and on this basis burdens continued to be shared. Any group suffering a crisis still had the same tax allotment as before, and if certain members left the group the rest had to pay relatively more. Thus the system aggravated the difficulties of groups which were going downhill, and was undoubtedly one of the incentives stimulating investment in agriculture. Agriculture was less affected – as we shall see later – by the new economic trends of the century, and ended by being taxed relatively less heavily.

Finally one has to consider the effects on Italian production costs of the division of the peninsula into many tiny administrative units, each of which drew revenue from various forms of excise. For instance, the *Consulta a S.C.C.R. Maestà* (7 June 1732), Chapter 81, shows clearly that if a merchant in Milan wanted raw silk from Cremona he had to pay customs duties three times, at the gates of the city of Cremona, then at those of Lodi and finally at those of Milan.

[1] Cf., for example, the significant fact noted by Simone Giogalli in 1671: 'Foreign goods are cheaper . . . here I may say that the amounts which the wool merchants have to pay their workmen are exorbitant, so that if these were scaled down and if public taxes could be regulated, cloth could be sold at more reasonable prices and consequently exported in larger quantities' (*Scrittura*, p. 16). In Venice, too, the representatives of the Collegio del Lanificio requested in 1678 (3 June, A.S.V., S. Mr. sez. Comm., b. 125, fasc. iv) 'that the regulations on wages should be removed, and that the merchant, knowing the worth of his workman, should reward him in accordance with his output and with the amount previously arranged between them'. On 21 May 1723 the *Compagnia della Nuova Institutione*, in a letter addressed to the *Cinque Savii alla Mercanzia* (A.S.V., S. Mr., sez. Comm. b. 125, fasc. iv), pointed out that 'the workers are a great burden. Apart from the disproportionate wages, both punctuality and obedience are lacking. Wool entrusted to hired workers is not safe. Work takes too long and is badly done. The weavers are even more disobedient than the others, and can

Recent research has illustrated the extreme rigidity of the Italian labour market and wage structures during this period. The workers' organizations succeeded in imposing wage levels which were disproportionate to the productivity of the labour itself.[1] Disastrous epidemics, like those of 1630 and 1657, destroyed nearly a third of the population, and by thus suddenly reducing the available labour supply, they strengthened the bargaining powers of workers' associations.

This was not the only misfortune Italy suffered. Guild rigidity, taxation and excessive production costs – aggravated by other more or less exogenous factors[2] – put Italian exports at a disadvantage

only be made to work at all by punishments and deductions from their wages. The number of holidays is a third difficulty.' Concerning Milan, the *Replica dei possessori*, of 1640, states that 'so many other taxes on the necessities of human life make the common people sell their labour dear'. In connection with the factors which kept wages high, Rossi in his *Relazione* (1641), notes also that, due to 'the wars in Lombardy and Piedmont, many people left work and went off into the army'.

[1] For details see D. Sella, *Salari e lavora nell'edilizia Lombarda* (Paria, 1968).

[2] The most important among the other factors was the mercantilist policy of France and England especially. This policy took the form of high import duties for some products. To quote an example: the case of Genoese velvets, about which a Genoese report of 11 July 1651 reveals that 'the French, to make good terms for their cloths and to exclude ours, have imposed a tax of 100 gold crowns *del sole* for every chest of our velvets. Thus, as ours turn out much dearer there is less demand for them' (A.S.G., Sala 50–1, Scansia 67, *Arte della seta* 1432–1771, b. 161). In other instances the mercantilist policy of the great competing countries was to give tax relief to their own local businessmen, thus encouraging their competition against the less-favoured Italian producers, both in local markets and in others. It is worth recording, for example, that the French mercantilist policy also produced instances of dumping. The *Compagnia della Nuova Institutione* in Venice in May 1723 showed that 'French manufacturers are at present causing the greatest trouble. If it is true, as it appears, that the King is giving a bounty of a gold doubloon for every piece of cloth which is sent to the Levantine markets, as well as exempting it from all duties, then we need look no further for the reason why it is sold in Constantinople at such low prices' (A.S.V., S. Mr., sez. Comm., b. 125).

I believe that another factor which must often have had a widespread influence in inflating the level of costs was the formation of monopolies, which we glimpse from time to time, especially in the supply of primary materials, particularly Spanish wool, oil and dyes.

For the moment it is impossible to say anything about the influence of interest rates. It is very likely that – except in Genoa – interest rates in Italy

compared with foreign competitors. Meanwhile, a combination of other unfortunate circumstances made it more difficult to export goods and services to several traditional Italian markets. In the seventeenth century Spain entered a phase of secular economic decline,[1] and Germany was devastated by the Thirty Years' War.[2] Likewise the ancient hostilities with the Turks became more damaging to Italian exports, given the presence of the Dutch, English and French, ready to step in wherever the Italians found themselves in difficulty.[3] Meanwhile, the development of the Atlantic trade routes progressively and irreversibly eliminated the Italians from the international trade in spices and tropical products.

Thus, the Italian economy experienced a drastic decline in exports protracted over the years and getting progressively worse; a prolonged withdrawal of investment from industry, banking and shipping; and the tendency of industry to desert traditional urban centres for new rural or semi-rural ones. This last tendency in its turn was due to the following causes: labour costs were less in

were higher than in Holland. But they do not appear to have been higher than in England or France. However, little is known on this subject, and we need several further studies before being able to formulate reliable hypotheses.

[1] See above chaps. 5 and 6.

[2] See for instance the following testimony from Genoa in 1651: 'The long German wars, bringing unheard of havoc and desolation, have almost devoured the inhabitants and their wealth. Everybody knows that the famous fairs of Frankfurt, Leipzig, and other places, where formerly we sold many of our silken cloths, have now in these times almost completely ceased. Here in Genoa were the houses of many German firms, Fortimbac, Brocco, and others, who are now wholly ruined and unable to continue' (A.S.G., Sala 50–1, Scansia 67, *Arte della Seta* 1432–1771, b. 161). From Milan in 1641: 'There is also the disastrous effect of the wars in France, Flanders, and Germany. These provinces are in some cases cut off from trade because the passes are blocked, while others are disturbed or even wrecked internally by the war. Consequently they have not been able to receive gold and silk goods, so much of which came from this market' (*Relazione* of Rossi). The same report also observes that freight rates had greatly increased owing to conditions of war: 'as for transport to Flanders and Germany . . . the price has gone up so much that what formerly cost 20 crowns now costs 60. The difficulties of the roads and the longer routes which have to be used are a further handicap.'

[3] Among many examples see the relationship between Genoa and the Turks described by Giacchero, *Storia economica*, (op. cit.), pp. 40 ff.

minor centres than in major ones;[1] and in the minor centres and in the countryside it was easier to evade both the tax officers[2] and the guild restrictions.[3]

As has already been stated Italy suffered greatly in 1630 and 1657 from plague. If one admits that it would have been impossible for Italy to keep her ancient sources of revenue or to find new ones, then a long, slow decline of her total population might have been a solution for the economic problems of the seventeenth century. But a drastic and rapid fall in population, provoked by plague, had the effect of raising wages and putting Italian exports in an even more difficult position. Moreover, in the long run, after the plague, population expanded again. Recent calculations show that, in 1600, Italy's population must have been about 12 million. At the end of the century, it was about 13 million.[4] But by the end of the seventeenth century Italy no longer had her industries nor her banking and shipping interests. Thus she began her career as a country at once depressed and overpopulated.

The key point around which all Italian misfortunes from the end of the sixteenth century revolved was the country's inability to maintain its exports. Between 1620 and 1700 the silver content of the Genoese lira fell by 30 per cent, that of the Milanese lira by 20 per cent and that of the Venetian lira by 15 per cent.[5] These

---

[1] For Genoa, cf. *Relazione dell'Ecc. Giunta del Traffico* of 10 November 1675: 'the weavers living on the Rivieras ask rather less than the Genoese for their work' (A.S.G., Sala 50-1, Scansia 67, *Traffico ed Arti*, Misc. b. 160). For Venice, cf. the report of the representatives of the Collegio del Lanificio of 3 June 1678 (A.S.V., S. Mr., b. 125).

[2] See for example the observations in *Consulta a S.C.C.R. Maestà* (7 June 1732), Chapter 52.

[3] See the documents cited in the two previous notes.

[4] C. M. Cipolla, 'Four centuries of Italian demographic development', in *Population in History*, ed. D. E. C. Eversley and D. V. Glass (London, 1965), p. 573.

[5] Cf. C. M. Cipolla, *Le avventure della lira* (Milan, 1958), pp. 63–4. Meanwhile English money had maintained its own metallic content completely unchanged (A. E. Feaveryear, *The Pound Sterling*, Oxford–London, 1932, p. 350). French money, on the other hand, during the Thirty Years' War, suffered a drop in metallic content of around 30 per cent. But it stayed unchanged between 1602 and 1640 and then from 1644 to 1689 (R. Sedillot, *Le franc*, Paris, 1953, p. 77).

devaluations could at least temporarily alleviate the situation by making Italian goods cost less in terms of foreign money, but operations on coinage are never in the long run capable of altering the essential facts concerning production and investment. The effective foreign demand for Italian goods and services gave way, and this had a multiple negative effect on home demand also. Due to the prolonged contraction of effective global demand (both internal and external), prices of goods, despite the devaluation of money, showed a secular tendency to diminish.

In all Italian markets the prices of manufactured goods tended to fall much more than those of agricultural products.[1] This itself was due to two things: first, to the fact that home demand for agricultural products (i.e. for essential foodstuffs) must have had a lower income elasticity than the demand for manufactured products; and secondly, the fact that, while foreign demand for Italian manufactures and services was contracting, on the other hand foreign demand for Italian agricultural products was rising.

In the long run, the scissor movement of industrial and agricultural prices, by greatly improving the position of agricultural prices relative to industrial, naturally had the effect of pushing available resources away from industry into agriculture. A new class of landed proprietors of a feudal character grew gradually stronger and imposed itself on the economic and social structure. In consequence, new values and new social hierarchies arose and strengthened the movement towards the countryside. The social and cultural processes which we are accustomed to see during phases of industrialization in underdeveloped countries were operating in reverse during the seventeenth century in Italy. This shows that they do not necessarily move in one direction only.

At the end of the seventeenth century, Italy was importing manufactured goods on a large scale from England, France and Holland. Exports were almost all primary products or partially

[1] For Milan, cf. A. de Maddalena, *Prezzi e aspetti di mercato in Milano durante il sec. XVII* (Milan, 1950); for Genoa, G. Calò, *Indagine sulla dinamica dei prezzi in Geneva durante il sec. XVII* (thesis presented to the Faculty of Economics and Commerce at the University of Genoa in 1957–8). For the movement of cereal prices in Tuscany and in the Veneto see G. Parenti, *Prezzi e mercato del grano a Siena 1546–1765* (Florence, 1942); and G. Lombardini, *Prezzi e mercato del grano a Bassano* (Venice, 1963).

worked goods – oil, grain, wine, wool and raw silk.[1] Italy had also been reduced to a passive role in maritime affairs. The great expansion of the free port of Leghorn during the seventeenth century directly reflected the victory of English shipping in the Mediterranean. At sea, too, conservatism and excessive labour costs had caused the Italians to fall behind in the race.

An English traveller wrote:

> I observed English Shipps going forth from Venice with Italian Shipps to have sayled into Syria and retorned to Venice twice, before the Italian Shipps made one retorne, whereof two reasons may be given, one that the Italians pay their Marriners by the day, how long soever the voyage lasteth, which makes them uppon the least storme, putt into harbors, whence only few wyndes can bring them out, whereas the English are payde by the voyage, and so beate out stormes at Sea, and are ready to take the first wynde any thing favourable unto them. The other

[1] For a general picture see R. Davis, 'Influences anglaises sur le déclin de Venise au XVII siècle', in *Aspetti e cause della decadenza economica veneziana nel secolo XVII* (Venice, 1961). There are numerous detailed references to this fundamental change in the economy of Italy in nearly all the documents already cited. For instance: Milan was reduced to importing cloths from France and England (Rossi: *Relazione*). It was also importing arms from France, and this fact, for a centre which had been famous for armament production, was really surprising: 'the instruments of war, swords and other equipment (a trade which once flourished so greatly in Milan) are now brought from France and other places, although it is war-time' (*Replica dei possessori del perticato*, cit., for the year 1640). Genoa, already famous for her silks, which she used to export all over Europe, had become an importer: so much so that on 5 December 1668 she had to adopt measures against the import of foreign silks which 'for variety and for beauty' had a far wider sale (A.S.G., Sala 50–1, Scansia 67, *Arte della Seta*, b. 161). Also for Genoa, see the import of cloth from France on behalf of the Genoese government itself in 1698, mentioned above, p. 135, n. 2.

Compared with the import of manufactured articles there was a tendency to export oil, grain, wool, and raw silk especially. Cf. H. Koenigsberger, 'English merchants in Naples and Sicily in the seventeenth century', *English Hist. Review*, 62 (1947), pp. 304–26. Also de Rosa, *I cambi esteri*, cit., p. 62, who quotes a contemporary document saying that the export of oil to England was no longer paid for in cash: English merchants 'no longer buy it with money, but barter with cloths and salted fish'.

that Italian Shipps are heavy in sayling, and great of burthen, and the Governors & Mariners not very expert, nor bold. . . .[1]

From being a developed country, mainly importing primary products and exporting manufactured goods and services, Italy had become an underdeveloped country, mainly importing manufactured articles and services and exporting primary products.

When a country finds itself in the unfortunate position in which Italy was at the beginning of the seventeenth century, sooner or later various spontaneous or induced forces start a process of readjustment. The steps necessary to restore equilibrium can be of several types: developing new industries, searching for new markets, lowering certain types of consumption, reducing the discrepancy between internal and international price levels, and so on. If the country succeeds in developing new industries and in opening new markets, then both employment levels and standards of living can, for the most part, be maintained. Otherwise it has to accustom itself to a drastic reduction in the standard of living and level of employment. Nowadays, when a country begins, like Italy at the beginning of the seventeenth century, to show the symptoms of a fully matured economy, it tries, by using massive investment, to keep up production, to redirect available resources and to conquer new markets. Such programmes can involve inflationary pressures dangerous to the schemes themselves. The story of seventeenth-century Italy is, however, a good example of the destructive effect of a process of readjustment abandoned to automatic long-term deflation.

[1] *Fynes Moryson's Itinerary: Shakespeare's Europe*, ed. C. Hughes (London, 1903), p. 135. This evidence is confirmed by the excellent study of U. Tucci, 'Sur la pratique vénitienne de la navigation au XVI siècle', *Annales, économies, sociétés, civilisations*, 13 (1958), pp. 72–86.

EIGHT

Some Reflections on the Decline
of the Ottoman Empire[1]

BERNARD LEWIS

The decline of great empires has always been a subject of fascinated interest, and in our own day has a new poignancy, both for those who rejoice and for those who weep at the passing of Imperial greatness. The decline of the Ottoman Empire has also received its share of attention, though not of serious study.[2] The half-millennium of Ottoman history is still one of the most neglected of fields of study. Whereas recent research, both in Turkey and in the West, has increased our knowledge of the beginnings and of the end of the Empire, it has shed but little light on the processes of its decline. The modern Turkish historians, naturally enough, have devoted most of their attention to the early greatness and recent revival of their people, while such Western scholars as have discussed the subject have been content, in the main, to follow the analysis of the Ottoman historians themselves. Often, too, they have been influenced by the national historiographical legends of the liberated former subject peoples of the Empire in Europe and Asia. These have tended to blame all the defects and shortcomings of their societies on the misrule of their fallen Imperial masters, and have generalized the admitted failings of Ottoman government in its last phases into an indictment of Ottoman civilization as a whole.

'The decline and fall of the Roman Empire', Professor Jones

[1] This article was published as chapter II of *The Emergence of Modern Turkey*, Oxford University Press for the Royal Institute of International Affairs, 1961. It is a revised and expanded version of an article which originally appeared in *Studia Islamica*, Vol. 9, 1958.

[2] An exception is the essay on the decay of the Ottoman 'Ruling Institution', incorporated in H. A. R. Gibb and Harold Bowen, *Islamic Society and the West*, I/i (1950), 173 ff.

has recently remarked, 'was the result of a complex of interacting causes which the historian disentangles at his peril.'[1] The peril is all the greater when, as with the Ottoman Empire, the essential preliminary work of detailed historical research is so little advanced. The great mass of Ottoman records for the seventeenth and eighteenth centuries are unpublished, almost untouched; even the chronicles have received only slight attention. The internal economic and social history in that period has hardly been studied at all, while the study of political history has progressed very little beyond the point to which it was brought by Hammer and Zinkeisen in the nineteenth century.

In what follows no attempt is made to cut through the complex web of cause, symptom and effect. What is offered is a broad classification and enumeration of some of the principal factors and processes which led to, or were part of, or were expressions of the decline of Ottoman government, society and civilization. They will be considered in three main groups – those relating to government, to economic and social life, and to moral, cultural and intellectual change.

In the first group we may include the familiar changes in the apparatus of government – the court, the bureaucracy, the judiciary, the armed forces, which form the main burden of the famous memorandum of Koçu Bey, presented to Murad IV in 1630.[2] If the first ten Sultans of the house of Osman astonish us with the spectacle of a series of able and intelligent men rare if not unique in the annals of dynastic succession, the remainder of the rulers of that line provides an even more astonishing series of incompetents,

[1] A. H. M. Jones, 'The Decline and Fall of the Roman Empire', *History* xl (1955), 226.

[2] Koçu Bey, an Ottoman official of Macedonian or Albanian birth, was recruited by the *devşirme* and joined the palace staff, where he became the intimate adviser of Sultan Murad IV (1623–40). The memorandum which he composed for the Sultan in 1630 on the state and prospects of the Ottoman Empire has been greatly admired both in Turkey and among Western scholars, and led Hammer to call Koçu Bey 'the Turkish Montesquieu'. On the editions and translations of his treatise see F. Babinger, *Die Geschichtsschreiber der Osmanen und ihre Werke* (1927), 184–5. A new edition was published in Istanbul in 1939. A German translation by W. F. Behrnauer appeared in *Zeitschrift der deutschen morgenländischen Gesellschaft*, xv (1861), 272 ff.

degenerates and misfits. Such a series as the latter is beyond the range of coincidence, and can be explained by a system of upbringing and selection which virtually precluded the emergence of an effective ruler. Similarly, the Grand Vezirate and other high offices, both political and religious, were filled and administered in such a way that what must surprise us is that they produced as many able and conscientious men as they did.

The breakdown in the apparatus of government affected not only the supreme instruments of sovereignty but also the whole of the bureaucratic and religious institutions all over the Empire. These suffered a catastrophic fall in efficiency and integrity, which was accentuated by the growing change in methods of recruitment, training and promotion. This deterioration is clearly discernible in the Ottoman archives, which reflect vividly and precisely the change from the meticulous, conscientious and strikingly efficient bureaucratic government of the sixteenth century to the neglect of the seventeenth and the collapse of the eighteenth centuries.[1] The same fall in professional and moral standards can be seen, though perhaps in less striking form, in the different ranks of the religious and judicial hierarchy.

Most striking of all was the decline of the Ottoman armed forces. The Empire could still draw on great reserves of loyal and valiant subjects, said Koçu Bey, writing in 1630. The Turkish soldier had suffered no loss of courage or morale, said Ali Paşa writing after the disastrous treaty of Küçük Kaynarca of 1774.[2] Yet the Ottoman armies, once the terror of Europe, ceased to frighten anyone but their own sovereigns and their own civil population, and suffered

[1] In the sixteenth century the records are careful, detailed and up to date; in the seventeenth and eighteenth centuries they become irregular, inaccurate and sketchy. Even the quality of the paper becomes poorer. In this general picture of falling standards, the carefully kept registers of the Köprülü interlude stand out the more significantly.

[2] Ali Paşa had served as governor of Trebizond, where he founded a *derebey* dynasty. Two questions, he tells us, had profoundly occupied his thoughts: why the Empire, from being so strong, had become so weak, and what was to be done to recover her former strength. His memorandum, still unpublished, is preserved in manuscript in Uppsala. A Swedish paraphrase was included by M. Norberg in *Turkiska Rikets Annaler* (Hernösand) v (1822), 1245 ff. See *EI²*, 'Ḏj̲ānikli 'Alī Pas̲h̲a' (by B. Lewis).

a long series of humiliating defeats at the hands of once despised enemies.

In the sixteenth century the Ottoman Empire reached the limits of its expansion, and came up against barriers which it could not pass. On the eastern border, despite the victories in the field of Selim I and Süleyman, the Ottoman armies could not advance into Persia. The new centralized monarchy of the Safavids, then at the peak of their power; the high plateau of Iran, posing new problems of logistics and calling for new and unfamiliar techniques; the difficulties of leading against a Muslim adversary an army whose traditions since its birth were of the holy war against the infidels – all these combined to halt the Ottoman forces at the frontiers of Iran, and cut them off from overland expansion into Central Asia or India.

In Eastern waters they encountered the stout ships of the Portuguese, whose shipbuilders and navigators, trained to meet the challenge of the Atlantic, were more than a match for the calm-water ships of the Ottomans. Stouter vessels, more guns, better seamanship were what defeated the successive attempts of the Ottomans to break out of the ring, and swept Muslim shipping from the waters of the Indian Ocean.

In the Crimea and the lands beyond it they were halted by Russia. In 1475 the Ottomans had conquered Kaffa. Part of the Crimean coast passed under direct Ottoman rule, the Giray Khans of the Tatars became Ottoman vassals, and in 1569 the Ottomans even launched a plan to open a canal between the Don and Volga and thus, by acquiring a shipping route to Central Asia, to break out out of the Portuguese noose.[1] But here too the Ottomans found their way blocked. At the same time as Western Europe was expanding by sea round Africa and into Asia, Eastern Europe was expanding by land across the steppe, southward and eastward towards the lands of Islam. In 1502 the once mighty Khanate of the Golden Horde was finally extinguished, and much of its territory absorbed by Russia. The successor Khanates of Kazan, Astrakhan

[1] On this project see the article of Inalcık, 'Osmanlı–Rus rekabetinin menşei ve Don–Volga kanali teşebbüsü (1569)', *Bell.* no. 46 (1948), 349–402. English version: 'The Origins of the Ottoman–Russian Rivalry and the Don–Volga Canal 1569', *A. Univ. Ank.*, i (1946–7), 47–107.

and Crimea lingered on for a while, but before long the Russians were able to conquer the first two, and to exercise a growing pressure on the third. The way was open to the Black Sea and the North Caucasus, the Caspian and western Siberia, where the advance of Russia barred and enclosed the Ottomans as did the Portuguese and their successors in the Eastern seas.

In Africa, desert, mountain and climate offered obstacles which there was no incentive to surmount, while in the Mediterranean, after a brief interval, naval supremacy was lost to the maritime countries of the West.[1]

But the classical area of Ottoman expansion had been in none of these. Since the first crossing of the Bosporus in the mid-fourteenth century, Europe had been the promised land of the Ottomans – the 'House of War' *par excellence*, in which the power and the glory of Islam were to be advanced by victorious battle against the infidel. On 27 September 1529, after conquering Hungary, the armies of Süleyman the Magnificent reached Vienna – and on 15 October they began to withdraw from the still unconquered city. The event was decisive. For another century and a half inconclusive warfare was waged for Hungary, and in 1683 yet another attempt, the last, was made against Vienna. But the cause was already lost. The Ottoman Empire had reached the line beyond which it could not advance, from which it could only withdraw. The valour of the Habsburg, as of the Safavid armies, no doubt played its part in stemming the Ottoman onslaught, but is insufficient as an explanation of why the defenders of Vienna were able to halt the victors of Kossovo, Varna, Nicopolis and Mohacs. There too we may perhaps find an explanation in the problems of a new and different terrain, calling for new techniques of warfare and especially of supply and transport.

[1] Lûtfi Paşa, writing after 1541, could already see the danger to Turkey of the growing naval power of Europe. He quoted with approval a remark by Kemalpaşazade (d. 1533–4) to Selim I: 'My Lord, you dwell in a city whose benefactor is the sea. If the sea is not safe no ships will come, and if no ship comes Istanbul perishes.' He himself had said to Sultan Süleyman: 'Under the previous Sultans there were many who ruled the land, but few who ruled the sea. In the conduct of naval warfare the infidels are ahead of us. We must overcome them' (Lûtfi Paşa, *Asafname*, ed. and tr. R. Tschudi (1910), text 32–3, trans. 26–7).

It was after the halting of the Ottoman advance that the lag began to appear between the standards of training and equipment of Ottoman and European armies. Initially, the backwardness of the Ottomans was relative rather than absolute. Once in the forefront of military science, they began to fall behind. The great technical and logistic developments in European armies in the seventeenth century were followed tardily and ineffectively by the Ottomans – in marked contrast with the speed and inventiveness with which they had accepted and adapted the European invention of artillery in the fifteenth century. One possible contributory factor to this change is the fall in the flow of European renegades and adventurers to Turkey – but to state this is to raise the further question of why Turkey had ceased to attract these men, and why the Turks made such little use of those who did come.

The decline in alertness, in readiness to accept new techniques, is an aspect – perhaps the most dangerous – of what became a general deterioration in professional and moral standards in the armed forces, parallel to that of the bureaucratic and religious classes, which we have already noted. It led directly to what must be accounted, in the Ottoman as in the Roman Empire, one of the principal causes of decline – the loss of territory to more powerful foreign enemies. Modern historians have rightly tended to put the loss of territory to invaders among the symptoms rather than the causes of weakness, but the effect of the steady draining away of manpower, revenue, and resources should not be underrated. For Koçu Bey and his successors, the causes of these changes for the worse lay in favouritism and corruption. The different presuppositions of our time may incline us to regard these less as causes than as symptoms, and to seek their motives and origin in vaster and deeper changes.

During the sixteenth century three major changes occurred, principally of external origin, which vitally affected the entire life of the Ottoman Empire. The first of these has already been mentioned – the halting of the Ottoman advance into Europe. This was an event comparable in some ways with the Closing of the Frontier in the United States – but with far more shattering impact. The Ottoman state had been born on the frontier between Islam and Byzantine Christendom; its leaders and armies had been march-warriors in the Holy War, carrying the sword and the faith of Islam into new lands. The Ottoman gazis and dervishes, like the pioneers and missionaries of the Americas, believed themselves to be bringing civilization and the true faith to peoples sunk in barbarism and unbelief – and like them reaped the familiar rewards of the frontier warrior and the colonist. For the Ottoman state, the frontier had provided work and recompense both for its men of the sword and its men of religion and, in a deeper sense, the very *raison d'être* of its statehood. True, by the sixteenth century that state had already evolved from a principality of march-warriors into an Empire, but the traditions of the frontier were still deeply rooted in the military, social and religious life of the Ottomans, and the virtual closing of the frontier to further expansion and colonization could not fail profoundly to affect them. The Ottoman systems of military organization, civil administration, taxation and land tenure were all geared to the needs of a society expanding by conquest and colonization into the lands of the infidel. They ceased to correspond to the different stresses of a frontier that was stationary or in retreat.[1]

While the great Ottoman war-machine, extended beyond its range, was grinding to a standstill in the plains of Hungary, the life and growth of the Ottoman Empire were being circumvented, on a far vaster scale, by the oceanic voyages of discovery of the Western maritime peoples, the ultimate effect of which was to turn the whole Eastern Mediterranean area, where the Empire was situated, into a backwater. In 1555 the Imperial ambassador in Constantinople, Ogier Ghiselin de Busbecq, one of the acutest European observers of Turkey, could still comment that the Western Europeans basely squandered their energies 'seeking the Indies and the Antipodes across vast fields of ocean, in search of gold', and abandoning the heart of Europe to imminent and almost

---

[1] The significance of the frontier and of the frontiersman in Ottoman government and society has been demonstrated by Paul Wittek. The whole question of the frontier as a cultural entity, with some reference to F. J. Turner's famous thesis on the significance of the frontier in American history, has been re-examined by Owen Lattimore in his 'The Frontier in History' (published in *Relazioni*, i, 105–38, of the Tenth International Congress of Historical Sciences, Rome, 1955).

certain conquest.[1] But in about 1580 an Ottoman geographer, in an account of the New World written for Murad III, gave warning of the dangers to the Islamic lands and the disturbance to Islamic trade resulting from the establishment of Europeans on the coasts of America, India, and the Persian Gulf; he advised the Sultan to open a canal through the isthmus of Suez and send a fleet 'to capture the ports of Hind and Sind and drive away the infidels'.[2] By 1625 another Ottoman observer, a certain Ömer Talib, could see the danger in a more pressing form:

> Now the Europeans have learnt to know the whole world; they send their ships everywhere and seize important ports. Formerly, the goods of India, Sind and China used to come to Suez, and were distributed by Muslims to all the world. But now these goods are carried on Portuguese, Dutch and English ships to Frangistan, and are spread all over the world from there. What they do not need themselves they bring to Istanbul and other Islamic lands, and sell it for five times the price, thus earning much money. For this reason gold and silver are becoming scarce in the lands of Islam. The Ottoman Empire must seize the shores of Yemen and the trade passing that way; otherwise before very long, the Europeans will rule over the lands of Islam.[3]

The effects on Middle Eastern trade of the circumnavigation of Africa were by no means as immediate and as catastrophic as was at one time believed. Right through the sixteenth century Eastern merchandise continued to reach the Ottoman Empire, coming by ship to Red Sea ports and Basra and overland across Persia, and European merchants came to Turkey to buy. But the volume of international trade passing this way was steadily decreasing. From the seventeenth century, the establishment of Dutch and British power in Asia and the transference of the routes of world trade to

---

[1] *The Turkish letters of Ogier Ghiselin de Busbecq*, tr. by C. T. Forster and F. H. B. Daniell (1881), i, 129–30.

[2] *Tarih al-Hind al-Garbi* (Constantinople, 1142/1729), fol. 6b ff.

[3] The observations of Ömer Talib, written on the margins of a manuscript of the *Tarih al-Hind al-Garbi* in Ankara (Maarif Library 10024), were published by A. Zeki Velidi Togan, *Bugünkü Türkili (Turkistan) ve Yakın Tarihi*, i (1947), p. 127.

the open ocean deprived Turkey of the greater part of her foreign commerce and left her, together with the countries over which she ruled, in a stagnant backwater through which the life-giving stream of world trade no longer flowed.[1]

The European voyages of discovery brought another more immediate blow, as violent as it was unexpected. The basic unit of currency of the Ottoman Empire had been the silver *akçe*, or asper, in which all the revenues and expenditures of the state had been calculated. Like other Mediterranean and European states, the Ottoman Empire suffered from a recurring shortage of precious metals, which at times threatened its silver-based monetary system. To meet these difficulties, the Ottoman Sultans resorted to such well-tried measures as controlling the silver mines, discouraging the export and encouraging the import of coin and bullion, extending the non-monetary sector of the state economy and alternately debasing and reissuing the currency.

This situation was suddenly transformed when the flow of precious metals from the New World reached the Eastern Mediterranean. American gold, and, to a far greater extent, American silver had already caused a price revolution and a financial crisis in Spain. From there it passed to Genoa and thence to Ragusa, where Spanish coins of American metal are first reported in the 1580s.[2] Thereafter the financial impact on Turkey of this sudden flow of cheap and plentiful silver from the West was immediate and catastrophic. The Ottoman rulers, accustomed to crises of shortage, were quite unable to understand or meet a crisis resulting from an excess of silver, and the traditional measures which they adopted only served to worsen the situation. In 1584 the asper was reduced from one-fifth to one-eighth of a dirham of silver – a measure of devaluation which unleashed a continuous financial crisis with far-reaching economic and social consequences. As the price of silver fell by 70 per cent, that of gold rose by 100 per cent; cheaply bought

[1] On these questions see the important studies of Köprülü in his additional notes to the Turkish translation of Barthold's *Muslim Culture* (*Islam Medeniyeti Tarihi*, 1940), pp. 255 ff. and Inalcık in *Bell.*, no. 60 (1951), pp. 661 ff.

[2] I am informed by Professor R. B. Serjeant that cheap silver of Portuguese provenance is reported slightly earlier in Southern Arabia, where it caused a drop in the rate of silver to gold.

silver coin by the million flowed from Europe to Turkey for quick and profitable re-sale, crowding out the traffic in commodities, draining the Turkish Empire of gold and accentuating the steep rise in the level of prices, which brought distress and then ruin to whole classes of the population. Before long there was a vast increase in coining, coin-clipping and the like; the rate of the asper fell from 60 to the ducat to over 200, and foreign coins, both gold and silver, drove the debased Ottoman issues even from the internal markets. Twice in the seventeenth century the Ottoman government tried to stem the inflationary tide by the issue of a new silver currency; first, the *para*, which appeared as a silver coin in the 1620s, then the piastre, or *kuruş*, which appeared in the 1680s, in imitation of the European dollar. Both followed the asper into debasement and devaluation.[1]

Precisely at this time of monetary and financial crisis, the government was compelled to embark on a great expansion in its salaried personnel and a great increase in expenditure in coin. When Mehmed the Conqueror had faced a monetary crisis, he had reduced the numbers of paid soldiers and increased the numbers of cavalry sipahis, whose services were rewarded with fiefs and not coin.[2] But in the changed conditions of warfare of the sixteenth and seventeenth centuries this had ceased to be possible. The greatly increased use of firearms and artillery necessitated the maintenance of ever larger paid professional armies, and reduced the relative importance of the feudal cavalryman. Both Koçu Bey and Hacı Halifa note and deplore the decline of the sipahis and the increase in the paid soldiery which, says Hacı Halifa, had increased from 48,000 in 1567 to

[1] The effects on wages, prices and currencies of the flow of American bullion, first studied for Spain in the classic monograph of Earl J. Hamilton (*American Treasure and the Price Revolution in Spain, 1501–1550*, 1934), were examined on a larger scale for the whole Mediterranean area in the great work of F. Braudel, *La Méditerranée et le monde méditerranéen a l'époque de Philippe II* (1949). Braudel's pointers on events in Turkey (especially pp. 393–4, 419–20, 637–43) were taken up and developed by Inalcık in his illuminating study, 'Osmanlı Imparatorluğunun Kuruluş ve Inkişafi devrinde Türkiye' nin Iktisadi Vaziyeti üzerinde bir tetkik münasebetile', *Bell.*, no. 60 (1951), 656 ff. See further the review of Braudel's book by Barkan in *Revue de la Faculté des Sciences Économiques de l'Université d'Istanbul*, xi (1949–50), 196–216.
[2] Inalcık, in *Bell.*, no. 60, 656 ff.

100,000 in about 1620.[1] Both writers are aware of the harmful financial and agrarian effects of this change. Understandably, they miss the point that the obsolescence of the sipahi had become inevitable, and that only the long-term professional soldier could serve the military needs of the time.

The price was appalling. Faced with a growing expenditure and a depreciating currency, the demands of the treasury became more and more insatiable. The underpaid and over-sized salaried personnel of the state—civil, military and religious—had growing difficulties in making ends meet, with the inevitable effects on their prestige, their honesty, and their further recruitment. Though the feudal cavalryman was no longer needed by the army, his disappearance was sorely felt in the countryside, as the old Ottoman agrarian system, of which he had once been the foundation, tottered and collapsed. In place of the sipahi, who resided in or near the fief in which he had a hereditary interest, palace favourites, parasites and speculators became the recipients of fiefs, sometimes accumulating great numbers of them, and thus becoming, in effect, absentee owners of great latifundia. Other fiefs reverted to the Imperial domain.[2] But the growing inefficiency and venality of the bureaucracy prevented the formation of any effective state system for the assessment and collection of taxes. Instead these tasks were given to tax-farmers, whose interposition and interception of revenues became in time a prescriptive and hereditary right, and added to the number of vast and neglected latifundia.

The shrinking economy of the Empire thus had to support an increasingly costly and cumbersome superstructure. The palace, the bureaucracy and the religious hierarchy, an army that in expenditure at least was modern, and a parasitic class of tax-farmers and absentee landlords – all this was far more than the medieval states or even the Roman Empire had tried to support; yet it rested

[1] *Düstur al-ʿAmal li-Islah al-Halal* (Ist., 1280/1863, as an appendix to the *Kavanin-i Al-i Osman* of Ayn-i Ali), pp. 131–2; German trans. by Behrnauer in *ZDMG*, xi (1857), 125. In this little treatise, written in about 1653, Hacı Halifa examines the causes of the financial and other troubles of the Ottoman Empire.

[2] From the late sixteenth century onwards the cadastral registers in the Ottoman archives show a steady decrease in the number of *timars*, and a corresponding increase in the extent of Imperial domain.

on an economy that was no more advanced than theirs. The technological level of agriculture remained primitive, and the social conditions of the Turkish countryside after the sixteenth century precluded the appearance of anything like the English gentleman-farmers of the seventeenth century whose experiments revolutionized English agriculture.

These developments are not peculiar to Turkey. The fall in money and rise of prices, the growing cost of government and warfare, the sale of offices and farming of taxes – all these are known in other Mediterranean and adjoining states, where they contributed to the rise of a new class of capitalists and financiers, with a growing and constructive influence on governments.

In Turkey too there were rich merchants and bankers, such as the Greek Michael Cantacuzenos and the Portuguese Jew Joseph Nasi – the Fugger of the Orient, as Braudel called him.[1] But they were never able to play anything like the financial, economic and political role of their European counterparts. Part of the cause of this must undoubtedly be found in the progressive stagnation of Ottoman trade, to which allusion has already been made. But that is not all. Most if not all of these merchants were Christians or Jews – tolerated but second-class subjects of the Muslim state. However great their economic power, they were politically penalized and socially segregated; they could obtain political power only by stealth, and exercise it only by intrigue, with demoralizing effect on all concerned. Despite the scale and extent of their financial operations, they were unable to create political conditions more favourable to commerce, or to build up any solid structure of banking and credit, and thus help the Ottoman government in its perennial financial straits. In England too finance and credit were at first in the hands of alien specialists, who have left their name in Lombard Street. But these were ousted in time by vigorous and pushful native rivals. In Turkey no such rivals arose, and in any case, in the general decline of the seventeenth century, even the Greek and Jewish merchant princes of Constantinople dwindled into insignificance. Fortunes were still made in Turkey, but their origin was not economic. Mostly they were political or fiscal in origin, obtained through the holding of public office. Nor

[1] Braudel, p. 567.

were they spent on investment or development, but consumed or hoarded, after the fashion of the time.

Reference has often been made to the technological backwardness of the Ottoman Empire – to its failure not only to invent, but even to respond to the inventions of others. While Europe swept forward in science and technology, the Ottomans were content to remain, in their agriculture, their industry and their transport, at the level of their medieval ancestors. Even their armed forces followed tardily and incompetently after the technological advances of their European enemies.

The problem of agriculture in the Ottoman Empire was more than one of technical backwardness, however. It was one of definite decline. Already during the reign of Süleyman the Magnificent, Lûtfi Paşa gave warning of the dangers of rural depopulation, and urged that the peasantry be protected by moderation in taxation and by regular censuses of village population, as a control on the competence of provincial government.[1] Koçu Bey reinforces these arguments; but by 1653 Hacı Halifa reports that people had begun to flock from the villages to the towns during the reign of Süleyman, and that in his own day there were derelict and abandoned villages all over the Empire.[2]

Much of this decline in agriculture can be attributed to the causes named by the Ottoman memorialists: the squeezing out of the feudal sipahis, the mainstay of the early Ottoman agrarian system, and their replacement by tax-farmers and others with no long-term interest in peasant welfare or land conservation, but only an immediate and short-term interest in taxes. Harsh, exorbitant and improvident taxation led to a decline in cultivation, which was sometimes permanent. The peasants, neglected and impoverished, were forced into the hands of money-lenders and speculators, and often driven off the land entirely. With the steady decline in

[1] Lûtfi Paşa, *Asafname*, ch. 4. Lûtfi Paşa's treaties, written after his dismissal from the office of Grand Vezir in 1541, sets forth rules on what a good Grand Vezir should do and, more urgently, on what he should avoid. In this booklet, written at a time when the Ottoman Empire was still at the height of its power and glory, the writer shows deep concern about its fate and welfare, and is already able to point to what, in later years, became the characteristic signs of Ottoman decline.

[2] Hacı Halifa, ch. 1.

bureaucratic efficiency during the seventeenth and eighteenth centuries, the former system of regular land surveys and population censuses was abandoned.[1] The central government ceased to exercise any check or control over agriculture and village affairs, which were left to the unchecked rapacity of the tax-farmers, the leaseholders, and the bailiffs of court nominees. During the seventeenth century some of the more permanently established lease-holders began to coalesce with the landowners into a new landed aristocracy – the *ayan-i memleket* or country notables, whose appearance and usurpation of some of the functions and authority of government were already noted at the time.[2]

While agriculture declined, industry fared little better. The corporative structure of the guilds fulfilled a useful social function in expressing and preserving the complex web of social loyalties and obligations of the old order, and also, though to a diminishing extent, in safeguarding the moral level and standards of craftsmanship of the artisan. Their economic effects, however, were restrictive and eventually destructive. A man's choice of profession was determined by habit and inheritance, the scope of his endeavour limited by primitive techniques and transport, his manner and speed of work fixed by guild rule and tradition; on the one hand a Sufi religious habit of passivity and surrender of self, on the other the swift fiscal retribution for any sign of prosperity, combined to keep industrial production primitive, static and inert, utterly unable to resist the competition of imported European manufactures.[3]

[1] See for example the list of *tapu* registers for the Arab provinces, given in B. Lewis, 'The Ottoman Archives as a Source for the History of the Arab Lands', *Journal of the Royal Asiatic Society* (1951), pp. 149 ff. The great majority of the registers listed there are of the sixteenth century. After 1600 the surveys became less and less frequent, and the resulting registers more and more slipshod.

[2] Cf. the remarks of Hüseyin Hezarfenn, writing in 1669 (R. Anhegger, 'Hezarfen Hüseyin Efendi'nin Osmanlı devlet teşkilâtına dâir mülâhazaları,' *Türkiyat Mecmuası*, x (1951–3), 372, 387. The *ayan-i vilayet* already appear occasionally in *Kanuns* of the sixteenth century (Barkan, *XV ve XVI inci asırlarda . . . Kanunlar*, i (1943), index).

[3] Sabri F. Ülgener, *Iktisadî Inhitat Tarihimizin Ahlak ve Zihniyet Meseleleri* (1951). Much light is thrown on these questions by Professor Ülgener's attempt to apply the methods of Weber and Sombart to the study of Ottoman social and economic history.

Some have sought the causes of this backwardness in Islam or in the Turkish race – explanations which do not satisfy, in view of the previous achievements of both. It may, however, be possible to find part of the explanation of Ottoman lack of receptivity – perhaps even of Ottoman decline – in certain evolving attitudes of mind, inherited by the Ottomans along with the classical Islamic civilization of which they had been the heirs and renovators.

Classical Islamic civilization, like others before and after it, including our own, was profoundly convinced of its superiority and self-sufficiency. In its earliest, primitive phase, Islam had been open to influences from the Hellenistic Orient, from Persia, even from India and China. Many works were translated into Arabic from Greek, Syriac and Persian.[1] But with the solitary exception of the late Latin chronicle of Orosius, not a single translation into a Muslim language is known of any Latin or Western work until the sixteenth century, when one or two historical and geographical works were translated into Turkish. For the Muslim of classical times, Frankish Europe was an outer darkness of barbarism and unbelief, from which the sunlit world of Islam had nothing to learn and little to fear. This view, though becoming outdated towards the end of the Middle Ages, was transmitted by the medieval Muslims to their Ottoman heirs, and was reinforced by the crushing victories of Ottoman arms over their European opponents. On the warlike but open frontier one could still exchange lessons with one's counterpart on the other side; through renegades and refugees new skills could still reach the Islamic Empire. But the willingness to learn these lessons was not there, and in time the sources also dried up. Masked by the still imposing military might of the Ottoman Empire, the peoples of Islam continued to cherish the dangerous but comfortable illusion of the immeasurable and immutable superiority of their own civilization to all others – an illusion from which they were slowly shaken by a series of humiliating military defeats.

In the military empire, at once feudal and bureaucratic, which they had created, the Muslims knew only four professions – government, war, religion and agriculture. Industry and trade were left to the non-Muslim conquered subjects, who continued to practise

[1] See further B. Lewis, 'The Muslim Discovery of Europe', *Bulletin of the School of Oriental and African Studies*, xx (1957), 415.

their inherited crafts. Thus the stigma of the infidel became attached
to the professions which the infidels followed, and remained so
attached even after many of the craftsmen had become Muslim.
Westerners and native Christians, bankers, merchants and craftsmen, were all involved in the general contempt which made the
Ottoman Muslim impervious to ideas or inventions of Christian
origin and unwilling to bend his own thoughts to the problems of
artisans and vile mechanics. Primitive techniques of production,
primitive means of transportation, chronic insecurity and social
penalization, combined to preclude any long-term or large-scale
undertakings, and to keep the Ottoman economy at the lowest
level of competence, initiative and morality.[1]

This apathy of the Ottoman ruling class is the more striking when
contrasted with the continuing vigour of their intellectual life. An
example of this may be seen in the group of writers who memori-
alized on the decline of the Empire, which they saw so clearly but
were powerless to stop. We may point also to the brilliant Ottoman
school of historiography, which reaches its peak of achievement in
the work of Naima (1655–1716); to the Ottoman traditions of
courtly and religious poetry, two of the greatest exponents of
which, Nedim and Şeyh Galib, lived in the eighteenth century; to
the Ottoman schools of architecture, miniature and music. It is
not until the end of the eighteenth century and the beginning of the
nineteenth that we can speak of a real breakdown in the cultural
and intellectual life of Turkey, resulting from the utter exhaustion
of the old traditions and the absence of new creative impulses.
And even then, behind the battered screen of courtly convention,
the simple folk arts and folk poetry of the Turks continued as
before.

In the late Middle Ages, the Ottoman Empire was the only state
in Europe which already possessed the territory, the cohesion, the
organization, the manpower and the resources to carry the new
apparatus of warfare, the crushing cost of which was outmoding the
city states and feudal principalities of medieval Europe, as surely as
modern weapons have outmoded the petty sovereignties of Europe
in our own day. In part perhaps because of that very primacy, it
failed to respond to the challenge which produced the nation-states

[1] Ülgener, pp. 193 ff.

of sixteenth-century Europe, and the great commercial and techno-logical efflorescence of which they were the scene.

Fundamentally, the Ottoman Empire had remained or reverted to a medieval state, with a medieval mentality and a medieval economy – but with the added burden of a bureaucracy and a standing army which no medieval state had ever had to bear. In a world of rapidly modernizing states it had little chance of survival.

The stages in the decline of Ottoman power and grandeur are well marked by public, international treaties. The first was the treaty of Sitvatorok, signed with Austria in November 1606. For the first time, this was not a truce dictated in Istanbul to the 'King of Vienna', but a treaty negotiated on the frontier and agreed with the 'Roman Emperor'. The Ottoman Sultan had at last consented to concede the Imperial title to the Habsburg monarch, and to treat with him as an equal.

The seventeenth century began with a concession of equality; it ended with a clear admission of defeat. In 1682 the Ottoman Empire, temporarily restored to health and vigour by the reforms of the Köprülü Vezirs, had launched one more major offensive, in the grand style, against its European enemies. The second failure before the walls of Vienna, in 1683, was decisive and final. The Austrians and their allies advanced rapidly into Ottoman territory in Hungary, Greece and the Black Sea coast, and the Austrian victories at the second battle of Mohacs in 1687 and at Zenta in 1697 sealed the defeat of the Turks. The peace treaty of Carlowitz, signed on 26 January 1699, marks the end of an epoch and the beginning of another. This was the first time that the Ottoman Empire signed a peace as the defeated power in a clearly decided war, and was compelled to cede extensive territories, long under Ottoman rule and regarded as part of the House of Islam, to the infidel enemy. It was a fateful opening to the eighteenth century.

By the treaty of Passarovitz of 1718, Turkey made further cessions of territory. Though the mutual suspicions of her enemies enabled her to recover some ground during the war of 1736–9, the recovery was of slight duration. A new humiliation came with the treaty of Küçük Kaynarca of 1774, after a war in which Russian troops had carried all before them and a Russian fleet had entered the Mediterranean and threatened the very coasts of Anatolia. By this treaty, the Sultan renounced not only conquered lands inhabited by Christian populations, but old Muslim territory in the Crimea;[1] he also conceded to the Russian Empress what became a virtual protectorate over his own Orthodox Christian subjects.

Thereafter there was a halt. Apart from the loss of Bukovina to Austria in 1775 and of Bessarabia to Russia in 1812, the Ottoman Empire made no important cessions to foreign powers until a century later, when the process was resumed with the loss of Bosnia and Herzegovina to Austria and of Batum and Kars to Russia in 1878. During this period the main threat to the unity and integrity of the Empire came from within.

The humiliations of Carlowitz, Passarowitz and later treaties further weakened the already waning authority of the central government over the provinces. Significantly, it was in the old Islamic territories in Asia and Africa that provincial independence first appeared and went farthest. These movements were in no sense expressions of popular or national opposition to Ottoman rule. Except in a few remote desert and mountain areas, such as Arabia, the Lebanon and Kurdistan, neither the leaders nor the followers were local, but were drawn from either the Ottoman or the Mamluk military classes. In neither case had they any roots in local soil – in neither could they count on any serious local support. Most of them were rebellious and adventurous pashas and officers, profiting from the remoteness and weakness of the Sultan's authority to intercept a larger share of the revenues of their provinces and to transform them into virtually independent principalities. Such were Ali Bey in Egypt, Ahmed Jezzar in Syria, and the Mamluk lords of Baghdad and Basra. They were no more concerned with the language and sentiments of their subjects than was a medieval European feudal magnate; far less with their welfare.

Rather different was the position in Anatolia, where the independent *derebeys* – valley-lords, as they were called – won virtual autonomy about the beginning of the eighteenth century. These too began as officers or agents and became vassals of the Sultan. Unlike

[1] By the terms of the treaty, the Sultan renounced his suzerainty over the Tatar Khanate of the Crimea, which became independent. The second stage was completed in 1783, when Russia annexed the Crimea, and the Khanate was extinguished.

the pashas in the Arab lands, however, they struck root among the peoples whom they ruled and from whom they had sprung, and formed genuine local dynasties, with strong local traditions and loyalties. Their financial and military obligations to the Porte came to be well defined and regulated, and evolved into a regular system of suzerainty and vassalage. Their close and intimate relationship with their territories and peoples seem to have had a beneficial effect on both.

In Rumelia, still the main centre and stronghold of the Empire and the home of its governing *elites*, the central government was able to maintain some measure of direct control. But there too the *ayan*, the new aristocracy of 'notables', were steadily taking over the functions of government, and by the end of the eighteenth century the notables of Rumelia, with their private armies, treasuries and courts of law, had rivalled the independence of the Anatolian valley-lords.

After each of the great military defeats of the eighteenth century, Ottoman statesmen and historians discussed with brutal frankness the decrepit state of the Empire and the abject performance of its armies. The treaty of Küçük Kaynarca and the subsequent annexation of the Crimea in particular gave rise to much heart-searching and discussion. Then, in 1787, a new war broke out between Turkey and Russia, joined in the following year by Austria. This time, distracted by events in Poland, Prussia, and France, the Russians and Austrians did not press the campaign as vigorously as previously, and in 1791–2 Turkey was able to make peace with Austria, at Sistova, and with Russia, at Jassy, on comparatively lenient terms.

During the war a new Sultan, Selim III, had been invested with the sword of Osman. Thirty-eight years of age at his accession, he was a man of greater ability and wider knowledge and experience than any who had emerged from the cage of princes in the Saray for a long time. Already as a young man he had entered, through his personal emissary Ishak Bey, into direct correspondence with the king of France, and showed a growing interest in European affairs. He was well aware that the respite of 1792 was due to difficulties elsewhere in Europe, and that there would be little time before Austria and Russia returned to the assault.

Selim's first problem was the modernization of the armed forces,

Q

NINE

The Dutch Economic Decline[1]

C. R. BOXER

J. C. Van Leur, whose death in the battle of the Java Sea (January 1942) was such a grievous loss to Indonesian historical studies, more than once protested against the common tendency of Dutch historians – and of others in their wake – to contrast the 'Golden Age' of the seventeenth century with the 'Periwig Period' (*Pruiken-tijd*) of the eighteenth, invariably to the disparagement and disadvantage of the latter. He argued that this contrast was the result of a legend spun by the 'revolutionary Patriots' of 1795 to use politically against the *ancien régime* in the Dutch Republic, and fostered by the nineteenth-century 'national romantics' in the literature they wrote about the Golden Age. That the northern Netherlands produced no painters like Rembrandt or poets like Vondel during the Periwig Period did not alter the fact that this despised era 'performed the great work of laying the foundations of modern *bourgeois* culture', in the Netherlands as elsewhere in Europe, Van Leur affirmed.[2]

With all due deference to so distinguished an authority, it seems to me that in some respects at any rate the traditional contrast between the achievements of the Golden Century and the relative stagnation of the Periwig Period is a valid one. It does not date from the times of the 'revolutionary Patriots' and 'national romantics', but was already being discussed and deplored in the mid-eighteenth century, both in the Dutch Republic and in the domain of the East India Company. 'We are living, thank God, in a flourishing century at Batavia', wrote the Governor-General and his council in 1649, but there is no trace of such confident

[1] This article was first published as chapter 10 of *The Dutch Seaborne Empire 1600–1800*, Hutchinson, 1965.
[2] J. C. Van Leur, *Indonesian Trade and Society*, pp. 266, 271, 288.

satisfaction in the correspondence of their successors a hundred years later.[1] The Dutch periodical press during the second half of the eighteenth century is full of complaints about the real or alleged decline of the national character and energy as compared with a century earlier. Admittedly, some dissenting voices were raised against this widely held belief. One of these critics pointed out (in 1769) that people who compared the past with the present always selected the best in former generations for comparison with the worst in the actual one. He argued that drunkenness, gluttony and disorderly brawling had considerably declined in the eighteenth century as compared with the seventeenth, and concluded: 'We dissemble more, but quarrel less.' In taking this line he anticipated by nearly two centuries a modern Dutch historian who wrote:

> We admire Erasmus who, in a turbulent period, described the conversation of friends in a beautiful garden as the height of civilized entertainment; yet we are disgusted with his eighteenth-century followers who put his theory into practice. We are anti-militarist but loathe the least military society in all Netherland history. There is something purely sentimental and irrational in the attitude of most Netherlanders towards this period.[2]

True enough, perhaps; but the pessimists of the Periwig Period and those who agree with them nowadays had – and have – some good and sufficient reasons for thinking that the glory had departed with the end of the Golden Century.

Rightly or wrongly, a declining population is often regarded as a symptom of national decay, and there were plenty of people in the United Provinces in 1780, including the Prince of Orange, who thought that the population was smaller than it had been a century previously. Unfortunately we have no reliable figures for the Dutch population as a whole in the seventeenth and eighteenth centures, and we have to depend on a few contemporary and

---

[1] Compare the reports of the Governor-General and Council dated 8 January and 31 December 1649 (De Jonge, *Opkomst*, Vol. VI, pp. 8–13) with those of 1750 (De Jonge, *Opkomst*, Vol. X, pp. 164–5).

[2] B. M. Vlekke, *Evolution of the Dutch Nation*, p. 241; J. de Vries, *De economische achteruitgang der Republick in de achttiende eeuw* (Amsterdam, 1958), p. 173, for the quotation of 1769.

conflicting estimates. Pieter de la Court, in his *Interest van Holland* of 1662, calculated the population of the United Provinces at a maximum of 2,400,000, but he admitted that this figure was only a very rough guess. A more common estimate was just about two million inhabitants, and this figure is accepted by most modern writers. I have not been able to find the source for it, nor any explanation of why this figure seems to have remained unchanged down to the end of the Dutch Republic; for nearly all authorities agree that this was the total in 1795. Yet in Western Europe as a whole there was a rapid rise in the population after the mid-eighteenth century. Why should the northern Netherlands have afforded an exception to this rule, particularly as they were not ravaged by disastrous wars nor decimated by outbreaks of plague during the Periwig Period?

The reasons given for the rapid population growth in Western Europe during the second half of the eighteenth century are that a decline in infant mortality was accompanied by couples marrying earlier in life and so having (other things being equal) more children. We do not know how far these two factors applied in the United Provinces, though an Englishman long resident in Holland referred in 1743 to 'the remarkable barrenness of the Dutch women', as if this was a well-known and uncontested fact.[1] More significant, perhaps, is the fact that the average yearly marriage-rate in Amsterdam during the period 1670–9 was almost exactly the same as that for the years 1794–1803, that is, 2,078 and 2,082, respectively. It is true that the average rate for the intervening years was sometimes higher, but it never exceeded 3,204 in any one year (1746), and the annual marriage-rate fluctuated between 2,100 and 2,500. In any event, it is clear that the population of Amsterdam, always the Republic's most populous and thriving city, increased rapidly between 1580 and 1660, but very slowly between 1662 (some 200,100 or 210,000 souls) and 1795 (some 217,000 or 221,000 souls). The number of houses in Amsterdam remained virtually the same between 1740 and 1795, which likewise indicates that there

---

[1] *A Description of Holland, or the present state of the United Provinces* (London, 1743), p. 97. The writer adds, with obvious exaggeration: 'In consequence, if this State had not constant and annual supplies of foreigners it would be impossible for it to subsist, and it would be dissolved in a very few years.'

was no substantial increase in the population during this period, despite Van der Oudermeulen's allegation to the contrary in 1795.[1]

In 1780 Amsterdam was still a thriving port with a great deal of overseas trade, and conditions in some other parts of the United Provinces were much worse in the second half of the eighteenth century. James Boswell wrote from Utrecht in 1764:

> Most of their principal towns are sadly decayed, and instead of finding every mortal employed, you meet with multitudes of poor creatures who are starving in idleness. Utrecht is remarkably ruined. There are whole lanes of wretches who have no other subsistence than potatoes, gin and stuff which they call tea and coffee; and what is worst of all, I believe they are so habituated to this life that they would not take work if it should be offered to them . . . you see, then, that things are very different here from what most people in England imagine. Were Sir William Temple to revisit these Provinces, he would scarcely believe the amazing alteration which they have undergone.

Boswell's testimony was echoed fourteen years later by the Dutch newspaper, *De Borger*, which stated (19 October 1778) that the economic decline of the nation had reached such a pitch that it seemed as if 'the body of the Commonwealth would shortly consist of little more than rentiers and beggars – the two kinds of people who are the least useful to the country.'[2]

Both Boswell and *De Borger* may have been laying on the dark colours a bit thick, but there is plenty of other contemporary evidence to suggest that the population of many provincial towns declined at this period, and that houses and streets were demolished to make room for gardens and meadows. This decline was by no means universal, and it seems to have been most marked in the small sea-towns of North Holland and of Zeeland, and in several of the

[1] Cf. J. de Bosch Kemper, *Armoede* (ed. 1851), statistical tables XI(c)–XI(t); H. Brugmans, *Opkomst en bloei van Amsterdam* (ed. 1944), pp. 88–9; Van der Oudermeulen's Memorandum of 1785 *apud* D. Van Hogendorp, *Stukken raakende de tegenwoordigen toestand der Bataafsche bezittingen in Oost-Indië* (The Hague and Delft, 1801), especially pp. 80–1, 290–1.

[2] F. A. Pottle (ed.), *Boswell in Holland, 1763–1764* (London, 1952), pp. 280–1; *De Borger*, 19 October 1778, *apud.* J. de Bosch Kemper, *Armoede* (ed. 1851), p. 357.

inland towns such as Utrecht, Haarlem, Leiden and Delft. What we do not know is where the surplus urban population (if there was one) went. It has been suggested that they may have gone to the peat moors of the north-eastern provinces, which were being developed at this time, and where new villages were being formed. It is significant that the population of the eastern province of Overijssel increased by nearly 90 per cent between 1675 and 1795; but this spectacular increase was almost certainly not reflected in any of the other provinces, and in most of them the population seems either to have stagnated or, perhaps, even to have decreased in some instances. It is unfortunate that Overijssel, the smallest and poorest of all the seven provinces, is the only one for which we have accurate population figures in the time of the Republic. Until further research is done in the demographic history of the other provinces, we cannot say whether the total population of the Dutch Republic increased or decreased between 1600 and 1800, in view of the conflicting and piecemeal nature of the available evidence.[1]

If there is considerable uncertainty concerning the total population of the United Provinces in the Periwig Period as compared with the Golden Century, there is less room for doubt that the second half of the eighteenth century revealed an unmistakable decline in industry in general, and in the fishing industry in particular, as compared with conditions a century earlier. The herring fishery, which was commonly termed a gold-mine of the United Provinces in the first half of the seventeenth century, still presented an impressive appearance in 1728, when a well-informed English resident in the Netherlands estimated that an average total of about 800 busses were employed in this fishery, making three voyages a year. Though this total was less than it had been a century earlier, the tonnage of the eighteenth-century vessels ranged from 30 to 50 tons, whereas they were only 20 to 30 in the earlier period. A

[1] J. de Vries, *Economische achteruitgang*, pp. 167–8, thinks that the population of the Netherlands as a whole, and not merely that of the province of Overijssel, increased between 1700 and 1795; but it seems to me that the weight of contemporary evidence indicates a stagnation or a decline for many places. The figures for Overijssel are derived from Slicher van Bath. Cf. also C. Wilson and Van der Woude's observations in *BMHGU*, Vol. 77, pp. 21, 22, 26.

modern Dutch authority estimates that the province of Holland alone provided a yearly maximum of about 500 herring busses in 1630, which had shrunk to 219 in 1730 – though here again allowance must be made for the increased tonnage. The same author states that, with the exception of Vlaardingen, the number of ships maintained by all the fishing towns decreased during the eighteenth century, the decline being particularly noticeable in Enkhuizen, which equipped between 200 and 400 busses in the closing years of the seventeenth century, but only 75 in 1731, and 56 in 1750. The decline was accelerated after 1756, and only about 150–180 busses were engaged in the annual Dutch herring fisheries on the eve of the Fourth English War (1780).

It was a similar story with the cod-fishery and even worse with the whale-fishery. The Dogger Bank cod-fishery still employed 200–300 vessels of 40–60 tons each in the year 1728, according to Onslow Burrish, but this total was apparently considerably less than it had been in the second half of the seventeenth century. The decline in the cod-fishery was more marked in the last thirty years of the eighteenth century and when the Republic collapsed in 1795, only 125 vessels were engaged in this occupation. The decline in the Arctic whale-fishery was equally marked, and although some good catches were occasionally made in the eighteenth century, the halcyon years of 1675–90 never returned. 'This trade, however,' wrote Onslow Burrish in 1728, 'is thought to be a kind of lottery, and is therefore undertaken by persons of overgrown fortunes, who if they fail this year, expect better luck the next, and do not feel the disappointment; but it is of undoubted and universal benefit to the State in general, as it promotes the increase of navigation, and the consumption of everything that depends on it.'[1]

The reasons for the decline of the Dutch deep-sea and coastal fisheries during the second half of the eighteenth century are not far to seek. The chief cause was increasing competition by the fishermen of neighbouring countries, principally England and Scotland, but also Denmark and Norway, not to mention the

[1] Onslow Burrish, *Batavia Illustrata, or a view of the policy and commerce of the United Provinces, particularly of Holland* (London, 1728), pp. 265–73. The other figures are taken from the section on the fisheries in J. de Vries, *Economische achteruitgang*, pp. 137–49, and the sources there quoted.

Flemish fishers from the Austrian Netherlands (Belgium). Hamburg became increasingly important as a staple market for the herring consumed in north Germany and Scandinavia. Most of these countries also adopted protectionist measures to foster their own fishing industries at the expense of the Dutch, the British government in particular making use of subsidies and premiums. The French government placed an embargo on the importation of Dutch herring in 1751, and the Austrian Netherlands, Denmark and Prussia followed this example in 1766, 1774 and 1775 respectively. There was also less demand for herring in eighteenty-century Europe, owing to a change in dietary habits, and by the end of this period the demand could be satisfied by a total of 300 European herring-busses, whereas at one time 500 Dutch busses had barely sufficed. But the quality and technical excellence of the Dutch herring fisheries and packers retained their primacy down to the end, and in 1780 about half of the total European demand for cured herring was still supplied by the Dutch. The reasons for the parallel decline in the Dutch cod-fishery are less clear, although increasing competition by English and French fishers off the Newfoundland Banks and by Flemings nearer home from Ostend and Nieuwpoort obviously had a good deal to do with it.

The decline in the Dutch fisheries inevitably affected to a greater or lesser extent the numerous ancillary trades and occupations with which they were closely connected. These included the timber trade with the Baltic, which provided the wood for building and repairing the busses; the salt trade with Portugal and France, which provided the salt for curing the herring; 'the carpenters, caulkers, smiths, ropemakers and sailmakers, with the coopers, who make the prodigious number of casks used for package of the herrings; the net-makers, and all other little trades who furnish the several instruments necessary in the manufactory', as Onslow Burrish noted in 1728. He calculated that in this way the herring fisheries alone gave 'employment and subsistence to thirty thousand families at least, not including that vast number of people, who get their living by the necessary consumption of all kinds of clothing and provision that they occasion'. When the whaling, cod, coastal and inland fisheries are added to the herring industry, we can see that a substantial proportion of Dutch labour was directly or indirectly concerned with the prosperity of these fisheries as a whole, even if we regard Pieter de la Court's estimate of 450,000 people as directly dependent on them in 1662 as somewhat exaggerated. The fisheries were doubly valued as a nursery of seamen and a source of employment for labour ashore; and this was why the winter cod-fishery in the North Sea was still maintained in the eighteenth century, although it gave little or no commercial profit, owing to the high cost of maintaining the ships and equipment in the stormy winter weather.

Another noticeable factor in the decline of the Dutch fisheries was the increasing shortage of deep-sea fishermen, of whom there had been no lack in the seventeenth century, by the unanimous testimony of Netherlanders and foreigners. The fisheries suffered grievously in the major wars in which the Republic was involved – from the ravages of the Dunkirkers between 1600 and 1645, from English attacks in the Anglo-Dutch wars, and, above all, from French corsairs in the War of 1701–13, when the herring fishery was virtually destroyed. But the intervening years of peace enabled a greater or lesser recovery to be made after each war, though it is probable that some fishing families did not return to the sea as their means of livelihood. The foreign fishing companies which tried to compete with the Dutch in the eighteenth century endeavoured to tempt experienced Dutch fishers into their employment, at any rate in their earlier years. It is uncertain how many succumbed to these temptations, but in 1756 the majority of skippers in the service of the recently founded Society of the Free British Fishery (1750–72) were mostly Dutchmen or Danes.[1]

The States-General periodically promulgated edicts forbidding Dutch merchant-seamen and fishers from taking service with foreign nations, but the frequent reiteration of such edicts implies that they were not well observed. We have no means of calculating how many Dutch fishers served abroad in defiance of these edicts, nor whether their absence was temporary or permanent. What is certain is that the manning of the Dutch fishing fleets became – and remained – a problem in the eighteenth century, which it had never been in the seventeenth. It has been reliably calculated that at the

[1] J. de Vries, *Economische achteruitgang*, pp. 137–49, for most of the above and what follows.

end of the eighteenth century the Dutch deep-sea and coastal fisheries together employed only two-thirds of the number which had been necessary for the herring-fishery alone in 1600. It is likewise certain that increasing numbers of Norwegians, Danes and North Germans helped to man Dutch fishing-vessels in the eighteenth century, just as they did in the States Navy, in the East Indiamen and in the merchant marine. It has been suggested that these (mostly raw) hands took the place of more experienced Dutch seamen who entered the foreign navies and merchant-ships, but we have no proof that this happened on any noteworthy scale. They certainly did not serve in any great numbers in English merchant-ships, which, save in war-time, seldom employed more than a few hundred foreigners all told.

Whatever the reasons, it is indisputable that the Dutch fisheries, though still nurseries of seamen, were not nearly so important in this respect in 1780 as they had been a century earlier. During the Nine Years War of 1689–97, the Dutch were able to send about 100 warships to sea every year manned with about 24,000 men, apart from the numerous privateers they fitted out and the thousands of sailors in the Indiamen and merchant-ships which sailed the Seven Seas with or without convoy. In August 1781, at a time when the whole of their seaborne trade and fisheries were virtually paralysed and thus many seamen should have been available for enlistment in the navy, it was only with great difficulty that the Dutch were able to send to sea the modest fleet of seventeen sail manned with 3,000 men, which fought so stoutly at Dogger Bank under Rear-Admiral Zoutman. By the end of this disastrous war they were barely able to secure 19,176 men out of the 30,046 they required for manning forty-six ships of the line and thirty-eight frigates. Only one conclusion can be drawn from this state of affairs, which is likewise reflected in the other evidence: the seafaring communities of Holland and Zeeland must have decreased considerably between 1680 and 1780.[1]

[1] Cf. C. R. Boxer, 'Sedentary workers and seafaring folk in the Dutch Republic', in J. S. Bromley & E. H. Kossmann (eds.), *Britain and the Netherlands*, Vol. II. For the paucity of foreign hands in English merchant-ships in the seventeenth and eighteenth centuries see R. Davis, *The Rise of the English Shipping Industry in the seventeenth and eighteenth centuries* (1962), p. 136.

This decline in the Dutch fisheries and in the numbers of the men employed therein was not regarded with indifference by those contemporaries who were aware of it, and who were in a position to attempt some remedial measures, even if these achieved no lasting results. Several protectionist measures, designed to help the Dutch herring-fishers, packers and dealers against their foreign competitors, were taken by the States of Holland in the second half of the eighteenth century, including the award of premiums and subsidies after the English example. The States of Zeeland went even further, and in 1759 awarded a cash premium to all fishing-vessels in that province. The results were disappointing if one may judge from the example of Zierickzee, which was one of the principal maritime Zeeland towns. This place maintained a fishing fleet of some forty sail in 1745, which had shrunk to seventeen or eighteen in 1785. This decline was paralleled in the number of merchant ships registered in the same port, which decreased from about sixty or seventy sail in 1760 to a mere fifteen, 'large and small', twenty-five years later. Corresponding figures for the other Zeeland sea-towns, such as Veere, Vlissingen and Middelburg, are lacking, though the last two ports still had an important share in the shipping trading to the East and West Indies, as well as Western Europe. But many of the smaller ports probably declined in the same way as Zierickzee. The 'dead towns' of Zeeland and North Holland, which have long formed one of the main tourist attractions in the Netherlands, date not from the nineteenth century but from the second half of the eighteenth.

As stated above, the Dutch herring-fishers, curers and packers maintained their technical superiority over their foreign competitors down to the end, even though they inevitably lost ground numerically, but the Dutch whaling industry declined both quantitatively and qualitatively. Whereas in the second half of the seventeenth century the Dutch had been the undisputed leaders in the whale fisheries, a century later they were overhauled and displaced by the English. The latter improved their catches by making longer voyages and using heavier ships, which could follow the whales deeper among the drifting ice-floes. They also introduced new and improved techniques, such as experimenting with mechanical harpoons which eventually displaced the hand-thrown variety. The

Dutch owners and whalers did not adopt these newfangled methods, or did so only belatedly; and they did not participate in the seal-hunting which the English and Germans exploited in conjunction with their whaling voyages.

This conservative and unenterprising mentality was also reflected in other and more important branches of Dutch trade and industry during the Periwig Period, contrasting with the enterprise and dynamism of the Dutch merchants and mariners in the Golden Century. We have had occasion to observe that the Dutch lost their seventeenth-century lead in maritime cartography and navigational techniques to their English and French rivals, and they were equally slow to adopt new and improved methods in shipbuilding. Stavorinus and Dirk van Hogendorp both criticized the directors of the Amsterdam chamber of the East India Company in the last quarter of the eighteenth century for their reluctance to build flush-decked instead of deep-waisted ships, although, as Stavorinus noted in 1774: 'It is incontrovertible that a flush-decked ship is much more able to withstand the force of the waves than a deep-waisted one.' There is also a remarkable contrast between the attitude of the directors and servants of the Dutch East India Company towards their English counterparts and rivals in the seventeenth as compared with the eighteenth centuries. Down to about 1670 the Dutch considered themselves as superior in energy and ability, as well as in capital and in material resources, to the English. Moreover, the English frequently admitted their relative inferiority. In the last quarter of the seventeenth century the relative attitudes of the two rivals begin to change. We find the English growing more aggressive and self-confident, and the Dutch becoming doubtful of their ability to compete on level terms with the English in places like the coast of Coromandel, where the VOC (the Dutch East India Company) did not enjoy unchallenged control of the sea as it did in Indonesian waters. The shift becomes still more noticeable in the eighteenth century, particularly in the second half, when the official correspondence of the VOC is full of lamentations about the superiority of the English and the threat they posed to the Dutch, even in Indonesia.

It is difficult to avoid the conclusion that the English had become in fact more enterprising and able than the Dutch in the East.

Admittedly their progress was mainly due to their now greatly superior capital resources and to the economic advantages they derived from their possession of Bengal and their domination of the China Trade. But there was evidently some truth in Dirk van Hogendorp's allegation that the employees of John Company were as a rule more able than those of Jan Companie, and this was just the opposite of the relative position of the two Companies in the first half of the seventeenth century. The reasons for this change require further investigation and research, but one contributory cause may have been the increasing tendency of the VOC to rely on uneducated 'louts from the heart of Germany', who had no particular incentive to work hard for Dutch directors and shareholders. Complaints of the real or alleged inferior calibre of the Company's servants always existed, but these allegations seem to have been more justified in the second half of the eighteenth century, as reflected in the reports of Nicholas Hartingh, the outstandingly capable Resident and Governor of North-east Java in the years 1746–61.[1]

The decline of the Dutch East India Company in the second half of the eighteenth century was, however, in some respects more apparent than real, for the volume of this trade in relation to the seaborne trade of the Republic as a whole actually increased in this period. This increase is reflected in the numbers of outward-bound East Indiamen, which are tabulated on p. 247.

Professor Brugmans has argued from these figures that the volume of VOC shipping virtually doubled between 1631 and 1780, but it seems to me that this deduction is not altogether warranted. It is obvious that the number of Indiamen sailing between the Netherlands and Java was doubled in this period, but the number of those engaged in the interport trade of Asia may have declined by just about as much. Whereas in the second half of the seventeenth century, from five to ten Indiamen, many of them of the largest size, sailed annually from Batavia to Nagasaki, in the

[1] For Hartingh's reports see J. de Jonge, *Opkomst*, Vol. X. Cf. also the previously quoted works of Van der Oudermeulen (1785), Dirk van Hogendorp (1801) and J. de Vries (1959), for relevant statistics and discussion of Dutch Merchant shipping and fishing fleets in the eighteenth century and the decay of some of the maritime towns.

second half of the eighteenth century they averaged only one or two. Similarly, the number of Dutch Indiamen engaged in the trade with India dwindled into relative insignificance in the period 1750–80, compared with a century earlier, while the trade to some regions, such as the Red Sea and the Persian Gulf, was abandoned altogether. Admittedly there were slight increases in other regions, such as the trade with Canton, and perhaps with Ceylon: but these did not compensate for the marked decline in the numbers of Dutch ships engaged in the interport trade of Asia from the Moluccas to Malabar as a whole.

THE OUTWARD-BOUND EAST INDIA FLEETS, 1611–1781

Period	Ships
1611–12–1620–1	117
1621–2 –1630–1	148
1631–2 –1640–1	151
1641–2 –1650–1	162
1651–2 –1660–1	226
1661–2 –1670–1	257
1671–2 –1680–1	219
1681–2 –1690–1	209
1691–2 –1700–1	241
1701–2 –1710–11	271
1711–12–1720–1	327
1721–2 –1730–1	379
1731–2 –1740–1	365
1741–2 –1750–1	315
1751–2 –1760–1	276
1761–2 –1770–1	303
1771–2 –1780–1	294

(from J. Brugmans, 'De VOC en de welvaart in de Republiek')

In 1640, for example, there were eighty-five Dutch Indiamen in Asian seas, exclusive of those on the point of sailing to or arriving from Europe. In 1743 this total had shrunk to forty-eight ships, nor was the decrease in numbers offset by any great increase in individual tonnage.[1]

[1] I. J. Brugmans, 'De Oost-Indische Compagnie en de welvaart in de Republiek (*Tijdschrift voor Geschiedenis*, Vol. 61, Groningen 1948), pp. 225–31;

During the Golden Century and in the Periwig Period, Dutch-men and their jealous trade rivals were both apt to claim that the Dutch East and West India Companies – more especially the former – were the chief pillar, prop and stay of the commercial prosperity of the United Provinces. This impression is not confirmed by such relevant figures as we have on this point, including those given by Van der Oudermeulen in 1785, who was one of the *Heeren* XVII, and one of those who advanced this claim. He gives the following figures for the value of Dutch seaborne trade on the eve of the Fourth English War:

Region	Millions of guilders
Trade with the East Indies	35
Trade with the West Indies and America	28
Trade with European countries	200

Of the European countries, he estimated the value of Dutch trade:

With England	42–4
With France	36–8
With the Baltic Region	55

On the other hand, we must remember that most of the goods imported by the Dutch from the East and West Indies were not consumed in the United Provinces but were re-exported to other European countries. The anonymous author of *A Description of Holland*, published in 1743, may have been exaggerating somewhat, but not much, when he wrote: 'At this day, for two or three millions of guilders in specie, which the Dutch Company sends to the East Indies, they bring home fifteen or sixteen millions in goods, of which the twelfth or fourteenth part is consumed amongst themselves; the rest is re-exported to the other countries of Europe, for which they are paid in money.' Van der Oudermeulen claimed in 1785 that 'three-quarters and seven-eighths' of the cargoes imported from East India were re-exported from the Netherlands, tea and coffee excepted, of which great amounts were consumed in

J. de Jonge, *Geschiedenis van het Nederlandsche Zeewezen*, Vol. I, pp. 799–805; Feenstra Kuiper, *Japan en de buitenwereld in de achttiende eeuw*, p. 23 n; J. S. Stavorinus, *Voyages to the East Indies*, Vol. III, p. 413, gives a total of thirty-seven Dutch ships in Eastern seas in 1768, exclusive of outward- or homeward-bound Indiamen.

Friesland and Groningen; 'so that one can certainly claim that our nation drives most of its East India trade with foreigners, to its own great advantage'. Unfortunately we cannot tell what was the proportion of colonial products in relation to the Dutch export trade with other European countries as a whole, but it must have been very considerable. Van der Oudermeulen was obviously guilty of special pleading when he argued that the collapse of the VOC would not merely be disastrous for the state but would adversely affect every individual Dutchman. The course of events in 1802–14, when the Netherlands were virtually without any trade with their former colonies, showed that this was not true. But it is likely that the Dutch East India Company contributed more to the general welfare of the United Provinces in the seventeenth and eighteenth centuries than Professor Brugmans is willing to allow. Apart from the thousands of men to whom the Company gave direct employment, it helped indirectly to maintain the 30,000 sailors who manned the Dutch merchant-ships engaged in the Baltic, Mediterranean and European Atlantic trades, in which the re-export of colonial goods such as spices, tea, coffee, tobacco and textiles played such a prominent part.[1]

There is another aspect of Dutch seaborne trade which we must glance at before briefly considering the developments in agriculture, industry and finance. This is the smuggling trade – above all, that with England. It is obviously impossible to ascertain the extent of this contraband trade, but it is certain that it helped to provide for the livelihood of thousands, particularly in the coastal towns of south Holland and Zeeland. For nearly the whole of the eighteenth century England was the best market for the sale of tea, and the heavy duties levied by the English government on this commodity inevitably encouraged smuggling on both sides of the North Sea. The war of 1780–4, and the passage of Pitt's Commutation Act in the last year, dealt a severe blow to the Zeeland maritime communities in this respect, as Van der Oudermeulen admitted in

---

[1] Cf. Van de Spiegel's 'Schets tot een vertoog over de intrinsique en relative magt der Republijk' of 1782 (ed. J. de Vries in the *Economisch Historisch Jaarboek*, Vol. XXVII, The Hague, 1958, pp. 81–100), and Van der Oudermeulen's Memorandum of 1785 in D. Van Hogendorp, *Stukken* (1801), pp. 37–400 especially pp. 127–275, 315–19.

R

1785. Dutch whalers long carried on a contraband trade with Iceland and other places, and the cod-fishers in the North Sea likewise indulged in smuggling nearer home. The burdensome network of excise duties which bore so heavily on the poorer classes in the United Provinces was, of course, a reason why many Dutch mariners were prepared to smuggle goods into Dutch ports as well as out of them; but humble sailors and fishermen were not the only or even the principal offenders in evading import and export duties. Merchants and shipowners did so on a considerable scale, and this was one of the reasons why the provincial admiralties were so often 'in the red', since their incomes depended largely on this uncertain and fluctuating source. Critics of these duties and of the excise network alleged that they not only kept up the cost of provisions, and thus the cost of living at home, but likewise encouraged foreigners to trade directly with each other instead of using the Dutch as middlemen, as they had done in the seventeenth century. A typical instance was afforded by the export of sugar, coffee and indigo from Bordeaux to Germany and the Baltic. Whereas at one time three-quarters of these commodities had been consigned via Amsterdam and one-quarter via Hamburg, by 1750–1 these proportions were exactly reversed.[1]

One of the numerous writers who deplored the decline of Dutch seaborne trade in 1780 alleged that the real trouble was that ship-owning had become increasingly separated from seafaring. In the seventeenth century many merchant-skippers had been owners or part-owners of their ships, and they had placed their sons and relatives aboard and furthered their prospects of promotion. They had also been actively concerned in the sale of the cargoes, and directly interested in the profits to be gained by advantageously disposing of the same for the owners or co-owners. 'Nowadays', this critic claimed, 'the ship owners are mostly merely in the business for carrying freight, and their cargoes belong mainly to foreigners, and they receive no profits for the transportation thereof, save only what they are paid for the freight.' He further alleged that the foreign correspondents or associates of these shipping firms or

[1] A. Kluit, *Iets over den laatsten Engelschen oorlog met de Republiek, en over Nederlands koophandel, dezelfs bloei, verval, en middelen van herstel* (Amsterdam, 1794), pp. 302–39, especially pp. 306–7.

partnerships (*rederijen*) often got their own nationals placed as deck-officers and skippers of such ships. These men, in their turn, enlisted, favoured and promoted their compatriots in preference to native-born Netherlanders. The latter, becoming discouraged at being passed over for promotion, either took to drink and debauchery or else left the sea-service in disgust.[1]

This writer, like most pamphleteers, was obviously overstating his case. It is evident that shipowning gradually became a full-time occupation in the northern Netherlands from the second half of the seventeenth century onwards, but this process was very far from completion in 1780. Several branches of the maritime trade, such as the timber and grain trade with the Baltic, were still largely conducted on the old footing, and skippers were still the merchants and factors of their cargoes. But it is equally evident – or so it seems to me – that foreign participation in ships sailing under the Dutch flag became much more noticeable at this time. Whereas during the Eighty Years' War Dutch shipowners and skippers had often traded in the Iberian Peninsula and elsewhere by masquerading as Hansa and Scandinavians, by 1780 the position was reversed. This malpractice was of long standing, and we find De Ruyter complaining about it in 1663, when he informed the Amsterdam Admiralty that he had found at Malaga several Hamburg ships provided with Dutch papers. Their skippers had openly boasted that for a few guilders they could easily bribe some burgher at Amsterdam who would swear on oath that the vessel was Amsterdam-owned, 'whereas in reality all the owners live at Hamburg'. De Ruyter urged the admiralty to stop this abuse, but it was even more prevalent over a century later. Kluit complained in 1794 that any Dutch burgher could claim he was the owner of a ship, and he did not have to produce proof of such a declaration. The inevitable result was that many foreign merchantmen sailed under Dutch flags and with Dutch ships' papers.[2]

[1] Anon, *Aanmerkingen op de bedenkingen van Mr G. Titsingh*, Amsterdam, 1780 (Pamphlet-Knuttel nr. 19465).
[2] G. Brandt, *Het leven en bedryf van den heere Michiel de Ruiter* (Amsterdam, 1687) pp. 263–4; g. Kluit, *Iets over den laatsten Engelschen oorlog* (1794), pp. 336–9. For the evolution of shipowning as an occupation in its own right in eighteenth-century England see R. Davis, *The Rise of the English Shipping Industry in the seventeenth and eighteenth centuries* (1962), pp. 81–109.

When due allowance is made for exaggeration by interested parties, it must, I think, be admitted that the sinews of Dutch maritime strength had weakened considerably during the eighteenth century. The best contemporary authorities – Van de Spiegel and Van der Oudermeulen – were agreed that in 1780 the Dutch merchant-fleet (including the East and West India Companies) still gave employment to some 30,000 or 40,000 mariners. At first glance this does not seem to indicate such a very great change from 1588, when the Vice-Admiral of the province of Holland boasted that he could mobilize 30,000 fighting sailors within a fortnight, or from 1688 when William III sailed from Hellevoetsluis to inaugurate the 'Glorious Revolution' in England. But in 1588 and 1688 the seafaring population of Zeeland and North Holland was undoubtedly greater than in 1780, and the Dutch Republic in its prime can hardly have disposed of much fewer than 80,000 qualified seamen – and the total may well have been more. Moreover, although these totals presumably included the foreign-born seamen then available in the Netherlands, we have reason to believe that their relative proportion was even higher in 1780 than it had been either one hundred or two hundred years previously.

If we turn from the sea to the soil of the northern Netherlands, we find that Dutch agriculture made a better showing than Dutch shipping in the 18th as compared with the 17th century. Although the commercial and financial interests of the Dutch Republic did more to shape its economic structure than did the agricultural sector, yet agriculture perhaps employed more hands than did either trade or industry. This was certainly true of the five land provinces (counting Friesland as one) in both the Golden Age and the Periwig Period, and it was probably true of Zeeland and south Holland as well in the second half of the eighteenth century. Dairy produce was the outstanding aspect of Dutch farming. It was calculated in 1740 that the North Quarter region of the province of Holland alone produced about 20 million pounds of cheese in an averagely good year. The year 1740, incidentally, was a disastrous one for Dutch agriculture, for an exceptionally severe winter in 1739–40 was followed by a wretched summer. The suffering among the working-classes was intense, and though its catastrophic effects cannot have been permanent, other people besides Stavorinus who were writing forty or fifty years later dated the decline of the United Provinces from then. Butter was another important Dutch dairy export, though this had to meet severe competition from Irish butter between 1666 and 1757 when the English government banned the importation of the latter, thus compelling the Irish farmers to expand their markets in Flanders, France and the Iberian Peninsula.

The raising of beef-cattle, horses, sheep and pigs was of much less importance than dairy farming, and there were widespread ravages by cattle-plague in 1713–23, 1744–56, and 1766–86, as well as localized outbreaks in the intervening years. The origin and cure of this disease were not scientifically understood, but the provincial States promulgated edicts enjoining various remedial or preventive measures. These injunctions were usually ignored by the peasants, partly from a distrust of the 'gentlemen' who promulgated them, and partly because they regarded the disease as a visitation of the wrath of God which it was impious to resist. In the last two decades of the eighteenth century a more reasonable attitude began to prevail as the result of efforts by a few progressive private farmers and by agricultural societies to encourage the inoculation of cattle against disease. Despite the ravages of cattle-plague, the losses were often more than made good after a few years by importation from abroad and by home breeding. Even in the poor and backward province of Overijssel, cattle raising increased between 1750 and 1800. On the other hand, the prevalence of cattle-plague did induce many farmers to turn wholly or partly from stock-raising to arable farming. In Groningen the switch was mainly to growing grain, in Holland to market gardening, and in Friesland to planting potatoes. In some districts sheep-folds increased for the same reason, and there were about 20,000 sheep on the island of Texel in the mid-eighteenth century.

The oppressive incidence of provincial taxation and the burden of the excise network were two reasons why a considerable number of farmers in north Holland left the land for other occupations in the first half of the eighteenth century. In the second half of this century there was a general rise in agricultural prices over most of Western Europe. This probably helped to offset the burden of taxation for the farmers and peasants in some of the United

Provinces and thus made life a bit easier for them. It certainly did so in Overijssel – the only province for which adequate statistics are available – where the rise in agrarian prices reduced the tax burden by about half. But this was not general, and elsewhere the increase in agricultural prices may have been more than offset by marked increases in provincial and municipal taxes and imports from about 1690 onwards.

Technical improvements in Dutch agriculture during the eighteenth century were introduced only tardily and incompletely, as compared with developments in contemporary France and England. The average Dutch farmer and peasant clung obstinately to the techniques employed by his seventeenth-century ancestors and regarded all innovations with suspicion. Peasants the world over were – and are – inherently conservative in their ideas, and the eighteenth-century Dutch peasant was no exception. The spreading of new ideas and techniques among the rural population was largely dependent on the interest and co-operation of the village school-master and the local *predikant*, neither of whom were usually of an inquiring turn of mind. Some of the larger landowners experimented with new agricultural instruments, such as Tull's sowing-machine, and between 1750 and 1784 a number of the more enterprising farmers and landowners formed societies for the improvement of agriculture after the French and English models. But the results of their propaganda, their experiments and their efforts only began to bear fruit in the closing years of the Republic. On balance, however, it is clear that agriculture in general, and market gardening and arable farming in particular, were relatively flourishing in the second half of the eighteenth century and more particularly in its last two decades, thus contrasting with the noticeable decline in fishing and industry. More land was reclaimed from sea and swamp during this period, but the greatest single cause for the relative prosperity in agriculture was the increase in prices for agrarian products.[1]

The undeniable decline in Dutch industry as a whole during the eighteenth century was not common to all branches, nor was the chronological sequence always the same. The textile industry was

[1] J. de Vries, *Economische acheruitgang*, pp. 150–66, and the sources there quoted, chief among whom is Slicher van Bath.

one of the first to suffer, being one of the most exposed to sharper foreign competition. Its decline can be dated from about 1730, although some sections of this industry were supported by the export requirements of the East India Company down to 1795. The cloth industry of Leiden, which had reached its highest point in 1671 with an annual production of 139,000 pieces, thereafter declined disastrously. In 1700 it produced only 85,000 pieces; in 1725, 72,000; in 1750, 54,000; in 1775, 41,000 and in 1795 a mere 29,000 pieces. Not surprisingly this decline in Leiden's greatest industry was reflected in a parallel shrinkage of the working-class population. Breweries, brandy-distilleries, sugar-refineries, salt- and soap-processing firms, dye-works, tobacco factories, oil-mills and diamond-cutting, all of which had flourished in the Golden Century, did not all decline in the Periwig Period, though some of them did, especially in the second half of the eighteenth century. The diamond-cutting industry maintained itself down to the last days of the Republic, as did the paper-making industry, largely owing to the high quality of these two products. The same applies to the high-quality velvets manufactured at Utrecht. Brandy-distilleries were still flourishing in 1771, when 85 per cent of this one-time 'national drink' was being exported to markets which included North America as well as the domains of the Dutch East and West India Companies. The dyeing and tobacco industries also held their own for most of the eighteenth century, although they declined in some localities. The famous Delft potteries, which reached their apogee in 1685–1725, declined thereafter, though not disastrously so. Brick- and tile-kilns continued to flourish, and their products were exported in ballast to the Baltic regions after the domestic demand had been satisfied. On the other hand, the train-oil industry inevitably declined with the decrease of the whale-fisheries.

Nowhere was the overall decline of Dutch industry in the years 1750–95 more clearly reflected than in shipbuilding. In the seventeenth century the Dutch shipwrights were kept fully employed in building, repairing and replacing ships for the fisheries, the navy, the European seaborne carrying trade and the two India Companies, apart from the vessels they built for sale or charter abroad. It has been calculated that there were then about 500 sea-going ships built yearly in the Republic, excluding those built on foreign account and the small craft used on inland waterways. Despite inevitable ups and downs, the shipbuilding industry remained a flourishing one for the first quarter of the eighteenth century, but it then began to taper off. Its decline became more noticeable after about 1750 and rapidly increased in the last quarter of the century. The Zaan region near Amsterdam, which was the seventeenth-century equivalent of what the Clyde became in Queen Victoria's reign, still had in 1707 over sixty yards where a total of 306 big and small vessels were under construction. In 1770 there were only twenty-five or thirty ships being built there; between 1790 and 1793 an average of only five yearly; and after 1793 only one. Rotterdam possessed twenty-three shipbuilding yards in 1650, and though these had shrunk to five by the end of the century, the position had improved again a hundred years later; but this recovery did not compensate for the catastrophic decline of the Zaan. Friesland actually recorded a marked increase in the number of ships during the eighteenth century, since 2,000 vessels were registered in that province in 1779, which was the largest number in any of the Seven Provinces. But the great majority of these craft were small coasters of under 80 tons, which were of little or no significance in the seaborne-trade of Europe.[1]

The reasons for the general decline of Dutch industries during the eighteenth century are fairly obvious. In comparison with their most dangerous competitors, France and England, the northern Netherlands were very poor in raw materials and their internal market was much smaller than in those two countries. During their period of prosperity in the Golden Century many Dutch industries besides the cloth industry of Leiden had expanded far beyond the demands of the home market and were primarily dependent on the export trade. When the protectionist measures adopted by neighbouring countries from the time of Colbert onwards effectively stimulated the consumption of their own manufactured goods at

[1] 'Dit blijkt te klarer, wanneer men overweegt, dat er in ons Land geen Provincie is, die meer reederijen heeft van smakken, koffen, galjooten en diergelijke vaartuigen dan Vriesland, zonder daarom commercie te hebben' (A. Kluit, op. cit., pp. 322–3). For the other facts and figures cf. J. de Vries, *Economische achteruitgang*, pp. 83-98.

the expense of Dutch exports, the Dutch industrialists could not fall back on an increased internal demand, nor was it possible greatly to increase their sales in the tropical dependencies. Moreover, the Dutch industries had originally been primarily finishing industries for the products of other countries, such as linen and woollen goods from England; but in course of time these countries made sufficient technical progress to undertake these finishing processes themselves. When the Industrial Revolution got under way in the second half of the eighteenth century, the Dutch were at a further disadvantage owing to their almost total want of coal and iron. The most important Dutch industry was the textile industry, and it was inevitably this which suffered most. With the exception of the Dutch Republic, it has been justly observed: 'Textiles were at the very heart of mercantile policy in all countries.'[1] The prohibitive duties placed on Dutch finished and manufactured cloth by England and France in the second half of the seventeenth century were successively followed by similar protectionist legislation in Russia, Prussia, Denmark, Norway and Spain in the first quarter of the eighteenth century. The resulting decline in the Dutch textile industry was unavoidable.

Apart from protectionist- and mercantilist-inspired legislation, one reason why foreign countries had been able to improve their industries at the expense of those of the Dutch was that they had enticed skilled labourers from the Netherlands in the early stages of developing their industries. In fact, the emigration of skilled labourers continued even after the foreign industries were functioning satisfactorily, because industrial unemployment in the northern Netherlands during the eighteenth century induced many workers to emigrate. We have no means of calculating how many, but in 1751 the States-General promulgated an edict forbidding the emigration of certain categories of skilled workmen, especially textile operatives, ropemakers and saw-mill workers. This was by no means the only example of such legislation, but there is no reason to suppose that these edicts were anything but futile and easily evaded by those people who wished to depart. Still less could the authorities prevent foreign workmen from taking service in

[1] E. F. Herkscher & E. F. Söderlund, *The Rise of Industry* (1953), *apud* J. de Vries, *Economische achteruitgang*, p. 101.

Dutch trades or factories to learn their respective techniques and then returning home to exploit their qualifications.

Another reason given by many contemporaries for the decline of Dutch industry in the second half of the eighteenth century was that the wages in the Seven Provinces, and more particularly in Holland, were higher than in most other countries. For instance, the weekly wage for calico-printers in Switzerland was the equivalent of Fl. 3.50 in 1766, of Fl. 3 at Augsburg in 1760 and Fl. 9–10 in Holland. On the other hand, there were wide variations between wage-rates in different regions of the Seven Provinces. In some places higher wages were paid in the country districts than in the towns. In other places the situation was reversed, and some Dutch industrialists shifted their factories from Holland to north Brabant and Overijssel, where local conditions permitted ruthless exploitation of the poor. 'People who know the peasants of Brabant', wrote an eyewitness in 1785, 'must acknowledge that they are deprived of all the comforts in life that are properly the part of human beings. They drink sour buttermilk or water, they eat potatoes and bread without butter or cheese, they are miserably clothed, they sleep on straw. A prisoner in Holland lives better than a peasant in Brabant.'[1]

It is difficult to say how far the allegedly 'high' wages of some Dutch skilled labourers formed a factor in the decline of Dutch industry. Just as farmers always complained about the weather, and merchants about crippling taxation or unfair foreign competition, so industrialists were apt to think that their own adequately paid labour force was being undercut by the sweated labour of foreign competitors. As late as the year 1740, an Englishman long resident in Holland, after noting that both the Dutch and the English had brought the arts of the gunsmith and the gun-founder to a high degree of perfection, added: 'As we have a considerable advantage over the Dutch in our Mediterranean and Levant passes, it were to be wished that our taxes were reduced, or that in the meantime our workmen would contrive to live lower, and work as cheap as

[1] B. M. Vlekke, *Evolution of the Dutch Nation*, pp. 259–60; J. de Vries, *Economische achteruitgang*, p. 107, for the differing wage-rates. The problem is examined more closely in C. Wilson, 'Taxation and the decline of empires', in *BMHGU*, Vol. 77, pp. 10–26.

the Dutch', in which event, he argued, the whole of the arms-trade with the Ottoman Empire and the Barbary States would fall into English hands.[1]

Whether workers in the Dutch arms-industry subsequently maintained their technical ability on a level with that of their English competitors, I do not know; but it is worth noting that it was just in the 1740s that British economic growth started accelerating and the first phase of the Industrial Revolution got under way. Forty years later the general decline of Dutch industry was lamented by a Netherlands industrialist in the following terms:

> One cannot refrain from observing that there are very few industries or trades here which are not in need of improvement; both as regards the form as also the means of their respective processes. Copper-smiths, brass-founders, workers in iron and steel and workmen of that kind, are all found to be rather unskilful, and, when their products are carefully compared with those of foreign workmen, they are found to be inferior. The workmanship here is clumsier, and the piece is usually much less well finished, than that made elsewhere; and one can presume that it comes more expensive because the foremen here have not been properly trained.

In the same year (1779) a leading Leiden cloth-manufacturer deplored the general lack of initiative among Dutch industrialists and employers, and their deep-rooted aversion to experimenting with new techniques and new methods.[2] What was good enough for their ancestors was good enough for them, and this seems to have been a marked trait of Dutch society in the closing decades of the Periwig Period, whether in the towns and fields of the northern Netherlands or in the hinterland of the Cape of Good Hope.

This lack of initiative and enterprise in so many Dutch industries, and to some extent in Dutch agriculture, afforded a striking contrast to the state of affairs a hundred years previously, when Dutch entrepreneurs, industrialists and technicians were in the van of commercial and technical progress in the Western World. As

[1] *A Description of Holland* (1743), pp. 236-7.
[2] J. de Vries, *Economische achteruitgang*, pp. 108–12.

Charles Wilson has rightly observed: 'The Dutch technician was to the seventeenth century what the Scotch engineer was to the nineteenth century, but in even wider fields of economic activity. He was to be found wherever profitable occupation offered and he was in demand wherever government or private enterprise was in need of technical or managerial skill.' A century later he was nothing of the kind, as a contributor to *De Koopman* ruefully acknowledged in 1775: 'We are no longer innate inventors, and originality is becoming increasingly rare with us here. Nowadays we only make copies, whereas formerly we only made originals.'[1] No doubt some allowance must be made for exaggeration in these and many other similar jeremiads published in Dutch periodicals during the second half of the eighteenth century; and we may recall here Captain James Cook's tribute to the skill and efficiency of the Batavian shipwrights in 1770. But I venture to suggest that contrary to what some recent writers have claimed, the Periwig Period in the United Provinces *was* a time of stagnation rather than of consolidation, when compared with the achievements of the Golden Century in most, though admittedly not in all, respects.

The contemporaries who bemoaned the economic decay of the Dutch Republic in the last half – more especially in the last quarter – of the eighteenth century were inclined to place the principal blame on the allegedly self-satisfied and short-sighted rentiers and capitalists, who preferred to invest their money abroad rather than in fostering industry and shipping at home and thus relieving unemployment. There was undoubtedly an attitude of '*je m'en fiche*'-ism in the Netherlands and its tropical possessions during the last quarter of the eighteenth century, which, if it existed at all a century earlier was not then nearly so marked. The periodical *De Borger* wrote of the prosperous rentiers of 1778: 'Each one says, "It will last my time and after me the deluge!" as our [French] neighbours' proverb has it, which we have taken over in deeds if not in words.' A few years later, Dirk van Hogendorp wrote from Java that the most popular maxim among his compatriots there was 'the going will be good as long as I live, and what happens after

[1] C. Wilson, *Holland and Britain* (London, 1945), pp. 14–18. The quotation from *De Koopman* of 1776 is *apud* J. de Vries, *Economische achteruitgang*, p. 63 of the notes and note (300).

my death won't worry me then'.[1] We have seen that some of these complaints were exaggerated (p. 236), and in any event the increase in unearned income from Dutch investment capital during the eighteenth century – Van de Spiegel estimated this surplus profit at a yearly total of 27 million florins in 1782 – offset to a great extent, or possibly even more than offset, the decline in other sectors of the national income, such as the fisheries, the textile and shipbuilding industries, and some branches of seaborne trade. Recent historical research on the reasons for the economic decline of the northern Netherlands in the second half of the eighteenth century has established that economic factors – many of them unavoidable, such as the development of industry and shipping in neighbouring countries – were primarily responsible for this. There were, however, some other subsidiary causes, which might, perhaps, have been mitigated or avoided altogether if the social structure of the Republic had been other than it actually was.

In the first place (as Johan de Vries has pointed out) there was the preponderantly commercial tradition inherited from the Golden Century, when the Dutch merchants dominated the seaborne trade of so much of the world, and almost came to believe that they had a God-given right to do so. The social prestige of the merchant was always much higher than that of the industrialist, or of most other people outside the ruling oligarchic circle; and this commercial tradition, prestige and inclination was not favourable for the development of an industrial mentality. People who made a fortune, or even a comfortable living, from industry or craftsmanship were apt to change over to a merchant's calling as soon as they had enough capital to do so, and to bring up their sons as merchants.

---

[1] *De Borger* of 19 October 1778, *apud* J. de Bosch Kemper, *Armoede* (ed. 1851), pp. 354–8, where the comparison between the energetic entrepreneurs of the seventeenth century and the slothful rentiers of the eighteenth is drawn at great if not altogether convincing length; E. de Perron-de Roos, 'Correspondentie van Dirk van Hogendorp', pp. 140–1, 144, 264–8. Cf. also Anon, *Nederlandsch India in haar tegenwoordig staat* (*c.* 1780), pp. 17–18, 48; *Nederlandsch–Indisch Plakaatboek*, Vol. XI, pp. 55-6, 226; F. de Haan, *Oud Batavia*, Vol. II, pp. 9–17, for some typical examples of the prevailing corruption and cynicism in the Dutch East India Company at this period, which it would be very easy to multiply, and which are much more convincing than the denunciations of the rentiers in the fatherland.

The decentralized structure of the government of the Republic and the inter-provincial jealousies of the self-styled 'United Provinces', which had not greatly hindered their economic growth in the Golden Century, became greater obstacles in the changed circumstances of the eighteenth century, when foreign competition was more effective. The financial contributions of the various provinces to the 'generality', which had been fixed during the period 1609–21, remained unaltered down to the end of the Republic, despite the abortive efforts of some statesmen to revise them in accordance with the changing circumstances. Political divisions and mutual mistrust between the pro- and anti-Orange factions in the second half of the eighteenth century also meant that sensible suggestions for reform put up by one side were automatically rejected or side-tracked by the other. Inter-provincial jealousies sometimes prevented agreement from being reached on the improvement of roads or canals crossing provincial (or even municipal) boundaries. Corruption and nepotism among the regent-oligarchs had certainly existed in the seventeenth century, but did not impair their efficiency to the same extent as occurred with their descendants in the Periwig Period, when 'contracts of correspondence' became the rule rather than the exception.

The common late-eighteenth-century allegation that Dutch capitalists and rentiers who invested part of their capital in English and French funds were thereby helping the Republic's most dangerous competitors was probably unjustified. These countries would have developed their trade and industry even without the aid of Dutch capital. England was also an exporter of capital, though admittedly not on the same scale as the Dutch. Johan de Vries has pointed out that England was able to bear the financial burden of the War of American Independence without undue difficulty, even at a time when the Dutch recalled part of their capital from London. He argues that the real adverse repercussion of the practice of investing in foreign countries, which Dutch capitalists developed in the eighteenth century, was that it continued longer into the nineteenth century than was economically justifiable.[1]

Whether some forms of the economic decline of the Dutch Republic could have been prevented or not, by 1780 the process

[1] J. de Vries, *Economische achteruitgang*, pp. 172–80.

had gone far enough for all to see. The merchant-bankers and the wealthy rentiers might never have 'had it so good', but the conditions of the poor seems to have been even worse than it was a century previously, particularly in the inland towns. Boswell's description of Utrecht in 1764 (p. 238) anticipated an observation by Luzac twenty years later: 'Nobody who has any feeling, and some love for his fatherland, can walk through the inland towns with dry eyes.' In 1792 another eyewitness deposed: 'Everywhere we look attentively around us we find the sad truth confirmed that the well-being of that class of people who lead a working life is steadily declining.' The general rise in the cost of living during the second half of the eighteenth century was certainly one reason for this, as the Zeeland blue-stocking, Betje Wolff, noted in 1778. Increasing poverty was evident not only among the declining working-class population of towns such as Leiden, Delft and Zaandam, but in the rural province of Overijssel, where the growth in population between 1675 and 1767 was accompanied by a speedier increase in poverty. The result was not only a greater gulf between rich and poor but also a greater gulf between the upper and the lower middle classes in the towns.[1]

Despite the increasing religious tolerance and the declining religious bigotry; despite the efforts of such bodies as the Economic Branch of the Holland Society of Sciences to improve social and economic conditions by precept and example; despite the efforts of Betje Wolff and her sympathizers to educate and uplift the masses; despite the decrease in drinking gin and brandy and the increase in drinking coffee and tea – despite all these and other improving aspects of the Enlightenment which might be mentioned, I have no doubt that the land of Rembrandt, Vondel and De Ruyter was a better as well as a more stimulating place in which to live than was the land of Cornelis Troost, Bilderdijk and Zoutman.

[1] J. de Vries, *Economische achteruitgang*, pp. 170–2.

TEN

Economic and Institutional Factors in the Decline of the Chinese Empire[1]

PING-TI HO

Not only were increased means of livelihood provided by a vastly expanding the more intensive agriculture; the employment opportunities offered by an immense domestic trade, by a highly lucrative if somewhat limited foreign commerce, and by some newly rising industries and crafts throughout the later Ming and early Ch'ing were also considerable. Ever since the latter half of the eighth century the influence of money had been increasingly felt, at least in the Yangtze regions, which, thanks to an incomparable network of rivers, lakes and canals, constituted a vast single trading area.[2] The economic development of the Yangtze area was further stimulated by the continual influex of silver from the Europeans and the Japanese after the early sixteenth century.[3] True, the Yangtze area and the south-east coast were not representative of

[1] This article was first published as a section of chapter IX of *Studies on the Population of China, 1368–1953*, Harvard University Press, 1959.

[2] On the rise of money economy in China, see Ch'üan Han-sheng, 'Chung-ku tzu-jan ching-chi' (Natural Economy in Medieval China), *Bulletin of the Institute of History and Philology, Academia Sinica*, vol. X, and his 'T'ang-Sung cheng-fu sui-ju yü huo-pi ching-chi ti kuan-hsi' (The Relationship between Public Revenue and Money Economy during the T'ang and Sung Periods), ibid., vol. XX.

[3] During the period 1573–1644 the total Mexican dollars imported into China through legal trade alone is estimated by a cautious modern economic historian to have definitely exceeded 100,000,000. Japan is estimated to have exported more than 70,000,000 taels of silver to China during the period 1601–47. See Liang Fang-chung, 'Ming-tai kuo-chi mao-i yü yin ti shu-ch'u-ju' (International Trade and Silver Movements during the Ming period), *Chung,kuo she-hui-ching-chi-shih chi-k'an* (Chinese Social and Economic History Review), vol. VI, no. 2.

the whole country. But when the south-east coast was brought into the sphere of a worldwide commercial revolution, the effects reached far into inland China. The commutation of labour services, which by 1600 had become nationwide, is one of the eloquent testimonials to the increasing influence of money. Although the majority of the people were engaged in subsistence farming, as they still are today, there were relatively few localities that did not depend to some extent on the supply of goods and products of neighbouring or distant regions.

Whatever the institutional and ethical checks on the growth of capital, the late Ming period witnessed the rise of great merchants. The unusually observant Hsieh Chao-che, *chin-shih* of 1602, later governor of Kwangsi and author of the famous cyclopedia *Wu-tsa-tsu*, gives the following account:

> The rich men of the empire in the regions south of the Yangtze are from Hui-chou (southern Anhwei), in the regions north of the river from Shansi. The great merchants of Hui-chou take fisheries and salt as their occupation and have amassed fortunes amounting to one million taels of silver. Others with a fortune of two or three hundred thousands can only rank as middle merchants. The Shansi merchants are engaged in salt, or silk, or reselling, or grain. Their wealth even exceeds that of the former.[1]

In fact, many regions in later Ming times boasted resourceful long-distance merchants. People of the congested islands in the Tung-t'ing Lake in the heart of the lower Yangtze delta, for example, were driven by economic necessity to trade in practically every part of the country and for a time vied with the Hui-chou merchants in wealth. Merchants of the central Shensi area, while active in trading almost everywhere, specialized in transporting and selling grains to garrisons along the Great Wall, in the salt trade in the Huai River region, in the cotton cloth trade in southern Kiangsu, and in the tea trade with various vassal peoples along the thousand-mile western frontier stretching from Kokonor to the Szechwan-Tibet border.[1] The southern Fukien ports, Ch'üan-chou

[1] Hsieh Chao-che, *Wu-tsa-tsu* (1795 Japanese ed.), 4.25b.
[2] Fu I-ling, *Ming-Ch'ing shih-tai shang-jen chi shang-yeh tzu-pen* (Peking, 1956), chs. 3, 5.

S

and Chang-chou, which handled the bulk of the Sino-Portuguese trade in the sixteenth century, probably produced some of the largest individual fortunes.[1]

As inter-regional merchants became more numerous, they gradually established guildhalls in commercial centres. In the early Ch'ing period there were guildhalls in Peking established by money-lenders from Shao-hsing in Chekiang, wholesale dye merchants from P'ing-yao in Shansi, large tobacco dealers from Chi-shan, Chiang-hsien and Wen-hsi in Shansi, grain and vegetable-oil merchants from Lin-hsiang and Lin-fen in Shansi, silk merchants from Nanking and Cantonese merchants who specialized in various exotic and subtropical products.[2] From the late seventeenth century the accounts in local histories of guildhalls established by distant merchants became more and more common, which indicated the continual development of the inter-regional trade.

The dimensions of individual and aggregate merchant fortunes were growing along with the volume of inter-regional trade. It has been estimated that some of the Hui-chou salt merchants of the eighteenth century had individual fortunes exceeding 10,000,000 taels and that the aggregate profit reaped by some three hundred salt merchant families of the Yang-chou area in the period 1750–1800 was in the neighbourhood of 250,000,000 taels.[3] It was known to the Western merchant community in Canton during the early nineteenth century that the Wu family, under the leadership and management of the famous Howqua, had built up through foreign trade a fortune of 26,000,000 Mexican dollars.[4] Commercial capital had made giant strides since China's first contacts with the Europeans.

A sampling of the biographies in the histories of Hui-chou prefecture reveals that the Hui-chou merchants, though their headquarters were in the cities along the lower Yangtze, carried on trade

[1] Fu I-ling, *Ming-Ch'ing shih-tai shang-jen chi shang-yeh tzu-yen*, ch. 4.
[2] Shigeshi Kato, *Shina keizaishi kenkyū* (Studies in Chinese Economic History) (Tōyō Bunko, 1953), vol. II. pp. 557–84.
[3] Ping-ti Ho, 'The Salt Merchants of Yang-chou: A Study of Commercial Capitalism in Eighteenth-Century China', *Harvard Journal of Asiatic Studies*, vol. XVII, nos. 1, 2, June 1954.
[4] W. C. Hunter, *The 'Fan Kwae' at Canton before Treaty Days, 1825–1844* (Shanghai, 1911), p. 48.

with various parts of north and central China, Yunnan, Kweichow, Szechwan and even the remote aboriginal districts and Indochina.[1] In the national capital alone there were 187 tea stores in 1789–91 and 200 in 1801 which were owned and operated by merchants of She-hsien, the capital city of Hui-chou prefecture.[2] So ubiquitous were the Hui-chou merchants that there was a common saying: 'No market is without people of Hui-chou.'[3] The radius of the trading activities of these and other comparable merchant bodies is one indication of the increasingly mobile character of the national economy. The fact that it was trade as well as agriculture that sustained the local population and made its multiplication possible is well attested by various local histories, particularly those of the active trading areas, such as Hui-chou, a number of counties in Shansi, Shensi and Kansu, the lower Yangtze counties, the Ningpo and Shao-hsing areas in Chekiang, Chang-chou and Ch'üan-chou in southern Fukien, and the Canton area. Even people of the poor and backward western Hupei highlands depended to a substantial degree on trading with Szechwan as a means of livelihood.[4]

The inter-regional and local trade consisted of an exchange of a few staple commodities, like grains, salt, fish, drugs, timber, hard-wares, potteries and cloths, and of a number of luxury and artistic goods of quality for the consumption of the ruling classes. The quantity of internal trade in late Ming and early Ch'ing China, although not unusual according to modern Western standards, certainly left a profound impression upon the Jesuits of the seventeenth and eighteenth centuries. In fact, few modern scholars are in a better position to compare the dimensions of the domestic trade of early Ch'ing China with that of early modern Europe than were the Jesuits, who, knowing both about equally well, measured the Chinese economy with the standards of pre-industrial Europe.

Du Halde, whose famous description of China may well be regarded as the synthesis of seventeenth- and early eighteenth-century Jesuit works on China, said of Chinese commerce:

[1] *Hui-chou FC* (1827 ed.), 9–12, *passim*.
[2] *She-hsien hui-kuan lu* (1834 second revised ed.), list of donators to the public cemetery for the poor people of She-hsien who died in Peking, pp. 12a–15a.
[3] *Tien-yeh hsü-chih lu*, undated manuscript, a manual for pawnshop apprentices, written by a native of Hui-chou, preface.
[4] Various nineteenth-century western Hupei local histories.

The riches peculiar to each province, and the facility of conveying merchandise, by means of rivers and canals, have rendered the domestic trade of the empire always very flourishing. . . . The inland trade of China is so great that the commerce of all Europe is not to be compared therewith; the provinces being like so many kingdoms, which communicate to each other their respective productions. This tends to unite the several inhabitants among themselves, and makes plenty reign in all cities.[1]

This generalization probably referred only to the vast Yangtze area, but it can nevertheless be applied to many other parts of China. The trade of mountainous Fukien during the late sixteenth century was described by the educational commissioner Wang Shih-mao:

There is not a single day that the silk fabrics of Fu-chou, the gauze of Chang-chou, the indigo of Ch'üan-chou, the ironwares of Fu-chou and Yen-p'ing, the oranges of Fu-chou and Chang-chou, the lichee nuts of Fu-chou and Hsing-hua, the cane sugar of Ch'üan-chou and Chang-chou, and the paper products of Shun-ch'ang are not shipped along the watershed of P'u-ch'eng and Hsiao-kuan to Kiangsu and Chekiang like running water. The quantity of these things shipped by seafaring junks is still harder to reckon.[2]

Wang's description of the large quantities of commodities shipped along the difficult mountain pass of northern Fukien is borne out by the later Jesuit testimony that in the watershed at P'u-ch'eng there were 'eight or ten thousand porters attending to the barks, who get their livelihood by going continually backwards and forwards across these mountains',[3] Wang's comment on the large coastal trade between Fukien ports and the lower Yangtze area is also corroborated by other sources. The demand of remote markets for Fukien sugar was so great that by the late sixteenth century a considerable percentage of the rice paddies in

[1] P. J. B. Du Halde, *A Description of the Empire of China and Chinese Tartary* (London, 1738), vol. I, pp. 333-4.
[2] Wang Shih-mao, *Min-pu-shu* (TSCC ed.), p. 12.
[3] Du Halde, *A Description*, I, p. 85.

the Ch'üan-chou area had been turned into sugar-cane fields.[1] Throughout the late Ming and early Ch'ing annually 'hundreds and thousands of junks' discharged sugar in Shanghai and went back to southern Fukien ports with full loads of raw cotton which were made into cotton cloth locally.[2]

Even in landlocked north China the inter-regional trade was very lively. Despite the lack of cheap water transportation in many northern areas, daily necessities as well as luxury goods from distant regions were carried by wheelbarrows, carts, mules and asses. 'The prodigious multitudes of people' and 'astonishing multitudes of asses and mules' engaged in the shipping of commodities in north China never failed to impress those Jesuits commissioned by the K'ang-hsi Emperor as imperial cartographers.[3] Silk and cotton fabrics of various kinds and luxury goods from the lower Yangtze region and Chekian were to be found in practically every northern provincial town, including the late Ming military posts along the Great Wall. Generally speaking, it was the technologically advanced south-east that supplied the inland Yangtze and northern provinces with finished products, for which the recipients paid in rice, cotton and other raw materials.[4] Even in westernmost Yunnan bordering Burma, trade in precious and common metals, ivory, precious stones and jades, silk and cotton fabrics was constantly going on during the late Ming.[5] In fact, so great was the volume of China's inter-regional trade that for centuries it consistently impressed the Europeans.

This growing internal trade stimulated industries and crafts and made possible regional specialization in commercial crops. In the late Ming and early Ch'ing, rural industries and crafts of regional importance were so numerous that it is possible here to mention only a few outstanding ones. The pottery or porcelain industry of Ching-te-chen in northern Kiangsi expanded greatly during the sixteenth century, thanks to increasing government demand for

[1] Ch'en Mao-jen, *Ch'üan-nan tsa chih* (TSCC ed.), A.7.

[2] Ch'u Yüan, *Mu-mien p'u* (*Shang-hai chang-ku ts'ung-shu* ed.), p. 11b.

[3] Du Halde, *A Description*, I, pp. 47–53.

[4] Fujii Hiroshi, 'A Study of the Hsin-an (Hui-chou) Merchants, I', *Toyo Gakuho*, June 1953. This first instalment is a study of the inter-regional trade in general and is by far the most useful work of its kind.

[5] Hsieh Chao-che, *Tien-lüeh* (early seventeenth-century ed.), 4.15b.

high-quality porcelains and the investment of the Hui-chou merchants in privately owned kilns.[1] By the K'ang-hsi period (1662–1722), when Chinese porcelain 'had materially altered' the artistic tastes of the English aristocracy,[2] the Ching-te borough had about five hundred porcelain furnaces working day and night to meet the national and foreign demand. At night, with its flame and smoke, this township, which stretched one and a half leagues along a river, looked like 'a great city all on fire, or a vast furnace with a great many vent-holes'. Since all the provisions and fuel had to be supplied by the surrounding districts, the cost of living in this industrial town was high. Yet, in the words of a contemporary Jesuit and longtime resident, 'it is the refuge of an infinite number of poor families, who . . . find employment here for youths and weakly persons; there are none, even to the lame and blind, but get their living here by grinding colours.'[3]

Another outstanding industry was cotton textiles, in the Sung-chiang area, of which Shanghai was a rising city. Thanks to an early start and to its moist climate, Sung-chiang was the Lancashire of early modern China. Although an enormous quantity of cotton was grown locally, Sung-chiang in the seventeenth and eighteenth centuries depended on remote northern provinces like Honan and western Shantung for the supply of raw cotton. The Jesuits reckoned that in the late seventeenth century there were in the Shanghai area alone '200,000 weavers of calicoes'.[4] Since at least three spinners were needed to supply the yarn for one weaver,[5] the total number of spinners must have been several times larger. Cloth of many grades and designs was made to meet the varied demands of the people of Shansi, Shensi, the Peking area, Hupei, Hunan, Kaingsi, Kwangtung and Kwangsi.[6] Contemporaries remarked that Sung-chiang clothed and capped the whole nation. The Su-chou area was also an important textile centre, supplying much of western Shantung with its finished products.

The area around Nanking, from which the name of the famous

[1] Fujii, 'Hui-chou Merchants', pp. 23–4.

[2] G. M. Trevelyan, *English Social History* (New York, 1946), p. 216.

[3] Du Halde, *A Description*, I, pp. 80–1.   [4] Ibid., I, p. 73.

[5] Yen Chun-p'ing, *Chung-kuo mien-fang-chih shih-kao* (Peking, 1955), ch. 2.

[6] Yeh Meng-chu, *Yüeh-shih pien* (*Shang-hai chang-ku ts'ung-shu* ed.), 1.5a–6a.

cotton fabric nankeen was derived, produced cloth of high-quality which was exported to the West from Canton. Exports increased constantly until over one million pieces were being exported annually to Great Britain and the United States during the early nineteenth century. H. B. Morse, a New Englander and the famous historian of the Chinese Customs, said:

> Cotton manufactures in 1905 constituted 44 per cent of the value (excluding opium) of all [China's] foreign imports, but in this industry the West could compete with cheap Asiatic labour only after the development springing from the inventions of Richard Arkwright and Eli Whitney, and in the eighteenth and early nineteenth centuries the movement of cotton cloth was from China to the West, in the shape of nankeens to provide small-clothes for our grandfathers.[1]

From the late sixteenth century Sung-chiang was subject to increasing competition from the rising cotton textile centres in north China. The low plain area of north China could produce cotton at lower cost and in larger quantity than the densely popu-lated lower Yangtze region. This increased production of raw cotton in turn stimulated spinning and weaving, which were becoming very important rural industries in north China. The rapid development of the cotton industry in southern Pei-chihli, or modern Hopei, greatly impressed the Christian prime minister Hsü Kuang-sh'i (1562–1633), a native of Shanghai, who estimated that the cotton cloth produced by Su-ning country alone amounted to one-tenth of the cloth produced by the entire Sung-chiang prefecture.[2] In the course of the seventeenth century many northern districts became regionally famous for their finished cotton products, although few could vie with Sung-chiang in skill and quality. Towards the end of the seventeenth century the Hankow area had already deprived Sung-chiang of much of its old market in the north-west and the south-west.[3]

[1] H. B. Morse, *The Trade and Administration of China* (New York, 1920), pp. 309–10.
[2] Hsü Kuang-ch'i, *Nung-cheng ch'üan-shu* (1843 ed.), 35.13a–13b.
[3] Fujii, 'Hui-chou Merchants', p. 15.

Cotton cultivation, which had been extensive in the Ming period, further expanded under the repeated exhortations of the early Ch'ing emperors. Many counties in southern and western Chihli, western Shantung, Honan, the Wei River valley in Shensi, the Fen River valley in Shansi, the Hupei lowlands and central Szechwan derived a major portion of their incomes from cotton.[1] Cotton spinning and weaving became a common rural industry even in Yunnan and Kweichow. A great many people must have made their living partly or entirely on the growing of cotton or cotton spinning and weaving.

The cotton growing was by no means the only example of farming for profit. Thanks to the expanding economy and the nationwide grain trade, many areas became specialized in one or a number of commercial crops which found ready markets elsewhere. The economy of the mountainous south-western corner of Kaingsi, the middle Fu River valley in Szechwan, the Lei-chou peninsula and the north coastal region of Hainan Island, the Hsün and Yü river valleys in Kwangsi, the Mi-lo area in Yunnan and many more scattered and relatively backward areas, had been revolutionized by a single crop, the peanut, in the course of the eighteenth century.[2] Since the late Ming sugar cane and indigo had helped to transform the economy of many southern regions, particularly Fukien, Kwangtung and southern Kiangsi. Many counties in Szechwan also benefited from extensive sugar cane cultivation. In 1727 the governor of Kwangsi, in a memorial protesting the extensive purchase of Kwangsi rice by the people of Kwangtung, attributed the rice shortage in Kwangtung to the fact that a considerable portion of its good farmland had been devoted to such commercial crops as fruits, sugar cane, tobacco and indigo.[3]

Tobacco, one of the most profitable crops introduced into China

[1] This generalization is based on Nishijima Sadao, 'The Extension of Cotton Cultivation during the Ming Period', *Shigaku Zasshi*, vol. 57, nos. 4–5 (1948) and the present author's sampling of Ch'ing local histories.

[2] *Kiangsi TC* (1880 ed.), 49; *T'ung-ch'üan FC* (1786 ed.), 3.7b; *Kao-chou* (1827 ed.), 3.63a; *Lien-chou FC* (1756 ed.), 7.1b; *Lei-chou FC* (1811 ed.), 2.49b; T'an Ts'ui, *Tien-hai yü-heng chih* (preface dated 1804, TSCC ed.), 10.73–74, 11.85; *Po-po HC* (1832 ed.), 12.21b; *Kuei-hsien chih* (1893 ed.), 1.2a; *Mi-lo CC* (1738 ed.), 23.50a.

[3] Fujii, 'Hui-chou Merchants', *passim*. The memorial is cited on p. 44.

during the late Ming period, had brought wealth to many localities, particularly Lan-chou in Kansu, P'u-ch'eng and Lung-yen in Fukien, north-eastern and south-eastern Kiangsi, Chi-ning in Shantung and north-eastern Chihli near the strategic pass of Shan-hai-kuan.[1] The extent to which rice paddies and good farmland were converted to tobacco farms so alarmed some provincial authorities that they brought about several imperial decrees prohibiting the cultivation of tobacco in the eighteenth century. But as an early nineteenth-century Manchu poet pointed out, repeated government prohibitions could not in the long run compete with a 200 per cent profit, which accounted for a continual conversion of cereal-growing land into tobacco farms in the Lan-chou area.[2] It was estimated by an early nineteenth-century official in Fukien that in some Fukien counties tobacco occupied some 60 or 70 per cent of the farmland.[3] In 1829 an able scholar and economic expert testified that in Chi-ning county in Shantung tobacco was monopolized by six local families who employed more than four thousand workers and annually grossed about two million taels.[4]

Many areas, such as the Ch'eng-tu plain in Szechwan, Heng-yang in Hunan and Han-chung in southern Shensi, were regionally if not nationally famous for their tobacco production.[5] The people of Jui-chin, a hilly district in south-eastern Kiangsi, said that, despite the loss of good farmland to tobacco, every spring the sight of the green tobacco leaves in the fields gave them assurance, because tobacco meant ready cash with which rice and other necessities could easily be bought from northern Kiangsi. This county furnishes one of the best examples of the extent to which self-sustaining agriculture had given way to specialized commercial farming in many areas. By the nineteenth century, perhaps much earlier, none of the cereal crops was grown there on any significant scale and the new staples were all commercial crops – tobacco, tea oil, an

[1] For a short study of the major tobacco-producing areas in the Ch'ing, see Wang Hsin, *Ch'ing-yen lu* (1805 ed.), 8, *passim*.
[2] Shu Wei, *P'ing-shui-chai shih-chi* (TSCC ed.), 6.63.
[3] Liang Chang-chü, *T'ui-an sui-pi* (*Ch'ing-tai pi-chi ts'ung-k'an* ed.), 8.8b–9a.
[4] Pao Shih-ch'en, *An-wu ssu-chung*, 6.
[5] *Ch'eng-tu HC* (1815 ed.), 6.38a; *Chin-t'ang HC* (1811 ed.), 3; Huang pen-chi, *Hu-nan fang-wu chih* (1845 ed.), 3.4b–5a; *HCCSWP*, 36.22a–22b.

indispensable ingredient for curing tobacco, peanuts and ginger.[1]

A well-travelled European during the 1840s commented on the general state of commerce:

> One excellent reason why the Chinese care little about foreign commerce is that their internal trade is so extensive. . . . This trade consists principally in the exchange of grain, salt, metal, and other natural and artificial production of various provinces. . . . China is a country so vast, so rich, so varied, that its internal trade alone would suffice abundantly to occupy that part of the nation which can be devoted to mercantile operations. There are in all great towns important commercial establishments, into which, as into reservoirs, the merchandise of all the provinces discharges itself. To these vast storehouses people flock from all parts of the Empire, and there is a constant bustle going on about them – a feverish activity that would scarcely be seen in the most important cities of Europe.[2]

From this and earlier Jesuit comments it becomes clear that the early Ch'ing economy, if somewhat less variegated than that of Europe, was reasonably complex and able to meet both the basic and the more sophisticated demands of the nation.

However, even during the period of steady economic growth there were inherent weaknesses in the traditional Chinese economy. It was capable of small gains but incapable of innovations in either the institutional or the technological sense. Institutionally, despite the availability of commercial capital on a gigantic scale (witness the Yang-chou salt merchants and the Canton Hong merchants), the traditional Chinese economy failed to develop a genuine capitalistic system such as characterized the Europe of the seventeenth and eighteenth centuries. The reasons were many and varied. In the first place, by far the easiest and surest way to acquire wealth was to buy the privilege of selling a few staples with universal

---

[1] *Jui-chin HC* (1603 ed.) lacks reference to these commercial crops and also lacks the confident tone as to the state of the local economy. The change in the economy of the locality brought about by commercial crops is described in the 1872 edition, 2.37b–45b.

[2] M. Huc, *A Journey through the Chinese Empire* (New York, 1855), vol. II, p. 129.

demand, like salt and tea, which were under government monopoly. The activities of the Hong merchants, and of other powerful
merchant groups, also partook of the nature of tax-farming rather
than genuine private enterprise.

Secondly, the profit and wealth accruing to these merchant
princes was not reinvested in new commercial or industrial enterprises but was diverted to various non-economic uses. Ordinary
commercial and industrial investments were less profitable than
money-lending and tax-farming in the broad sense. Furthermore,
the cultural and social values peculiar to the traditional Chinese
society fostered this economic pattern. In a society where the
primary standard of prestige was not money but scholarly attain-
ment, official position or literary achievement, rich merchants preferred to buy official ranks and titles for themselves, encourage their
sons to become degree-holders and officials, patronize artists and
men of letters, cultivate the expensive hobbies of the *élite*, or simply
consume or squander their wealth in conspicuous ways. Consequently, up to a certain point wealth not only failed to beget more
wealth; it could hardly remain concentrated in the same family for
more than two or three generations.[1]

Thirdly, the lack of primogeniture and the working of the clan
system proved to be great levelling factors in the Chinese economy.
The virtue of sharing one's wealth with one's immediate and
remote kinsmen had been so highly extolled since the rise of Neo-
Confucianism in the eleventh and twelfth centuries that few
wealthy men in traditional China could escape the influence of this
teaching.[2] Business management, in the last analysis, was an extension of familism and was filled with nepotism, inefficiencies and
irrationalities. These immensely rich individuals not only failed to
develop a capitalistic system; they seldom if ever acquired that
acquisitive and competitive spirit which is the very soul of the
capitalistic system.

Fourthly, the Confucian cultural and political system rewarded
only the learned and studious. Technological inventions were

[1] For a more systematic explanation of traditional China's failure to develop
a capitalistic system and her difficulties in capital accumulation, see Ho, 'Salt
Merchants of Yang-chou', last section.
[2] Ho, 'Salt Merchants', and Fu I-ling, *Ming-Ch'ing shang-jen*, pp. 171–3.

viewed as minor contrivances unworthy of the dignity of scholars. Despite the budding scientific spirit in Chu Hsi's philosophy, China failed to develop a system of experimental science; moral philosophy always reigned supreme. Major technological inventions are seldom accidental and are necessarily based on scientific knowledge; hence traditional China could not produce a major technological revolution, which depends as much on the application of scientific knowledge to practical industrial problems as on a co-ordination of various economic and institutional factors. By the last quarter of the eighteenth century there was every indication that the Chinese economy, at its prevailing technological level, could no longer gainfully sustain an ever-increasing population without overstraining itself. The economy during the first half of the nineteenth century became so strained and the standard of living for the majority of the nation deteriorated so rapidly that a series of uprisings occurred, culminating in the Taiping Rebellion.

Finally, throughout the Ch'ing by far the most powerful control over the economy was exerted by the State, through the bureaucracy. Such key enterprises as the salt trade and foreign commerce were jointly undertaken by the bureaucracy and a few individuals who were resourceful enough to assume the financial responsibility demanded by the State. Even in the late Ch'ing and early Republican periods the few new industrial enterprises launched by the Chinese were almost invariably financed by bureaucratic capitalists. In the cotton textile industry, for example, out of a total of twenty-six mills established between 1890 and 1913, nine were established by active and retired high officials, ten by mixed groups of officials and individuals with official titles, and seven by the new breed of treaty-port compradores, practically all of whom had official connections.[1] It is common knowledge that after the founding of the Nationalist government in 1927 a few top-ranking bureaucrats who enjoyed Chiang Kai-shek's confidence exerted ever more powerful control over the modern sector of the national economy through the incomparably superior apparatus of four major modern banks. Genuine capitalism based on private enterprise never had a chance of success in modern China, which could only choose between bureaucratic capitalism and bureaucratic collectivism.

[1] Yen Chung-p'ing, pp. 152–5.

In the midst of the storms and stresses of the middle nineteenth century, the Chinese economy came into full contact with the Western economy. Western technology, which could be the answer to China's economic ills, was adopted piecemeal only after prolonged resistance from the scholar-official class who had a vested interest in the Confucian system.

Appendix

As has been written, 'Development is not a theory, it is an historical process.' The same can be said of decline. This implies two corollaries. First: the totemistic worship of technical analytical tools may powerfully help us as long as we limit our analysis to the surface of economic affairs, but may easily blind us to the cultural context of economic activity and the relation of economics to the whole. One has to go beyond and behind capital-output ratios, productivity coefficients, marginal returns, production functions and the like and try to identify the socio-cultural forces that condition both the economic variables and their parameters. Secondly: although we may not resist the temptation of drawing grandiose parallels among different historical cases of decline, we must constantly remind ourselves that each decline is a story of its own, which to be fully comprehended must be studied in its historical individuality and on its own human terms.

The essays that are reproduced in the pages above are a good antidote to the dangerous generalizations of the preceding Introduction. The interested reader will find in any library large numbers of books and articles on the declines of Rome, Byzantium, the Arabs, Spain, Italy, the Netherlands, as well as on the dynastic cycles of China, the fall of the Mayas, of the Aztecs, etc. With reference to only those cases of decline that are considered in this volume, I give here a short and selected list of works that may usefully be consulted in addition to the works reproduced or cited in the preceding pages.

Bibliography

On the Late Roman Empire:

M. L. ROSTOVTZEFF, *Social and Economic History of the Roman Empire*, Oxford, 1957

A. H. M. JONES, *The Later Roman Empire*, Oxford, 1964

J. VOGT, *The Decline of Rome*, London, 1967

F. M. WALBANK, *The Awful Revolution. The Decline of the Roman Empire in the West*, Liverpool, 1969

On the Late Byzantine Empire:

P. GRENIER, *L'Empire Byzantin*, Paris, 1904

A. M. ANDREADES, 'The Economic Life of the Byzantine Empire', in N. H. BAYNES & H. L. B. MOSS (eds.), *Byzantium*, Oxford, 1948

P. CHARANIS, 'Economic Factors in the Decline of the Byzantine Empire', in *Journal of Economic History*, 13 (1953)

G. OSTROGORSKY, *History of the Byzantine State*, Oxford, 1956

C. DIEHL, *Byzantium: Greatness and Decline*, New Brunswick, 1957

I. SAVCENKO, 'The Decline of Byzantium seen through the eyes of its intellectuals', in *Dumbarton Oaks Papers*, 15 (1961)

J. M. HUSSEY (ed.), *The Byzantine Empire*, The Cambridge Medieval History, vol. 4, Cambridge, 1966–7

On the Late Arab Empire:

C. CAHEN, 'Les facteurs économiques et sociaux dans l'ankylose culturelle de l'Islam', in R. BRUNSVICK & G. E. VON GRÜNEBAUM (eds.), *Classicisme et declin culturel dans l'histoire de l'Islam*, Paris, 1958

J. J. SAUNDERS, 'The Problem of Islamic Decadence', in *Journal of World History*, 7 (1963)

On the Decline of the Ottoman Empire:

N. T. JORGA, *Les causes de la catastrophe de l'Empire Ottoman*, Paris, 1913

T. STOIANOVICH, 'Factors in the Decline of Ottoman Society in the Balkans', in *Slavic Review*, 21 (1962)

P. COLES, *The Ottoman Impact on Europe*, London, 1968, chap. 5

On the Decline of Spain:

E. J. HAMILTON, 'The Decline of Spain', in *The Economic History Review*, 8 (1938)

I. OLAGÜE, *La decadencia española*, San Sebastian, 1939

A. ULLASTRES, 'Notas sobra España y su economia en el siglo XVII', in *Anales de Economia*, 8 (1948)

V. PALACIO ATARD, *Derrota, agotamento, decadencia en la España del siglo XVII*, Madrid, 1949

M. SCHWARZMANN, 'Background factors in Spanish economic decline', in *Explorations in Entrepreneurial History*, 3 (1951)

R. TREVOR DAVIS, *Spain in decline 1621–1700*, London, 1957

A. DOMINGUEZ ORTIS, *La sociedad española en el siglo XVII*, Madrid, 1963

J. GENTIL DA SILVA, *En Espagne, développement économique, subsistance, déclin*, Paris, 1965

On the Decline of Italy:

S. PUGLIESE, *Condizioni economiche e finanziarie della Lombardia nella prima meta del sec. XVIII*, Turin, 1924

A. FANFANI, *Storia del lavoro in Italia dalla metá del sec. XV agli inizi del XVIII*, Milan, 1943

G. LUZZATTO, 'I primi secoli dell' eta' moderna', in *Per una storia economica d'Italia*, Bari, 1957

D. SELLA, *Commerci e industrie a Venezia nel secolo XVII*, Venice, 1961

On the Decline of The Netherlands:

C. WILSON, 'The Decline of the Netherlands', in *The Economic History Review*, 9 (1939)

VV. AA. *Algemene Geschiedenis der Nederlanden*, Utrecht, 1949–58, vols. 6 and 7

J. DE VRIES, *De economische achteruitgang*, Amsterdam, 1959

C. WILSON, *The Dutch Republic*, London, 1968, chap. 13

P. JEANNIN, *L'Europe du Nord-Ouest et du Nord aux XVIIᵉ et XVIIIᵉ siècles*, Paris, 1969, chap. 13